■

"This book is essential reading for anyone who cares about children and the tragic nature of current foster care practices. It will break your heart and, I hope, motivate you to run, not walk, to your city social agencies and courts and howl for reform. I wish I could give a copy of this book to every person who rages against crime and wants vengeance. Criminals are made, not born, and many of them are the desperate victims of terrible child care practices."

—Eda LeShan, author of
*In Search of Myself and Other Children*

■

"Louise Armstrong, whose penetrating investigations broke the silence on incest and domestic violence, now takes her close scrutiny to the foster care system, exposing its bureaucratic scandals while celebrating the genuine bonds of human love. Her thorough research, intelligence and compassion make *SOLOMON SAYS* an important book not only for service providers but any reader who cares about the passions and purpose of the American family."

—Mary Kay Blakely, author of
*Wake Me When It's Over*

■

"There could be no better guide through the Dickensian world of foster care and child protection than Louise Armstrong. This is an important book."

—Ann Jones, author of
*Women Who Kill*

(more . . .)

———————— ■ ————————

"Reading this book is like being lost, then suddenly found. A disheartening welter of frustration and contradiction becomes simple, clearer, and therefore manageable. Here is light shone into the heart of darkness; here is caring, focused and organized; here is patient guidance to profound understanding. Louise Armstrong's *SOLOMON SAYS: A SPEAKOUT ON FOSTER CARE* is a congress of urgent voices providing perspective and direction for meaningful action."

—Ruby Dee

———————— ■ ————————

"Eloquent . . . shows us what life is like when the State is Daddy. If you care about children, you should read this book."

—Andrea Dworkin, author of
*Letters from a War Zone*

———————— ■ ————————

"A humanizing, street-level tour of the broken lives of foster children . . . a call to action."

—Thomas J. Downey,
U.S. House of Representatives

———————— ■ ————————

"Provides enormous insight into our troubled foster care system. This disturbing yet fascinating book is highly recommended."

—Glenn M. Hester, President,
National Association of Former Foster Children

# What Does *Foster Care* Mean?

———————————— ■ ————————————

Listen to the voices of experience . . .

KIM, foster child: "The social workers would take things away from you, privileges, if you didn't participate in group therapy. . . . It wasn't like the girls who lived in this home had discipline problems. Their parents were nuts, or poor, or had sicknesses, or their parents abused them, incest. . . . It was just that they needed somewhere to live."

KELLY, "unfit" mother whose children were placed in foster care because she had no money—and who was then ordered to pay child support: "I was not even allowed to see my children. I had to pay child support payments to welfare for not letting me see my kids."

MARK, a caseworker: "There's a lot of cases where I really don't believe that the mother was bad to the children. . . . I'm very confused about why the children were removed."

TRACY, an "incorrigible" foster child and self-made success: "God, I hope that your book can change the system! Not that I'm holding my breath . . ."

———————————— ■ ————————————

# SOLOMON SAYS

## A Speakout on Foster Care

Louise Armstrong

**POCKET BOOKS**

New York  London  Toronto  Sydney  Tokyo

*For Tom*

An *Original* Publication of POCKET BOOKS

POCKET BOOKS, a division of Simon & Schuster Inc.
1230 Avenue of the Americas, New York, NY 10020

ISBN: 0-671-65782-8

First Pocket Books trade paperback printing November 1989

10  9  8  7  6  5  4  3  2  1

POCKET and colophon are trademarks of
Simon & Schuster Inc.

Printed in the U.S.A.

# CONTENTS

Acknowledgments                              ix
Note to the Reader                           xi

Setting Out: An Introduction                  1
A "Not-Story"                                23
Complications I                              31
"Falling in Love"                            39
Complications II                             53
The Permanency-Planning Worker               57
The "Unfit" Mother                           67
He Who "Makes Trouble"                       85

vii

Complications III                        103
"You Are Troubled"                       109
Flamboyant                               125
To Cut and to Run                        137
Complications IV                         149
Laura Speaks                             161
La Madre                                 169
The Great Leveler                        177
Mal-treatment                            187
A Professional's View                    211
Complications. Again.                    221
One Solomon Says                         227
Emerging: An Afterword                   243

   Notes                                 267

# ACKNOWLEDGMENTS

It is an irony of a book such as this—where all names besides those of professionals must be changed—that it is then impossible to publicly thank the very people whose contributions provide the book's essence: those whose voices you will hear, whose lives you will enter. Still (in the spirit of "you know who you are"), I would like to express my deep gratitude to the many women, men, children who did choose to speak with me, in the hope it would make the reality of the world of foster care accessible; the hope that speaking might help others; might lead to change.

Professionals whose assistance or testimony was invaluable include William Grimm, Janet Fink, Kathy Kosnoff, Ira Schwartz, Mary Dean, Arletta Walker, Dr. C. A. Cowardin, Judy Watts, Glenn and Carla Hester, the Honorable Elaine Slobod, John Cameron, Lawrence Lebowitz, Chris Hansen, Mark Hardin, Debra Ratterman, Kim Storm, Pat Peterson, Donna Mac-

Namara, Sgt. Teddy Daigle, Richard Ducote, Alfred Kadushin, Judith A. Martin, Mary Lee Allen, Alice Williams, Jim Peters, Janet Dinsmore, Diane Shust, Trudee Able-Peterson. I must also express my debt to those whose studies and writings informed my journey: Michael Wald, David Fanshel, Ruth Hubbell, Trudy Festinger, Joseph Goldstein / Anna Freud / Albert J. Solnit, Linda Gordon, Elizabeth Pleck, Jeanne M. Giovannini / Rosina M. Becerra, Richard J. Gelles, Murray A. Straus, Patrick Murphy.

# NOTE TO THE READER

This book is the story of my journey into the world of foster care—my travels among those whose lives have been intimately touched by state intervention; whether as children or, in the case of parents and foster parents, caseworkers or other professionals, as adults.

Each of the voices is the voice of a real person, not a composite. Each of the stories sticks to the truth of the person's experience, which experience I have verified to the best of anyone's ability, given the general closure of records. Obviously, the testimony has been edited for space, sequence of events, and coherence.

I have written this as a personal-journey book because any visit to the world of foster care is, inevitably, a deeply personal one: it is bound to tap into each person's own childhood as well as each person's sense of what childhood should be; to tap into each person's memory of family and each person's ideal of what family should be; each person's level of ease or dis-ease with the relationship of the state to the family.

I have kept my citation of sources to a minimum, largely for comfortable reading, but also because so very much exists in the professional literature on foster care/child welfare that one could say almost anything, find a citation for it, and thus "validate" it. This might get someone an advanced degree, but it will not get the reader even one degree closer to a feel for the reality, the textural truth, of the world of foster care.*

---

*I use the term *foster care* to refer to all children in state care—whether in foster family care, group homes, or residential or treatment facilities.

# SOLOMON SAYS

# SETTING
# OUT:
# AN
# INTRODUCTION

On November 2, 1987, six-year-old Lisa Steinberg was found comatose and brain-dead in the New York City apartment of attorney Joel Steinberg and the woman who had lived with him for twelve years, Hedda Nussbaum, whom Steinberg had chronically and severely battered.

Steinberg was charged with abusing the child, endangering her welfare, and with her murder. Pictures of him, hangdog, unshaven, being escorted to jail, appeared in the press—alongside pictures of the sweetly smiling, now-dead white child, Lisa.

The public was inflamed. In a frenzy of outrage, the cry went up: Why hadn't someone *done* something? Why hadn't neighbors reported their suspicions of abuse? Neighbors claimed they *had* reported them. Well then—why hadn't Social Services investigated? And what about the teachers at Lisa's Greenwich Village school? Why hadn't *they* noticed any signs of Lisa's abuse? Why hadn't *they* notified Protective Services?

1

Accusatory fingers jabbed in all directions. The news media both reflected and fed the outcry for weeks, until the drone of the legal machinery diminished to a procedural hum, and little Lisa took her place as a legendary landmark: a symbol of our moral outrage toward the abuse of children; our passion for the rescue of innocence.

"Do something!"

This same public outcry could have been heard more than a hundred years earlier, also in New York City, over the plight of little Mary Ellen Wilson. The legend of Mary Ellen has a number of versions. In an oft-recited one, she was brutally beaten by the man and woman with whom she was living. The abuse was discovered by a church worker and, since there were then no laws to protect children—as there were to protect animals—her case was brought before the court as seeking the protection of a "member of the animal kingdom."

On April 10, 1874, the *New York Times* quoted the child as saying:

"My mother and father are dead. I don't know how old I am. I have no recollection of a time when I did not live with the Connellys. I call Mrs. Connelly Mama. I have never had but one pair of shoes, but I cannot recollect when that was. . . . Mama has been in the habit of whipping and beating me almost every day. She used to whip me with a twist whip . . . a raw hide. The whip always left a black and blue mark on my body. I now have also a cut on the left side of my forehead which she made with the scissors. She struck me with the scissors and cut me. . . . Mama never said anything to me when she whipped me."

The uproar over Mary Ellen led to the creation of the Society for the Prevention of Cruelty to Children, and to the empowerment of other private child-rescuing agencies, such as the Boston Children's Aid Society, the Children's Mission, and the sweetly named New England Home for Little Wanderers, to remove children from their parents. These agencies' primary attentions were toward children living in what then (as perhaps now) was perceived to be the moral contagion of poverty: children thus thought to be at risk of *pre*delinquency. Their goals were mixed: as much to punish indigent ("idle") parents as to rescue children. In 1909, legislation was passed in Massachusetts to provide protection of children deprived of "proper physical care" because of "the neglect, crime, cruelty, insanity, drunkenness or other vice of their parents."[1]

Ironically, these child-rescuing agencies were the granddaddies of state, city, and county protective services—such as New York City's Special Services for Children (SSC), against which, in 1987, the public railed for the failure to protect little Lisa.

By the time the Lisa Steinberg tragedy occurred the imperative was everywhere: "Do you know a child who is being abused? Call this 800-number." Over and over, the public was being told to watch, to listen, to act, to report: being told that "help is available."

Yet in bizarre counterpoint to both the cries of "do something" and to the admonitions to report were headlines like these: "CHILD INJURED BY FOSTER PARENT." "CHILD AGENCY SUED FOR NEGLIGENCE." "ABUSED FOSTER CHILDREN SUE STATE OFFICIALS."

Explanations were reiterated in the system's defense, until they took on an incantatory cast: underfunding, understaffing, overburdening of caseworkers, caseworker burnout, caseworker turnover, poor training . . .

By 1988, child welfare/child protection had become such a politically hot subject that New York State, for example, had task forces and "brain trusts" at virtually every high level of state government: Assemblyman Albert Vann was chair of the New York Assembly Committee on Children and Families, with his own personal advisory group, informally called his "brain trust"; Chief Justice Sol Wachtler presided over the New York State Permanent Judiciary Commission on Justice for Children; the governor had an Interagency Task Force on Children and Families.

These, along with hundreds of other individuals and groups doing child welfare research, publicly or privately funded, government run or university affiliated, are meant to serve child welfare as wise King Solomons. But King Solomon's task had been a relatively straightforward one: Two women came to him, each claiming to be the mother of a particular infant; each claiming the other had smothered her own infant to death in her sleep. At which, King Solomon offered to settle the matter by dividing the remaining infant in half. One woman saw that as a fair solution. The other cried out in protest: better to give the child up than that! It was she, said Solomon, who must be the real mother.

What this says, of course, is that a "real" mother will value her child's well-being over all else.

Even this apparently straightforward case of to whom a child "really" belongs, however, allows for a contradictory viewpoint. In *The Caucasian Chalk Circle*, playwright Bertolt Brecht posed the question afresh. In his scenario, the birth mother was the selfish, greedy wife of a local governor in the imaginary land of Grusinia. There is an uprising: The Palace Guard mutinies. The governor is taken off to be killed. His wife, more concerned with saving her expensive clothes than anything, neglects to remember to take her infant when she flees. It is a peasant girl, Grusha, who watches over the child, escapes with it, manages to protect it. On Grusha's eventual return to Grusinia, the old regime has been restored. The governor's wife now demands the return of her child. In court, the matter comes before a buffoonlike justice (Brecht's stand-in for the wise old king). His decision? That the child belongs to the one who has taken care of it, Grusha.

These instances, these judgments, though, are child's play (as it were) in comparison to the dilemmas raised by late-twentieth-century child welfare/child protection policy and machinery.

What if Solomon's mandate had been to determine not who was the real mother, but rather what was in the best interests of the child? What if, once the case came under his scrutiny, he had set his minions to doing a home study of the woman who was the real mother, an examination of her means, her living arrangements? What if these minions suggested to Solomon that this woman had acted negligently toward the child in even allowing the circumstance that raised the dispute? What if her housing was found to be inadequate? What if his power included taking the infant into state care until the real mother was, in the terminology of his minions, rehabilitated (which would include: fulfilling her "goal plan"; securing adequate housing; having plenty of food in her refrigerator; taking parenting classes; going for counseling)?

At this point, we move into Brecht's scenario: The infant is placed with a foster mother, nurtured and raised by her for (let's say) eighteen months. During this time, the "real" mom has somehow managed to jump hurdles of ever-increasing height. Let's say she's gone from being on welfare to a steady job with the phone company, an apartment, has given up her boyfriend, and eschews even wine with dinner. She has visited the child in the designated office once a week for an hour, as directed. But the baby is now calling the foster mother Mama; does not remember the "real" mother as Mother (despite the one hour a week). To whom does this child "belong"?

Add to this for Solomon an entrenched system that, for all its language of benevolence and good intentions, has a history of imperatives that are entirely contrary and less savory: imperatives deriving from strong race, class, and gender bias.

Even assuming real and heartfelt concern for children's "best interests," now add on: underlying presuppositions from which the "shoulds" derive. What "should" a satisfactory childhood be like? (How many people do you know who had a satisfactory childhood?) At what level of "unsatisfactory" is it in the child's real interest that the state intervene? At what point (and for what reasons) is it in the state's compelling interest to intervene? All of these mega-questions invite inquiry that might appear to have the trappings of neutrality, of scientific consideration. Yet Solomon's response will be profoundly influenced not only by his class and cultural bias (and that of his minions), but by the resonance of his personal memories (and theirs): the wished-fors, and the should-have-beens.

All of this helps explain why the subject of protecting children is incredibly prone to abstraction and romance: why conversations that begin with the tragic death of a child like Lisa Steinberg will tend to wind up with cries about emotional "neglect" and psychological "neglect."

Now stir well and mix in another inseparable question, one that allows for even more galactic dialogue: What is it we truly want childhood to be so as to produce the optimum chance of children becoming the adults we, as a society, desire?[2] If what you desire is a warrior culture, then brutalizing and oppressing children might prove suitably hardening and might make them societally useful adults. If what you desire is women accustomed and acquiescent to sexual exploitation, then the routine sexual exploitation of girl children might be advantageous as well. The question of what really makes for a successful adult in our culture is apt to produce rancorous bickering among people of varying degrees of candor: Is it the ability to trust (in a corporate environment)? A mastery of "sharing and taking turns" (in an intensely competitive industry)?

Add, for our Solomon, the fact that you now have a well-established rule that the entire "Solomonic" system and all events and decisions are so "confidential" that they can even be withheld from or misrepresented to Solomon himself (not to mention the general public) . . . It is enough to make any wise old king take early retirement.

* * *

I set out on this journey into the world of foster care with this simple-seeming question: What is the experiential reality behind the words *foster care system*? What is the texture, the feel, for those whose lives have been intimately touched by state intervention?

Literature on child welfare abounds, God knows. Much of it is on the level of psychological shoulds: optimal conditions for child development; the question of psychological "bonding"; the "best interests of children."[3] Much of it reports on studies: some showing the results of foster care are not as bad as we'd thought;[4] at least one seeming to show there is no significant developmental difference apparent between children removed to foster care and those remaining in the home, even when the home situations are comparable.[5] There are studies that attempt to codify the characteristics of parents who abuse or neglect. And studies showing that these characteristics apply 70 percent of the time to parents who do not abuse or neglect.[6] There are studies providing evidence that abuse is generationally transmitted. And studies showing the evidence is that it is not. There is research attempting to show that the child him/herself plays a role in the abuse: is more difficult, irritating, fussier, etc. And research suggesting these traits are, rather, the *result* of abuse.

In fact, the world of child welfare is liberally littered with language that no one knows the precise meaning of. *"Neglect* and *abuse* are terms used to describe a wide variety of behaviors that have in common only certain effects on the child."[7] Which means that what a caseworker perceives as abuse and neglect may not be experienced that way by the child. Or that a child may experience damage from treatment that is imperceptible to anyone else as abuse or neglect.

Another large segment of the literature has to do with considerations of law, and of rights: the rights of the parent, of the foster parent, the rights of the child. The latter, particularly, exhibits a tendency common to considerations of children-in-the-abstract: an anthemlike idealization. For instance, how can the state "assure for each child a chance to be a member of a family where he feels wanted and where he will have the opportunity, on a continuing basis, not only to receive and return affection, but also to express anger and learn to manage his aggression"?[8] How can the state possibly assure all of that? And for each child? (On the evidence, even God is still practicing.)

I began to harbor an uneasiness, reading: All this "should-ism" about children seemed more about the shoulds of childhood itself. Few adults that I know would nod in recognition at all of that "feeling wanted" and "affection" as a reality of their own childhoods. And most adults that I know, faced with a long flight seated next to (or behind) a two-year-old who had learned to "express anger" but was only in the blueprint stages of "managing his aggression," would find themselves rethinking the entire issue of child abuse.

The literature was thoughtful. It was scholarly, and laudably well intentioned. And it was bizarrely—distanced. The more I read, the more I got the sense that it was actively designed to elude any persons not already trained to a professionalism in which part of the bargain was an agreement to agree not to question too closely what all this was really about: what all this was really for.

The very language took on the flourish of decoration, rather than substantive meaning. Place any weight on the meaning, and the words themselves collapsed. In what sense is the state, using its power to remove a child as a threat to coerce changed behavior, offering a "service"? In what sense is the mother whose child is being removed a "client"? In what sense is the child, reacting to the cruelty of a parent, and thus perhaps labeled "emotionally troubled" (and perhaps ordered to do time in a residential treatment center from which she can only gain release by agreeing she is "sick" and completing irrelevant tasks to prove she is "well"), a "client"?

All sense of real children, real women—mothers and foster mothers*—was excised from most of the literature.

To say this is not to question the human caring and true concern of the researchers and authors but merely to suggest that there is a curious sense of dislocation when, on the one hand, the

---

*The entire emphasis of the literature on foster care/child welfare is on women, as mothers, as foster mothers. Where the male adult in the home is the abuser, the entire focus of the case as recorded is nonetheless on the mother as the "client" from whom the child was removed (due to neglect and failure to protect). It is she who is the object of "rehabilitation." "The disproportionate visibility of females in the maltreatment of children is emphasized further by the relative absence of males. Martin (1984) reviewed sixty-six studies of child abuse published during a five-year period and confirmed the absence of attention given to abusive fathers. Only two of the sixty-six studies focused on fathers. Apparently, the mother is regarded as the primary responsible parent even in situations in which the male parent is the abuser."[9]

language is of lofty intentions for children and families—and, on the other, the nitty-gritty is tables, scales, percentiles, and estimated (as opposed to hard) data. It is to suggest that there is a sense of unreality to the juxtaposition of the language of passionate caring about children and the startling fact that no one knows how many children are really in state care under various labels, various systems—foster care, mental health, education, juvenile justice; nor how many are placed out of their home state. As one researcher was to say to me about Minnesota: "We know to a one how many chickens we send out of state. But we don't know how many children we send out of state."

What I hoped to do was set out with as much background knowledge as possible tucked in my mental suitcase. Because literature rains everywhere in the atmosphere like a permanent shower of confetti, I hoped for one authoritative source; one comprehensive work. Surely someone had tried to make order out of what was known.

It was with a sense of excitement, then, that I read that a classic text on the subject, *The Child Welfare System,* coauthored by Professor Alfred Kadushin (who has taught at the School of Social Work, University of Wisconsin at Madison, since 1950) and Professor Judith Martin, had just been updated and published in a new edition.

Go quickly, I thought. Order it. It was published by Macmillan. My local bookstore said they couldn't order it. I should call the Yale Co-op bookstore. They said *they* couldn't order it because no price was listed.

They suggested I call Macmillan directly, gave me an 800-number, and advised me to be prepared to be put on hold for sixty or seventy minutes.

I called. I was put on hold. The young woman who finally came to the call told me I could not order the book because no price had been listed. The book, she explained, was only meant to be sold in bulk order.

"Let me see if I have this right. You mean I cannot now, nor ever, possibly, nohow, buy this book?"

"I'm afraid not."

"Are you sure you have published it? Or is it printed as a secret document for 'eyes only'?"

Silence. A bewildered silence.

"Look. I really, really want this book. I want to read it. If you like, I will promise to return it. I'll promise to pay for it and return it. I'll . . ."

Finally, the woman at the other end of the phone line gave me—another 800-number.

This one called a computer. The computer told me if I wanted such and such, to press so and so numbers immediately; if I wanted thus and such, to press these numbers immediately; if I wanted this and that, to press . . .

My wit was too slow. I lost the computer game; put in more coins; tried again.

This time I pressed this and such numbers and got a live operator. I threw myself upon her as though she were the proverbial pond in the Sahara. She told me the name of a person I should speak with. If he was out, she said, I could leave a message with the "message center."

She was gone before I could ask how. Ah, but it came clear. A recording answered the ring. It told me that to leave a message with the message center I should press these and those numbers. My call would be returned.

Hanging up, I felt that I had been on a treasure hunt at summer camp and somehow gotten separated from all other campers and counselors. I did not feel much hope that either my message or I would ever be found.

It was! My call was returned by a real person. I was told the price: $36.40. I gave my credit card number. Astounding. The book arrived by United Parcel the very next day.

The volume was worth every bit of the trouble. I have relied on it heavily (though hardly exclusively) as background. If I tell you that for just one chapter of 51 pages, the bibliographical reference lists 190 sources, and for a 101-page chapter there are close to 500 sources listed, you will understand the scope of my gratitude. It is also pleasantly and intelligently written.

However, I mention this chase for another reason. It stood as a metaphor for all my attempts to get hard information: the sense that I was being blockaded. At every step of the way, early on, the thought forced itself on me: It would be easier to research the daily activities of the National Security Council than to research the child welfare system. In many ways, if you do more than accept the surface as presented, child welfare as a system—at least on the state level—feels like a covert operation.

The first thing you notice on entering the *official* world of foster care is the sense that you are decidedly unwelcome. Your footsteps echo as you move along silent, labyrinthine corridors.

The only other sound is of doors quietly clicking shut at your approach.

"We cannot help you. That is confidential." "I'm sorry. All that information is privileged."

Occasionally, you encounter a friendly soul who would enjoy talking with you, who thinks the questions you ask are worth the asking. He or she rushes off excitedly to clear it with superiors. That is the last you ever see or hear of that person.

The paranoia is palpable, and not surprising considering that states are facing a continuous barrage of suits against them: for wrongful removal; for failure to remove; for the gross maltreatment of numbers of children while in state care; for (in the case of New York City) the failure to place children they have removed anywhere at all. Indeed, in March of 1988, the Supreme Court agreed to decide whether public officials may be sued when their alleged gross negligence permits a child to be abused by a parent. (The Seventh U.S. Circuit Court of Appeals had thrown out the suit against the Winnebago County, Wisconsin, Department of Social Services and two of its employees the year before.)*

Nor does the constant barrage of what the system terms "anecdotal horror stories" in the media encourage those in the system to want to talk.

The reason they *need* not talk is the word *confidentiality:* this, along with *privileged information,* is such an ingrained idea in the world of child welfare that it is like rain and wind, something that is there and taken for a given. I asked numerous family law experts where the notion of confidentiality had come from: The very question seemed to take them by surprise; none, that I spoke with, had the answer to hand. Some suggested, however, that it is very closely tied to the precept that the treatment of juvenile offenders and of dependent and neglected children should occur in a court deemed nonadversarial. That this court would be avuncular (as well as paternal), there to deal wisely and

---

*DeShaney v. Winnebago County Department of Social Services 109 S. Ct. 998 (1989). U.S.L.W. 4218 (February 22, 1989). According to Chris Hansen, associate director, Children's Rights Project, ACLU, "The court held that where a child is not in state custody, the state has no general constitutional duty to protect the child from possible harm by his parents." In a personal communication, William L. Grimm, National Center for Youth Law, writes: "The Court in *DeShaney* explicitly rejects the following argument:

'Having actually undertaken to protect Joshua from this danger [from abuse at his father's hands]—which petitioner concedes the State played no part in creating—the State acquired an affirmative duty, enforceable through the Due Process Clause, to do so in a reasonably competent fashion. . . . We reject this argument.' 109 S. Ct. at 1004."

well, to "save" the child. Thus there was no need for due process for children; nor was there any need for the public to know what had been done to the child or what the child (or the court) had done, or why.

I will return to the issue of confidentiality later. However, no one of whom I inquired even bothered to pretend that the "best interests" at stake in this secrecy, at least in the late-twentieth-century world of child welfare, were the best interests of anyone other than the state. (I will leave it to you, the reader, to decide whether you think that the stories told in this book by those whose lives have been touched by the foster care system involve situations that could be called nonadversarial.)

Occasionally, the paranoia bordered on the comical. At one point, rather than disturb myself to go to the library, I called the protective services department of my own state to ask what the reporting laws were: information that not only should be but is commonly available to the public (who, after all, are among those asked to report suspected neglect and abuse).

A pause filled with suspicion met my inquiry. Then: "Why do you want to know?"

When I explained that I was writing about protective services and foster care, I was transferred to someone higher up; and from there to someone higher up still—who was on vacation.

Once in a while, though, as with some children in state care, I fell through a crack—and found myself granted an appointment. So it was that, perhaps because he had only been on the job a short while and had not yet caught the spirit of things, an Official with Special Services for Children in New York City agreed to see me.*

The interior of the building at 80 Lafayette Street is grim-institutional. Emerging from the elevator, I immediately sense myself in another universe; one of a "they," the executors of power. The faces of those at the desks outside offices are unsmiling, impassive. The endless ringing of telephones adds to the atmosphere of constant crisis and weary response.

The Official explains to me that he, in fact, has just had a crisis. A state facility has been closed and a great number of severely retarded children must be placed. The state does not

---

*I will not name this Official for two reasons: (1) with the high rate of administrative turnover at this agency, he most likely will not be there by the time of publication; (2) if he is still there, it is as well there remains someone with his bent toward candor.

have to deal with them. The city agency is where the buck stops: they are not allowed to refuse these children.*

When I say something about the system seeming always to be in crisis, he explains to me that New York City has major intractable social problems. He expands on that to say that the system tends to blame victims as ogres as a way to distract attention from structural problems. He speaks of how the well-intentioned people who focus on child abuse and neglect become part of the problem.

(Later, in response to my unavoidable question as to why, then, he is working here, he explains he has taken this job because—what is the alternative? Do nothing? At least one can try to make changes, do good.)

He admonishes me not to individualize the problem—not to look for individual "ogres" in the case-by-case area of abuse—but to deal with the broad political and economic problems. It is because people are dealing with the wrong problem, he says, that they are coming up with the wrong solution.

When I mention that the *public,* at least, seems to have the impression that child abuse *is* the problem, and protective services, the removal to state care at least temporarily, the solution, he grows restive. "The public just doesn't understand," he says. "The system serves a police function. Do they really want the entire resources of the state used to turn homes upside down?" His point? "We're dealing with a welfare issue. This is a system that regulates poor people. . . . It seeks to control potential violence. It targets an underclass. Foster care misses the point. It's a bogus system."

Certainly, the history of the state's role as super-parent bears this out. From its inception, the doctrine that gives the state the *right* to intervene and remove children—*parens patriae*—was as undemocratic in spirit as in practice.

It can be traced back to fourteenth-century England, where it was asserted as the "sovereign's responsibility toward the property and later the person of the insane."[10] It was then extended to include children of property: "The King as political father and guardian of his kingdom, has the protection of all his subjects, and of their lands and goods: and he is bound, in a most peculiar

---

*More than a year later, this crisis would lead to this crisis: "20 Retarded Children Shunted to Squalid Foster Care Homes." (*New York Times,* 29 March 1989, A-1, B-4.)

manner, to take care of those who, by reason of their imbecility and want of understanding, are incapable of taking care of themselves."[11] The sovereign's concern, of course, was not the children but the property the children were "of."

The doctrine, then, was quite blunt: "The rich indeed," said Lord Blackstone, "were left at their own option, whether they will breed up their children to be ornaments or disgraces to their family."[12] The full attention of the state was directed toward the children of the poor.

In the Colonies, as well, the first statutes focused entirely on parental poverty: on children who were poor, orphaned, illegitimate. The first system of foster care was indenture. Children were bound out in involuntary servitude (that they might get "necessary instruction in trades and useful arts," of course).

With the passage of the Constitutional Amendment of 1865 prohibiting involuntary servitude for blacks, the question of its constitutionality as regarding children came up. The solution was to—rename it: the Placing Out System.

The mid-1800s in New York City saw an "infestation" of vagrant children, estimated at about ten thousand.[13] Charles Loring Brace, the first secretary of the Children's Aid Society, came up with the idea of draining the city of these children by shipping them out west where there was a need for their labor (i.e., Placing them Out). Once out west, the children were then placed on what was effectively an auction block. The difference between this and indenture? The children, travel weary and a couple of thousand miles from anything familiar, had to nod their assent to the stranger who spoke for them.

The development of Societies for the Prevention of Cruelty to Children in the last quarter of the nineteenth century signaled an adherence to the original intent of *parens patriae:* the legalized, coercive removal of children from the suspect poor. However, almost from the beginning there was a tension between the police function implied by *parens patriae* and a social work approach. It was a battle of attitude and orientation. But attitudes and orientations are expressed in language: and it soon became clear that language could be co-opted: that the coercive intent of the state in its police power guise could be formulated in the language of care and concern.

The establishment of the first juvenile court in 1899 both confirmed the state's powers and outfitted them in the language of benevolence. This court was said to be for the child's own "salvation." In a landmark case in 1905, the court stated,

"Whether the child deserves to be saved by the state is no more a question for a jury than whether the father, if able to save it, ought to save it."[14]

It was people of good conscience, of feeling for children, who supported all this good-news language for children. And—because it is always possible to do bad in the name of doing good—it was people of good conscience, of feeling for children, who would spend the next eighty years fighting the system that had been set up in the name of care and concern.

Children had become a commodity.

As public support for the "rescue" of poor children gained ground, and as states became willing to provide funds for services related to managing the problem of "predelinquent" children, a decidedly entrepreneurial spirit enveloped the issue. "Reform" schools were developed. (Who could be against reform?) And "industrial" schools. (Who could be against industry?)

Coincidentally, the industrial schools gained much in popularity as a place for children at exactly the time when child labor laws were being enacted; when unions were forming. As industrial schools would open, the proprietors would contract with small businesses for the services of their young wards. Industrial schools became workhouses sprayed with linguistic cologne.[15]

The dichotomy between punishing the poor, preventing predelinquency (in reality preventive detention)—and the nobler, more lyrical hyperbole that exists today about what should be for children—can be found then. Even as statutes were enacted that authorized removal of children growing up in idleness, mendicancy, and vice, a White House Conference on Dependent Children in 1909 stated:

"[H]ome life is the highest and finest product of civilization. It is the great molding force of mind and character. Children should not be deprived of it except for urgent and compelling reasons. Children of parents of worthy character, suffering from temporary misfortune, and children of reasonably efficient and deserving mothers who are without the support of the normal breadwinner, should, as a rule, be kept with their parents, such aid being given as may be necessary to maintain suitable homes for the rearing of children."[16]

In other words, then as now, what was being said (rather than remove children, offer economic and other assistance to help poor women cope) was entirely other than what was being done (removing "neglected" children).

It was the 1935 Social Security Act that first provided federal monies to the states for the care of dependent and neglected children (Aid to Dependent Children: Title IV-E).

By then, SPCCs had largely faded from the picture and the slack been taken up by public welfare agencies. From 1920 to the early 1960s, the issue of children, child neglect, child abuse, largely faded from public consciousness—before exploding again. Why?

As Kadushin and Martin say, "The roller coaster history of child maltreatment as a social problem deserving of public attention requires some explanation. It exemplifies the general finding that programs in favor of children serve a variety of needs only one of which, and not necessarily one of prime importance, is the concern for children."[17]

In 1962, the band struck up again. Child abuse was rediscovered. Why?

It was in that year that C. Henry Kempe, a pediatrician, published his findings about what he termed the "battered child syndrome." That in itself, however, might have been no more than a nine-day wonder had other forces supporting the escalation of the issue not been at work. Certainly, the sixties being an era of social activism and concern for the rights of the less powerful members of society helped. As did the fact that the Children's Bureau, a Federal agency established in 1912, had fallen comatose in the past years of disinterest in children's issues, and was in danger of being vaporized. "Battered children" gave them an issue to take into their purview.

Politicians embraced the issue as well. It was an issue that allowed for no apparent opposition. Who is *for* battered children?

Renewed interest was also, Kadushin and Martin tell us, "the consequence of the social distance between those who labeled the problem, namely middle-class professionals, and those who were most frequently labeled as child-abusers, relatively politically powerless lower-class families."[18]

Perhaps the most important component was that the issue of battered children (which quickly segued into the issue of child abuse) was sanitized by being placed in a medical category; seen as a "social illness." In that, the rush to the fore of experts on children—pediatricians, psychologists, and psychiatrists—played a role. But also "government more readily adopts issues which are constructed as a social illness [and therefore require only that individuals be 'treated' and 'cured'], than issues which confront long-established power arrangements."[19]

From start-up, the newly vaunted issue of child abuse focused almost entirely on mothers as abusers, with only the odd socially disadvantaged male thrown in. Since, as has been often recited, the longest-established power arrangement in the family has been that fathers held all the power, and since it was perceived that these were only poor folks we were talking about anyway, nobody thought to get nervous.

The identification of the problem as one of medical "deviance" for which "help" was being offered greased the path for expanding state intervention, for aggressive outreach and case-finding, and for calls to the public to report suspected abuse and neglect. The word *neglect* was extended beyond physical neglect to include psychological, emotional, and even moral neglect.

Nineteen sixty-two was also the year the Social Security Act required each state to extend its child welfare services to every political subdivision of the state.

"Do something!"

By the 1970s, however, it began to be clear that nobody at all knew what "somethings" were being done.

As best anyone could determine by estimating, there were some five hundred thousand children in state care in 1977.[20] But no one really knew. Nor did they know where many of those children were. Children were revealed to be frequently placed out of their home state—sometimes in facilities that were exposed as inhumane and brutal. The phrase *foster care drift* appeared, to describe thousands of kids dumped or dragged into the system and picked up and put down in multiple placements—more or less at the whim of whichever individuals and agencies held power over them. Not only that, but there were multiple doors through which children could enter (and reenter) the system: An abused child might be labeled emotionally disturbed, and thus enter through the mental health system and be placed in a residential treatment facility; a child running away from parental abuse might enter through the juvenile justice system as a "status offender" (a status offense being an offense that would not be considered an offense if committed by an adult).

The federal government and members of Congress became upset. The federal government, after all, was paying more than 50 percent of the cost for children eligible under what was now called Aid to Families with Dependent Children (AFDC).

Along with others, Congressman George Miller (D-Cal.) began work on legislation that would bring about reform. The resulting legislation was the Adoption Assistance and Child Welfare Act of 1980 (P.L. 96-272). This was aimed at reducing the number of children in foster care and the amount of time children spent in such care. It aimed to assure that "reasonable efforts" would be made to keep mother and child together, and—failing that—"reasonable efforts" made, then, to reunite them.

In fact, the act requires the establishment of a statewide program of services to avoid unnecessary foster care, and reasonable efforts by the agency to prevent foster placements. It says that the state may not receive federal matching funds for any child coming into foster care without there has been a judicial finding that the agency has indeed made such reasonable efforts to prevent placement.

The act also requires there be a statewide program of services to aid in reunifying the family once the child has been removed. It requires there be a written case plan, wherein reunification is the goal. And it requires this plan to be reviewed by a court or administrative agency at least once every six months to insure that the plan is being implemented.

Within eighteen months after a child has been placed in care, the act requires a hearing to determine whether the child should be returned home, placed for adoption, or placed in another permanent home.

The penalty for noncompliance is loss of federal funds.

Hailed as the gateway to good news was the catchphrase *permanency planning*. This phrase, of course, suggests that the previous policy had been one of *im*permanency planning—and indeed, in one outstanding way that was true. Since the goal of state intervention has long been the family's reunification, it was believed that children and foster mothers should not become too attached. Thus, many children were routinely moved when it was thought that the placement was too agreeable. This legislation stated (again) that the goal of permanency planning was to reunite the family, or, failing that, to place the child in an adoptive home, or, failing that, to plan for long-term foster care.

One of the major requirements at the other end of the federal funding leash was that each state would implement and operate what was called, chillingly, an "inventory" of all children in the state's care for the previous six months. The idea of it was thrilling. At last it would be possible to have some real idea about what was really going on! How many kids, where they were, which kids, why.

Nearly eight years later, there would be total confusion among the states as to what constituted literal compliance with the act.

Some states would be found not compliant, while other states with exactly the same policies and practices would be found compliant. Such federal oversight as there was, was eccentric and entirely superficial, relying on the review of what the agencies wrote in the case record.

At a hearing of the House Select Committee on Children, Youth, and Families, on April 22, 1987, Congressman Miller asked Jane Burnley, associate commissioner of the Children's Bureau, DHHS (Department of Health and Human Services): "[W]hen we went back and we took a look at whether or not these reviews were being made and attempts were being made to keep the children out of foster care, in fact what we found was a very casual system. It was simply running children through . . . its system without that kind of intensive review. . . .

"But my question is whether or not you're looking at the paper that says there's a reasonable effort or whether or not you're looking behind the paper to see whether or not in fact that's what's taking place.

"And I suspect at this time, for whatever reason, we're looking to see whether on paper there is a procedure in place to expend reasonable efforts. But, in fact, that may not be taking place. . . ."

Ms. Burnley: "You are correct, we do not go beyond to look at whether or not ones [sic] reasonable efforts are indicated as part of the judicial determination that placement was necessary and continued placement in the home is contrary to the job [?] welfare."[21]

So states did not have to comply: They had to *appear* to comply. Judges could simply sign off on the agency's testimony that "reasonable efforts" had been made.

The labeling of children remained tied capriciously to a funding advantage. As Brian F. Cahill, chairman of the Public Policy Committee of the California Association of Services for Children, would testify before Miller's committee: "I'm particularly bothered . . . by our administration and specifically the Director of Social Services, who would love to dump all the delinquent kids [meaning those labeled delinquent—status offenders: truants, runaways] who are in the foster care system over to the youth authority system because she has to pay 95 percent of the non-Federal share to have those kids in foster care. It's a powerful incentive to say they're not abused and neglected, they're delinquent & therefore not eligible for foster care funding."[22] According to Cahill, the words *dependent, delinquent, mentally ill,*

*educationally handicapped* tell you nothing about the child—only
what service delivery door they came into the system through.
And the reason all these different service guys would not get
together is called *turf*. Coordinating services would threaten the
existing categorical funding streams; it would reduce the influ-
ence of the particular professional specialty. So the child welfare
industry is really several subindustries, each competitive, rather
than cooperative, with the others: child victims are commodities.

Eight years later, there still would be no "inventory" of
children in state care. Eight years later, no one knew how many
children were in care, or exactly why they were in care, or where
they were in care.

It is true that the *estimated* numbers had decreased by 1983
to 276,000. But from there the numbers began climbing again. It
is true that subsidizing adoption led to an increase in the number
of children adopted. But that led to reports that now there was
*adoptive* care drift, replacing foster care drift: that children were
being adopted, tossed back to the system; adopted; tossed
back . . .

It was also discovered that at the very minimum one out of
five children in the system was actually *re*entering the system
after having been "reunited."[23] There was an estimated 29 percent increase in the number of child deaths due to parental
maltreatment and abuse.[24]

Eight years later (May 12, 1988), Mary Lee Allen, director of
child welfare and mental health for the Children's Defense Fund,
testifying before Miller's committee, said, "It is still not possible
to do any comparative analysis of foster care and adoption data
among states even on such simple issues as the number of
children in care."[25]

Despite all the marvelous language, all the good intentions
framed by this legislation, the hundreds (if not thousands) of
"Solomons" attending the issue, the hundreds of thousands of
people working in the child welfare system at every level (from
federal to state and local—to private, to university)—still, on
April 22, 1987, Congressman Miller said, "Today, nearly seven
years after enactment of the reform law, we are revisiting the
continuing crisis in foster care of which I warned a decade ago."[26]

The reader may well be wondering, by now, as I was to
wonder often, what all this is for; what all this is about. Some
readers may even be reminded (as I am) of *The Hitchhiker's
Guide to the Galaxy* by Douglas Adams, in which, following the

destruction of the Earth, Arthur Dent and Ford Prefect escape to the Galaxy where—among numerous other adventures—they seek the Ultimate Answer to Life, the Universe, and Everything from a gigantic super-computer named Deep Thought. When the answer is delivered, it is—42. And Prefect and Dent are then forced to go in search of the Ultimate Question to which 42 is the Ultimate Answer.

The reader may also be wondering: What does all this really mean in terms of the human beings it affects? The trouble with all this information is not just that it is frustrating and depressing, but that it is vacant of all human and emotional content—even as the horror stories of individual children's torture and death in the home are all too filled with it.

My informational baggage packed as well as possible, I set out among people across the country whose lives had been intimately touched by the system: foster children, former foster children, foster mothers, child welfare professionals and personnel, biological mothers.

What was the system's personality? (Systems do have a personality, as do department stores, and companies, and even governmental bureaucracies under different regimes.)

When the state intervenes, taking over custody of a child in the role of super-parent, what is that parent like? How do its agents behave? How does the child experience that super-parent? How do those who provide surrogate care experience that super-parent? How does the parent, whose child is removed from her, experience that super-parent?

It was only by listening, I thought, that we could even begin to consider the larger questions: What is child "abuse"? What is child "neglect"? Why, if the goal is to reunify the family, is no distinction made? Clearly one can be more optimistic about that goal if one has a woman who is good to her children, but is economically extremely needy, than one can with a woman whose world-script is that her baby is possessed by a devil that needs to be roasted out of it in the microwave.

What is the level of intervention we can legitimately tolerate—under what circumstances—with what safeguards? Do we tolerate a system that targets only the poor? (Or do we tolerate it only so long as it does not *say* this is what it does?) Can the middle class stand the scrutiny of a system that does not do that? Can we bear the vast expense of removing children to state care—compared with the lesser expense of financing housing (say), so the family can remain together? (Or is that coddling the undeserving poor?)

Can we tolerate a system that operates virtually without public monitor, without review, without checks of any kind? Or can we only tolerate that so long as the system does not bother us, and continues to tell us it's all being fixed. It's better now. Honest.

Can we accept as the only evidence of what is going on the paper trail of a case: the so-called case history, reflecting entirely the caseworker's (or caseworkers') side of the story: his or her (or their) perceptions or biases, his or her covering up for personal shortcomings or pressures and time constraints? As the Official from SSC said to me: "What is a case history except a retrospective biography? I could write a case history on you that would make you look like a terrible person—simply by playing up your weaknesses."

If members of the public—members of families (defined here as adults with children legally in their custody and care)—are subject to state scrutiny, should (or shouldn't) the state, when it takes care and custody, be subject to public scrutiny?

In a sense, the stories in this book, the voices you will hear, taken together, comprise a what dunit: a different kind of mystery; one of real life, not fiction. The mystery of what is wrong in the way we are thinking about the problem posed by children who really do need intervention and help, that has allowed such a Byzantine and rudderless industry to develop.

These voices by no means represent every kind of story, certainly not the worst stories. People who have been deeply traumatized as children are not always articulate. Children who are murdered do not grow up and talk. I did not, for instance, go into prisons, though I was told that a large proportion of the prison population grew up in foster care (which does *not* mean that a large proportion of those who grow up in foster care wind up in prison).

I did not go into the very worst neighborhoods. I did not, as well, get any stories from Native Americans, though I was told stories that bordered on the grotesque. Recent immigrants, once spotlighted by the system, find themselves utterly helpless in the face of language barriers as well as poverty. Their stories are not included here; the language barriers were mine as well.

I listened to far more stories, far more people, than can be given voice here. There are, in the world of foster care, stories of every conceivable kind—from the magnificent women who have taken in and raised hundreds of children, to those adults who were brutalized in terrorist institutions during their childhood. I was not in search of the best or the worst, but of what was, and what was representative.

My goal was to allow the public to hear the voices of some of those previously buried under a rubble of abstractions, a deluge of tales of disaster; to allow the public into a conversation about what is said to be public policy—toward child abuse and neglect; about policy regarding the state's role, its responsibility, its accountability. To allow the public to feel intimate with the actual reality; to know what they were wishing for Lisa Steinberg when they cried out so passionately that "something" should have been done.

As Ira Schwartz, professor and director of the Center for Youth Policy at the School of Social Work, University of Michigan, was to say to me:

"The bottom line as far as I'm concerned is that the child welfare system has really run aground. . . . It's in very deep trouble, very serious policy and programmatic crisis in this country. And I think that organizations like the Child Welfare League of America and others are not sensitive to the depth of the crisis, the severity of it. And the kind of fundamental rethinking and refocusing that is necessary.

"I think we need to go back to some very basic assumptions that people have taken for granted. The whole business of abuse. What is child abuse? What is a 'substantiated' complaint? What is the role of protective services? A lot of the things that the system has kept hidden and secret, but has masked under the guise of professionalism, have given the lay person the impression that we're operating a system which is based on science. And it's really based on—not even art. So a lot of the basic assumptions need to be fundamentally reexamined—and in the public arena. Because over the past seventy-five years or so that the public child welfare system has been in existence in this country, it has largely been under the control and dominance of the professional community. And I think that's been a mistake.

"The public's been locked out of policy decisions. And I think that we suffered immensely as a result of that. The system has been largely unmonitored and unregulated—and has demonstrated a remarkable inability even to protect children, to guarantee their basic health and safety. So I think the whole thing is just chaos."[27]

With that in mind, I invite the reader along on this journey.

# A "NOT-STORY"

At eighteen, Kim is blond, with a pretty, intelligent face. She comes in carrying an obviously weighty, oversize shoulder bag. With her is her adoptive mother, Gerri, blond as well, in her late thirties, friendly and obviously self-confident. They are neither of them women anyone would associate with the words *foster care system* (or *state care,* or *out-of-home placement*). They haven't, they assure me, got much of a story at all.

"I lived with my mother, my father, and four sisters," Kim begins (when I ask what the not-story is). "When I was four years old, three of my sisters and me were put in a group home—a girls' home. I like to say it was poverty. My mother, it turned out later, was very sick. But I think they took us away from them because of the poverty. I think it was my mother who talked to them about putting us in Saint Catherine's. The first time. I was four.

23

"I was the youngest girl in the home. I don't remember much from that time—except that it wasn't that bad. They were nuns who took care of us at this time, so we lived in groups—one person took care of twelve of us.

"Okay. So when I was seven, my mother took me out. Two of my sisters were old enough to get out on their own at this time. And then my sixteen-year-old sister stayed.

"I was home for two years.

"And this was when my mother—let's see, how can I say this?—she's mentally insane."

Affirmatively, Gerri says, "She's crazy."

"I guess you'd classify her as a schizophrenic. I don't know. She abused us. She was—just not in this world. She heard voices."

Gerri, smiling at Kim: "She would try and get rid of the spirits. Say, 'You know the spirits are in you.' So she would try to drown you."

"Beat us," Kim adds. "At seven, what happened was she was mad because I wanted to spend a holiday with another family—like a volunteer family that I had met. She got mad and took me out anyway. I do remember going home sometimes. I was a child, you know. I wanted to be with my mother.

"So then I went to live with her for two years. By the time I was in the fourth grade of school, she became worse. This was like the height of her insanity. My father worked for an oil-rigging company, so he was always away. Every six months, he was home for a couple of weeks. And they fought. They beat the hell out of each other.

"I missed a lot of school during this time. I always had a lot of violence."

"Were you," I ask, "afraid of it?"

"No—uh, it's hard to explain. I always thought families were like that. I didn't know there was another way. I mean sometimes, when she did outrageous things, I thought, 'Oh God, that's weird.' Now that I look back, I know that people knew—just by the way they looked at me. How my teachers talked to me.

"So what happened was that finally my sister who was still in the group home told the worker that my mother was crazy, and that she needed to get me out. And the principal of my school had called up. I had missed weeks and weeks of school."

A pause occurs. Gerri prompts: "And they came and knocked on the door and she wouldn't open the door . . ."

"Yeah. They came a few days in a row. They came Wednesday, Thursday, Friday. And finally Saturday morning she went to the door, my mother, and opened it up. And they took her away. Two policemen. And the social worker came and got me. It was horrible. I didn't know what they were doin'."

I am thinking: "This, in the world of foster care, is some people's idea of a 'not-story.' "

"I thought I was going back to Saint Catherine's," Kim says. "And I said, 'Well, can I get some stuff for her?' And they said, 'No. They'll have everything for her.' Well, eventually we got evicted and everything I had was on the street, and I came back and got some of it."

What happened?

"They put her in a mental hospital. They put me in a temporary placement. It was in a really bad neighborhood. An all-black neighborhood. I went to an all-black school—there were only three or four white kids in the school. My fourth-grade year. And I had to fight. Stuff like that. It wasn't so bad because I was a kid—so I didn't think, 'Oh, this is bad for me.' It was just kids who came from the projects and everyday fistfights. I guess I was fortunate because I never really got a lot of flak from kids my age. Plus, I was a nice kid, so people liked me. But if I had been a problem child, I think everything would've been different.

"I only lived there a few months. And then they put me back in Saint Catherine's. When I went back they were in the process of taking all the nuns out and putting other people in. Let me explain. It was funded by Catholic Charities—then it went state.

"I was nine. And also at that time my father died. That was sad. And my mother—as I say, she was hopping around an institution at that time. She kept escaping."

Gerri: "She recently escaped from another one. Climbed down a tree."

"My father—I never really got to know him. When I lived those two years with my mother, he was injured. And he had to stay home for a couple of months. I got to know him a little bit at that time.

"But I had thought before he died that he was going to take me out of the home and I was going to live with him."

"What," I ask, "was the worst part of it?"

"There were so many—terrible—things about it. Loneliness. Frustration. See, I'm really one of the fortunate ones. Because I really lucked out in everything. As I was growin' up, I always had a lot of friends. People who cared about me. Outlets. So it isn't like I was really miserable. I was very fortunate. But some of the other girls—they rebelled against the system or whatever."

I ask what it was like, Saint Catherine's, the second time around.

"When I got older, I started to realize that the way they were running the place—we had privileges, and—if you got in a fight with somebody, you couldn't do certain things. Like you couldn't watch TV. Or you couldn't go to the store. Stuff like that.

" 'Privileges' were things you could do. And the thing that they were doin' there, like testing out different ways of doing things? One week, it was one way; and the next week, another. I really hated that.

"And every week we had like three meetings to go to. I hated that. First, we had a group meeting—the people who lived together. Then, they decided to do this thing where the student social workers would come in and on Wednesday nights we had a different meeting, with different people from different groups. Just to talk about 'our problems.'

"*They* were the problem. That's what I could never understand. Week after week—'I don't have anything to talk about. I don't want to talk.' And then they would take things away from you, privileges, if you didn't participate. Which I thought was wrong. You got a lot of flak about it if you didn't participate. Week after week, all these depressing things we'd talk about. It was so funny: it was like, 'Let's agree—everything you don't want to think about, we'll talk about.' They'd talk about their family situations—a fight they got into with their friend. That was a lot of to-do. If you had an argument with somebody, you brought it up in a group meeting. 'You used my brush and I'm mad at you.'

"And then we'd have our private meetings with the social workers. That was so funny. They'd sit down and—there's nothing I could say. I'd just sit there and laugh. 'I don't have any problems this week. I feel great.' I guess they were trying to do what they thought was best. And also, it wasn't like the girls who lived in this home were problem children, discipline problems. They had problems, like me—their parents were nuts, or poor, or—had sicknesses, or their parents abused them, incest—stuff that was *not* their problem. It was just that they needed somewhere to live."

Over and over, I was to hear of a system permeated by the illusion that counseling, therapy, is the solution to reality. Most often, it was *coercive* counseling: a demanded confession that you—the child—are the defective one; that *you* are emotionally damaged. If you do not admit this, do not confess it, the system is punitive. The issue seems to be power, even while the procedure is named help.

"When the state took over," Kim says, "a lot of changes happened. One was that they accepted people who were discipline problems. And I was getting caught in that. I was about as normal as I could be, given the situation. But the fact that they were gearing the system toward those girls was kind of strange. So I asked my social worker for a foster home.

"And Gerri had asked for a foster child."

It is nothing if not impressive, as I was to learn, how little "happy endings" had to do with a "plan," and how much to do with sheer luck: the child fortuitously endowed with charm, intelligence, spunk; the coincidental appearance of a compatible adult . . .

Why, I ask Gerri, were you looking for a foster child?

It was funny, she tells me. She had become accustomed to doing things every weekend with her sister's two kids. But then they had moved out of town. So she wound up with a lot of time on her hands on weekends when she wasn't working. (She is administrative level at a local industry.) She considered adopting a child, but—"This one wants you to be married, and this one wants you to be Catholic. There was always something."

Someone then told her about an agency in California that helped people adopt "special" kids. She called and discovered that the kids they meant were seriously handicapped. She said, "No, really, I'm not bucking for sainthood. I really wish I could. But I really can't do that by myself." So the agency suggested she call her state department of social services.

She says, "So I thought about that: What kind of kids would I get? And finally I said, 'Well, what could it hurt?' So I called. And it was really a strange coincidence because I got this woman who said, 'Well, I'll tell you what happens. When our kids become available for adoption, they've usually been in foster care, and the foster family has the first right of adoption.' And this was the first time I'd really heard about foster care. I said, 'Okay, why don't you tell me some more about that.' She said, 'What age are you interested in?' I said, 'Well, between four and eight.' She said, 'Have you thought of a little bit older?' I said, 'No. Not really. Why?' She said, 'The reason I say that is because tomorrow I'm scheduled to meet this little girl at Saint Catherine's who's just asked for a foster home. And everybody just raves about her. She's on grade level, and she's real smart. She wants to go into professional sports.' "

Gerri said she was interested. She made an appointment to talk with Kim at Saint Catherine's.

"Kim was so excited by my coming," Gerri says teasingly, "that she overslept. She was still asleep when I got there." She looks fondly at Kim. "Little did I know—that was an omen! Yes. Kim sleeps very well."

While she was waiting for Kim to get herself together, Gerri spoke with the social worker. "She was real nice, kind of normal. A lot of the ones I met were so far from normal. Extremely strange. I'm a kind of normal person. I don't make a lot of demands. I'm independent. I don't need somebody to tell me every move to make at home to do stuff. I just found them really very peculiar. But this woman was a real down-to-earth person. She couldn't say enough good stuff about Kim.

"So then I met Kim, and she was this little bean pole. And she says, 'Well, do you want to know my story?'

"I said, 'Not really. Unless you want to tell me.' 'Well, it's like this and this and this . . .' Just the cutest little teenager. Just adorable."

Before Kim moved in, not only did she have a social worker, but one was assigned to Gerri, and there was a pre–foster care worker, then a preadoptive worker. Gerri had to attend training classes, which she found dismal. "This worker—she said, 'The book says this.' No personal commitment to the program, to the book itself, to what she was training. And they come to your house—maybe twice. First of all, what the hell could they see? I could be insane. I could be anything, but I could behave normally for one hour. Twice.

"In my case, I don't think they have too many single people. And so right there, there's suspicion. Am I a lesbian? Am I afraid I'll never get married, so I have to go ahead and have a kid by any means?"

To Kim, Gerri says, "And then we never heard from a social worker—after you moved in—for about a year."

"I remember it was months and months," Kim says. "And then there was this big scare. There were two or three cases where the foster kids were killed. And that's why they started checking up on foster homes. So one day a social worker came by and stayed about five minutes. She never talked to me alone.

"But there were so many social workers. They were always changing. You always had to uproot in all these situations. Every time you'd talk to a new person, they'd sit there saying, 'Tell me your story.' I can't remember any of my social workers' names. They never meant anything to me. I hated most of them. The majority of them were—to me—unstable. And the student social workers—I guess they were taking classes and they took us for examples. 'Let's analyze your situation.' I didn't like that at all. It was like being a mouse in a biology class."

Gerri says, "Every time I saw them talking with a kid, you could see them thinking, 'Okay, how am I gonna word this in my report?' Everything came down to documentation. And they analyze, they analyze every move these kids make. And they *presume* to have the answer for why the kid did everything.

"I remember reading the case records, and everything in there was so cold. Every time they gave her an aspirin, they had to write down that they gave her an aspirin at this time. They write it down and then they turn it over to the next social worker who came on that shift. 'Look what Kim did today.' You don't raise kids like that."

It turned out that, though Kim did not know it at the time, her father's relatives did try to get her, did want to raise her.

"I didn't find out until March of this year. I went to visit my father's family. I had never met anyone outside my immediate family. But when my father died, an uncle got in touch with me, and we wrote for a couple of years. When I was thirteen and moved in with Gerri, we got in contact again. I called him. And we wrote.

"And finally last year Gerri and I went up there. And I have a lot of family. I didn't know how much I have. I went to this uncle's house, and the aunt and uncle—they have three children. A boy my age, a girl a little bit older, and a younger boy. And they told me that when my father had died they wanted me to live up there with them. They had called down. They said that Saint Catherine's social workers said that I was taken care of. Financially.

"See, my father left me social security. Two hundred and fifty dollars a month. So—maybe it was the money. Why else?"

Gerri says, "That was a real fiasco. First of all, they never told me when I got her she was getting any money. After she had lived with me for about a month, I got these two checks— forwarded to me from Saint Catherine's. With a note attached, saying, 'These are Kim's social security payments. Please have the name and address of the recipient changed'—to me. I got on the phone and called the social worker I liked. 'Jane, what is this? I never knew Kim was getting social security.' *She* didn't know they were getting money for Kim. So she checks into it, and she says, 'Well, no, you can't be the recipient. The state still has to be the recipient.' So I said, 'Okay. Fine.' I wasn't looking to make the money, but to put it in a fund for her for later on. But they told me they would be the recipients.''

Peculiar?

''And on holidays,'' Kim says, ''I had nowhere to go. I think it's just horrible.'' Kim starts packing her cigarettes and her lighter into her huge, bulging bag. ''So you're going to find a lot more interesting stories than ours. Other people's situations, I'm sure, are so much worse.''

Gerri says, ''My friend was just saying, 'I don't understand how you two connected after all that.' Me too.''

''What in the world can you possibly have in there?'' I ask, as Kim gives a great shrug to position the strap of her bag on her shoulder.

''The thing about the big bag,'' Gerri says. ''When she lived with her mom and they used to get evicted a lot—one step ahead of the rent sheriff—and a lot of times her stuff was thrown out after a couple of weeks. So she was always losing her stuff. When she moved in with me, she'd saved everything since she got to Saint Catherine's. Every single thing. It was about two years before she could start weeding through that: 'Okay, well now I could throw away this. Now I could throw away this . . .' ''

A happy ending, then, to what—I was to learn—was an uncommonly straightforward story.

# COMPLICATIONS I

Among the first things one learns on the journey into the world of foster care is that it requires a patience with complications. Complications are normal to anyone's life, but they tend to take on a sort of spectacular complexity once magnified by the power of a bureaucracy, and by the personas of those who act to enforce that power.

From the viewpoint of a child, certainly, there is seldom any rationality to events. But frequently, I discovered, the same holds true for the adult observer. More often than not, the law governing outcomes seems the law of caprice. The overall image was of a giant game of whimsical dictates—somewhat like the children's game Simon Says ("Do this. Do that"). Only this one was called Solomon Says.

In many stories, as well, the cast of characters threatens to become utterly unwieldy. No forms besides pageant and spectacle seem to accommodate the number of players: but pageant and spectacle would seem inappropriate to what often is a quasi-Dickensian reality.

Charles Dickens, however, did not have to deal with the caseworker for the child, the caseworker for the biological parent, the caseworker for the foster parent, the caseworker who does home inspection; with the supervisors for each; with a sequence of placements of often multiple kinds; with a caseworker turnover that has Miss Jones abruptly becoming Miss Brown; and with any number of people who act facelessly, from behind a desk piled high with forms and regulations and case history folders.

To absorb the complications, one simply needs to take a break sometimes and return (and return again). This was the case with Pauline Mason.

I am in a hotel room in a small mid-Atlantic city. Pauline comes in—a slim, vigorous, smartly dressed black woman in her early fifties. She walks with a slight limp, with the use of a cane. This, she explains, is the result of a tumble she took in her late forties—while roller skating.

"Roller skating?"

"Oh, yeah! That was fun!"

"Pauline, you work?"

"Oh, yes. I have been employed in a senior clerical position for fifteen years." She adds, "Call me Pauli. That's what my friends do."

As we begin to talk, it becomes clear from Pauli's bearing, her easy manner, her genuine outrage at points, that Pauli has confidence in herself as a Respectable Citizen, a woman who holds her integrity and dignity dear.

"How," I ask, "did you first get involved with foster children?"

"See, I never *intended* to get involved. I have six children of my own, but they're all grown, out of the home. And I just wasn't accustomed to being alone. I needed companionship. So first I applied for adult foster care. I wanted to take in adult retarded people. With my hip, I wouldn't have to do as much for them physically. This is what I wanted—and it took me almost a year to get an application.

"This institution I applied to, they had retarded people they were trying to put in the community. And I wrote and I called and I called. They'd promise me they were going to send me one, and then they'd just forget it.

"So I took a day off from work and my son took me out there.

And they gave me the application, and to rush it the woman was gonna help me fill it out right there. See, that's why a lot of people just give up. The runarounds. They tell you they don't have enough foster people—but that's *why* they don't have enough.

"Anyway, they helped me fill out part of the application. Then they told me they needed three references. And they told me that they would prefer that one was from my doctor—they wanted professional people. So I had a dentist friend, and his wife was a doctor—they wrote me a reference. And my medical doctor. And then another girl, who grew up with my kids—who was teaching special education—she wrote me a glowing letter. And I sent all these things in. I got a physical. I sent that. I sent everything they said they needed.

"And then they said someone was supposed to come out to my home. And they never came. So I called. And the man I spoke with said it was the first he had ever heard of it. Then he said he would come out and see me. Meanwhile, the state also sent someone to evaluate my home, to see if I had a problem with cleanliness. All that was taken care of—everything they had asked for.

"So he comes out to my home and he pulls out all these same forms, asking me these same questions, and telling me that I had to have three letters of reference. And I said, 'What *for?* I've already sent all that stuff.' He say, 'Mrs. Mason, there is nothing in my folder. The first I heard of you was when you called my office.'

"So then I had to start bugging the woman who'd helped me fill out the forms the first time. You know: she had been out all week, and the papers were on her desk *someplace,* and she had to find time, and I had to just wait . . ."

What eventually got done, in the mysterious ways of the foster care world, was that Pauli's name was given to a hospital-affiliated institute (we will call it the Parker Institute), which had programs for caring for ill children and had recently started a foster care program—separate from the city foster care program—to deal exclusively with what are called special-needs children. (In the common currency of child welfare, special-needs children can be anything from a child perceived to be emotionally troubled because of abuse, to an unconforming adolescent, to a young person with one or more physical disabilities. Wherever it is applied, the label prompts extra funds. However, the Parker

Institute's definition was stringent: it meant the seriously disturbed, the fragile, the handicapped.)

"So," Pauli says, "Parker called me. And the lady came and
told me they'd been given twenty children to place. These were
*children* now, and I'd asked for adults."

Nonetheless, Pauli agreed to take the training Parker offered:
in everything from artificial respiration to dealing with difficult
behavior firmly but not physically. She passed, and got a certifi-
cate as a specialized foster parent.

"It didn't matter," I ask, "that you were working?"

"No. With Parker you have to have another income. They
investigated that. You couldn't be in it for the money. I didn't
have a husband—so I had to have a job. Otherwise, they wouldn't
have considered me.

"See now, the city pays you $231 a month for a child—which
doesn't even pay room and board, although they put on the check
'room and board.' Parker paid $1,300 a child—and any extra you
incur, you just keep the receipt and they will reimburse you."

"Who funds Parker?"

"The state."

"So you mean that a program funded by the state pays $1,300
a month and a city program, also majorly funded by the state,
pays $231?"

"Yes."

Laughter.

"So I told them I couldn't take a child I would have to lift.
She said would I please wait. There would be kids that would
have mental or behavioral problems, but they would be able to
maneuver on their own. And that's the kind of kids they felt I
would be good with. So that is what I was waiting for."

In the meantime, however, there were (capital C) Complications:

"This girl that grew up with my children, Pat, she had two
kids, Dana and Ali, and she wasn't taking care of them. She had
never taken care of them: Most of the time, off and on, they had
been with me. And I did what I could for them. Half the time
they were in the home by themselves.

"Dana was raising her little brother. She was his mother. In
school, the kids called them old stinkies. The little boy went to
school with his pants hanging down to here and his rear showing
and no panties on underneath. They were just dirty and filthy—
that's when she *sent* them to school. Most of the time, she didn't.
She kept them out for one whole year.

"Finally I called the Department of Social Services. Her friends called. My daughter called. And none of this was done anonymously: We gave our names. We didn't care if she knew. We had done everything we could to help her. But we couldn't. So our concern had to be—for the children.

"One day she came to my house and she asked me to keep them overnight. And she let them stay two weeks. And she had not brought them a medical care card. She had not brought them any clothes. The little boy was sick; he had diarrhea, and he was having bowel movements on himself. And I had to go and buy him clothes.

"Ali had ringworms, and he had them so long that the ringworms had gotten into his bloodstream, and that's what was causing the diarrhea. Pat knew he had diarrhea—and she left.

"She did give us two prescriptions. My son had to go to the bank and get money to pay for them.

"When she finally came back, she was angry with me. 'Cause I told her she was wrong. She took them away and told them they better not come to my house.

"Then one day the kids called me. It was the weekend of George Washington's Birthday. They called Friday and asked could they spend the night. I said, 'Well, if you want to come, I'm in the house.' I said, 'Where's your mother? Does she know you're coming?' They said, 'Yes. She's at home. In her room. With her boyfriend.'

"So I told them, 'Okay, come on.'

"Well, during this time, her boyfriend beat her up. The police took her to the hospital. When she went to the hospital she had to have surgery—he had been beating her up a long time. Pat went into the hospital on Monday. I didn't hear from her till Thursday.

"Then I went up to the hospital to see her. She asked me, could she come to my house to recuperate. Because there was no heat in her house. And I told her okay, but she couldn't stay on. See, I didn't know how I could try to help these children— without helping their mother. How were they gonna feel if they knew their mother was sick and I didn't help her when she needed it?

"So while she was there, the man from Protective Services called me at work. He said he wanted to talk with Pat. I told him, 'She's at my house. You can talk to her, but call first and make an appointment.'

"So he went there and he told her he was gonna take the

children. He didn't want to leave them with me. He said it wasn't allowed. I wasn't a blood relative. Well—*wherever* they put them in foster homes they would not have been blood relatives. They wouldn't even have known the kids. And he started making all these excuses, giving different reasons—and I had told him I was licensed by Parker. He said, 'Well, but you're registered with the state.'

"I said if that was the problem, I'd give up Parker: 'I don't want you to take these kids and separate them.' 'Cause that's what they would have done. And they needed each other. Dana'd never been without Ali. Ali'd never been without his sister. She's the only mother he'd ever had.

"So in all this uproar, he finally decided to put the kids in my home if I could promise him that Pat would not take them out. I said, 'You don't have a problem there. She don't even *want* to take them out.'

"This was March. I'd had the kids since February.

"Then suddenly, on April the third, all these social workers started calling my job—asking me to take children."

"You mean," I say, "that on the one hand they didn't want to even leave kids with you that you'd known all their lives—and on the other they were after you to take foster kids?"

"Yeah! They heard I was interested in foster care and would I be interested in taking a child. And I tried to explain to them that I had these two kids—this wasn't settled yet. And I was registered with Parker Institute as a state foster parent, and I just couldn't do it right now. And they asked me could they call me at a later date, and I told them sure.

"Then this one lady called, asking me to take a little girl named Laura. I said to her the same thing. And she said they paid $14.35 a night. This was a special child with special problems. She said they pay $14.35 per night if the child has special problems. They pay $25.00 a night for two weeks. After the two weeks, if the problems were alleviated, they went back to the regular price—of $14.35.

"Now obviously if a child has had problems all her life, they're not gonna be cleared up in two weeks. But I didn't say anything. I told her things were just in too much of an uproar. I couldn't take any kids right now.

"So she said, 'All right.' Then she called me back. Her supervisor had told her to ask me could I take the child just for the weekend. So I told her, 'Sure. I will.' "

What Pauli found out later was that eleven-year-old Laura had been in the system a little over a year; that she had been in sixteen different placements, including two hospitals when they had no place else to put her, and numerous so-called sixty-day homes.

"And in some of these foster homes she had been raped. And they'd never pushed it. They never took it to court. They tried to cover it up. They say, 'Laura *accused* people of raping her when it wasn't true.' But they never investigated—so how would they know?"

"What was it like," I ask, "your first meeting with Laura?"

"It was after work—April third, so it wasn't dark, and the door was open. I saw them when they drove up. So I went to the door. And I saw this cute little girl—she really was—with all these braids in her hair.

"But she had all these cardboard boxes—all these great big cardboard boxes. And I was wondering to myself, 'Why are they bringing all this stuff when the child is only going to be here for a weekend?' What it turned out was that this was all of her worldly possessions. 'Cause she had been put out of another foster home, and they had no place else to put her or her things.

"What I did was I smiled at Laura and said hello. I knew that *I'd* have to be uncomfortable goin' in a strange place with strange people. So the social worker, Miss Bowers, told me—she didn't tell me anything about the child's problems—she say she was a nice child, and she was very helpful around the house.

"I say, 'All right.'

"And she told me this is her last day on the job.

"I say, 'If this is your last day on the job and I'm only supposed to keep the child for the weekend, who's gonna pick Laura up on Monday? How'm I supposed to get to work?'

"She say, 'Well, we left a note on the desk of the new social worker.' Left a note on the desk. And they don't get in till eight or eight-thirty—and I'm supposed to be at work at eight."

"What was Laura's reaction, coming in?"

"Well, what I did was—I thought that another child would be able to make her feel more comfortable than I would sitting there asking her a lot of questions. So I brought her in and we sat at the dining room table and we talked for a few minutes—not about anything personal. I introduced her to Ali; Dana wasn't there at the moment. And I said, 'You all talk together for a few moments. I gotta go upstairs.' And he made her comfortable. They started laughing. They sat there and they laughed and they talked and they got to know each other.

"Then—that was Friday—I let them have a slumber party. With my granddaughter and the little girl next door. I made these beds on the living room floor, to make it fun for them. And I gave them knickknacks and stuff and hot dogs and ice cream. They just had a good time.

"And meanwhile, I had sort of fallen in love with her."

As I was to quickly come to realize, that, in itself, usually signaled a major Complication.

(To be continued)

# "FALLING
# IN
# LOVE"

The context in which I would hear the phrases "falling in love with" a foster child or "becoming very attached to" a foster child was virtually always one in which such evidence as was made available to the foster mother strongly suggested there really was nothing much else for the child. And yet nothing gave the system so much leverage; nothing seemed to bring the threat of disaster down faster.

Why? It does not seem remarkable, after all, to "fall in love" with an essentially homeless and parentless child, even unexpectedly, without intending to: people unexpectedly "fall in love" with puppies in the dog pound all the time; people respond to notices of stray animals who need a home all the time.

If that same pup was being reasonably well cared for elsewhere, or could be within a reasonable period of time, and if one were only asked to care for it for a while as an emergency measure—one might become fond of it, but it would be most unusual to 'fall in love with' it.

But then—if the journey into the netherworld of foster care requires a tolerance for Complications, it also requires that one develop the skill to entertain six conflicting or murky thoughts before breakfast.

Children should be removed to be protected (Family unity must be preserved). Biological mothers should be offered "services" (Most of the services needed are not on the menu of the intervening agency). Foster parents should be nurturing, caring (They should not care to the point of taking independent initiative or action on behalf of the child, even when, in their perception, the child's real welfare is at stake).

Not only are distinctions not delineated between abuse and the far more amorphous *neglect,* but there is a failure to distinguish between the adult actively doing the abuse and the one who may be a victim herself: the situation in which the woman also is badly battered, for instance; the one in which a mother has only just learned that her child is being sexually abused by her husband or her ex-husband.

Even the seemingly clearer distinction between a voluntary placement by the mother and an involuntary court-ordered removal is easily blurred. It is far from unusual to hear of a single mother with a severe medical emergency placing her children temporarily while she has surgery, and getting out of the hospital only to find the placement is now court-ordered, involuntary—because her housing is now deemed inadequate, or some other fault has been ascribed to her by a caseworker and become part of the record, now that she has brought herself to the system's attention.[1]

A similar lack of clarity obtains when trying to understand the definition of the role of a foster mother. Despite tremendous linguistic ingenuity, the role continues to be best defined by what it is *not.* Though the child's room and board are nominally reimbursed, the foster mother is not salaried, and thus not an employee. For a while, the word *vendor* was tried: but again, there is no monetary purchase of product or service. Recently, because of the foster mother shortage, linguistic attempts have been made to paint the role with status: there is talk of foster mothers as "professionals"; of their role as part of the "treatment team." Much is said about foster parent "training."

There may be some few localities in the country where foster mothers and the system have reached a place of mutual respect and cooperation. From the testimony of foster mothers I spoke with around the country, though, the most relevant training would be akin to basic training in the military: training to take directives without question; to snap to and salute authority without hesitation; to perform tasks according to inflexible and sometimes mindless rules—or even according to the whim of a caseworker, who now assumes the status of your superior by virtue of being the agent of state power over you and the child. No shadow of complaint must cross your face. Ever. Or else.

I was shocked when I first heard that—for all the chronic handwringing about the shortage of foster homes for children—any contentiousness on the part of a foster mother was liable to trigger the threat that the child would be removed, and that the woman would be given no further foster children. "How Teutonic," I thought, "how bizarre." Yet why my surprise? The state really does have unfettered power, after all, unmonitored, unchecked, and subject to legal challenge only when gross results can be proved by one of the few legal services committed to the young, the poor, the powerless.

My dis-ease with the ruthlessness of this notion, then, was simply a by-product of my middle-class grounding. By middle class, here, I mean less an economic category than one that holds an ideation (or illusion) about rights, about autonomy, about one's standing as a citizen, and holds a belief that the welfare of children is what the system is all about.

Although the language requiring nonattachment has been modified, the imperative remains tacit in new category constructs in many parts of the country: there are temporary foster homes, long-term foster homes, and preadoptive homes. Thus, a child who has made a promising adjustment in a temporary foster home can—should the system decide this is the 'permanency plan'—be summarily moved to a long-term foster home. Just because.

Clearly, anyone who responds to a publicized emergency by offering to take in a child temporarily had best not become too invested in what becomes of that child afterward.

By tradition, the state has removed children from the poor and placed them with the working class. It has offered them for adoption to the middle class, but—despite public service announcements indicating that the need for foster parents is class-indiscriminate—the state has been wary of placing its wards with those who might feel they have the right to challenge its assumptions, its dictates, its acts.

In 1987, New York City had a crisis of what were called boarder babies: infants simply abandoned in hospitals, who remained there for months, even years. Much publicity brought thousands of white middle- and upper-middle-class families, who would never before have thought of being foster parents, to offer their help.

What happens when a well-regarded professional woman, and upper-middle-class (as defined by education, standing in the community, as well as by joint income), wanders into the foster care system?

Molly is married to a prominent attorney, and has two children of her own; a spacious New York City co-op; a full-time housekeeper. Molly remembers 1987:

"New York City had an enormous population of—*healthy* boarder babies. I'm making that distinction as opposed to a lot of other children—AIDS babies, drug-addicted babies, handicapped—who were living in hospitals. And nothing was done to find them placements. They were there for a variety of reasons—from their mothers walked out without taking the baby, to women who were homeless and either not permitted to take them, or, in many cases, had no place to take them. They were there for months. Some children were there over a year.

"My husband and I have two children of our own, and the last thing we wanted in our life was another child. But—seeing so many of these babies was just breaking me down. Actually, it was my husband who said, 'Why don't we take a child? Because we can give it a home until they reunite him or her with her family.'

"So we went through the regular procedure to become foster parents with an agency in New York. And we were given a little girl—at the time we got her she was thirteen months old. And my expectation was that, once they had actually placed the child in foster care, then, to meet their mandate, they would go out and look for relatives. We hoped they'd find a kindly grandmother, happy to embrace her granddaughter.

"So we took this beautiful little girl, Nikki, home—a child of white skin, but classified as Hispanic. She, it turned out, had gone home at some point, but then had been brought back to the hospital with pneumonia—and was never picked up. We were also told at the time that her mother was a drug addict and had had a previous child, a nine-year-old, whom she had given up. And the father, who was not her husband, and was not the father

of the previous child, had visited the baby one or two times at
the beginning in the hospital—and then disappeared.

"The day we picked her up, the city social worker was
supposed to deliver her from the hospital to the foster care agency
where we were waiting. After waiting there five or six hours with
one of our children, they finally decided we'd go to the hospital
and pick her up—because the city child protection workers had
gotten screwed up.

"So at that time I talked to several people in the hospital who
had been doting on this baby who'd been there so long, and were
very happy to see her leave. They said there hadn't been much
contact with her family at all.

"We took her home, and at the beginning, of course, developmentally, she was in nowhere-land—because she hadn't had
any opportunity. She couldn't walk. She couldn't talk.

"And through contact with our children, this baby flowered
amazingly. To begin with, she didn't even crawl. Because—the
way the children were living in this hospital was—they were
living in cages. When the babies got old enough to maybe walk
or get out of their cribs, which were made of metal, the hospital
put a top piece on it. So we're talking about *no* opportunities.

"Anyway, she started to walk and talk within six weeks. It
was amazing."

"What," I ask, "was the agency like?"

"The child welfare agency was—the opposite of helpful, in
several ways. The caseworker that was assigned to the baby had
her own agenda. For example—this is from the first visit—her
questions to me had to do with things that were age-inappropri-
ate. She might as well have been talking about an eight-year-old.
They sounded as if they were from a handbook somewhere, but
she'd read the wrong chapter. She didn't see the baby in front of
her. One of the questions had to do with whether her toilet
training had been completed. Well—certainly any kind of current
thinking is you don't even start to train a child until after two
because they don't have the muscular control. To say nothing of
*this* child.

"Now when we'd picked Nikki up at the hospital on a Friday
night, she'd had to be given a full medical checkup before she
left. And then we were told that we were required to take her
back on Monday—to the agency—for a medical checkup. That
was the agency policy.

"So we brought her back, and suddenly they were preparing
to give her a full set of inoculations. And I said, 'This child has

lived in a hospital all her life. I think she's *had* these inoculations.
We should check the records before we subject her to this.'

"They were astounded, upset: 'Call the top supervisor!'—
that I would even suggest they check. And babies get feverish,
fretful, from these shots. And I didn't even know if there were
medical repercussions from double-dosing.

"They wanted us to sign a form saying that for all her medical
needs we would bring her back to the agency, or if it was the
weekend, take her to an emergency room at the city hospital.
This was not a city or state regulation: this was their own policy.
And I said to them, 'I'd rather not do that.' It's a three-hour wait
every time you go down to the agency. I said our children had a
doctor who was chief of pediatrics at one of the major city
university hospitals. And that I would prefer to treat Nikki as I
did my other children. And that—made them crazy.

"At one point, a midlevel supervisor threatened me. They
were going to take the baby away because I was refusing her
proper medical attention.

"It was at that level of communication."

From the outset, then, it is obvious that the world of foster
care is not the world as most of us take the world to be. What
sense can be made of the idea that an agency under contract to
New York City's child welfare system, self-described as in permanent crisis, would require that each child it places be brought
to its waiting room for every sniffle, each sore throat or earache?
Or be brought to the emergency room of a city hospital, to wait
with the slashed, the victimized, the truly desperate, when a
competent physician is immediately available? Mightn't it make
more sense to require a pediatrician's report after each visit?
Phone access to that pediatrician?

"Anyway," Molly continues, "we subsequently learned that
Nikki's mother was a heroin addict, *not* a young woman; and
furthermore, she was in jail for selling. And they located Nikki's
father, who turned out to be a man of about sixty. He told me he
didn't want this child, he couldn't take care of her, it wasn't a
man's job to take care of her, he didn't want any responsibility
for taking care of her. And that maybe he had some relatives in
Puerto Rico who might take care of her. He certainly did not
wish to take her home—that's why he'd left her alone in the
hospital for most of her life.

"But he agreed to visit every two weeks with the child—at the agency.

"The point is that the agency agenda was to get him to take her home."

That is the goal, after all, reunifying the family.

"What," I ask, "was the visiting like?"

"The way they scheduled a visit was that they sent you a postcard—which often arrived after the date, but sometimes on the day—saying you will come in at X hour. Nothing was ever scheduled except between nine and five on Monday through Friday—and we were two working people. But here we were trying to put Nikki first in everything; we went along with it— which turned everybody's life upside down.

"The father did speak some English, but he either hadn't indicated that to agency workers or they hadn't noticed. They got one of their people to be the English/Spanish interpreter—for Nikki—who spoke *no* language.

"The first visit, the interpreter was a young woman, about eighteen, smiling and talking to Nikki in Spanish. And Nikki was responding. And the social worker said to us, 'Isn't it lovely! She understands Spanish!' I mean, fine—would you like to smile and talk to her in Russian?

"She was then classified as needing a Spanish home because this was her language."

How curious. It is entirely reasonable that members of the black and Hispanic communities should be passionate in their concern that black and Hispanic children be placed in homes that are culturally compatible: that this would be a severe political pressure point on the system. It is too easy to envision what might happen otherwise: the removal of children from minority homes for placement with white America. It is a should, however, that—like so much else I was to see in the world of child welfare—is easily corrupted when codified; when no one is looking at the real child, the real circumstance. The fact is that Nikki had no one for thirteen months. And now a match had been made that seemed entirely satisfactory to the child, and that was becoming enormously emotionally important to Molly and her family.

"After a while," Molly says, "the baby would—cry. Someone else could hold her, but they had to be carefully introduced. But the agency had its own procedure—pluck her away and carry her upstairs. And I became known as a troublemaker—because I insisted on accompanying her for the first few minutes—until she quieted down.

"These insensitivities—they sound minor. But they're not minor to someone who is one year old. Sometimes the father made the visits, and sometimes he didn't. He never told anybody ahead of time what his plans were. So we'd show up. And he wouldn't.

"Another thing about the agency—we were planning to go away for a five-day trip to Pennsylvania, and naturally we were planning to take Nikki. And they refused us permission because that was leaving the state. So our whole family has now become hostage—to the system.

"One of the things I noticed when her father did show up was he got angry at her very quickly—for instance, if she dropped a toy on the floor.

"Meanwhile, needless to say, my husband and I became very attached to her. The children were referring to her as their sister. And so we went back to the agency and we said, 'We would like to be considered as adoptive parents.' We were very afraid that they were going to take her and put her in what they call a preadoptive home. We were not considered adoptive parents, and also we were supposedly not suitable because we weren't Hispanic. This is a blue-eyed child, by the way. Not that I cared. We'd said we would foster a child of any race. Nikki just happened to turn up who she was.

"After we declared our willingness to adopt the baby, they started putting a great deal of pressure on the father to take her, and we were becoming very alarmed. Because we knew he didn't want her; we also thought from the way he dealt with her he couldn't handle her. We just thought it would be a disaster.

"We also knew something that had been dropped—that he had an apartment in the city, but he had nothing in it except a mattress on the floor. Which either meant he lived that way, or indicated he didn't live in New York. And I think his erratic visit schedule in fact had to do with when he came to New York every few weeks.

"I was at court in the waiting area outside the hearing rooms several times. [There would be only one hearing, but it was always postponed.] And you hear all kinds of stories—on both sides. There are natural mothers sobbing because they've lost their children. And maybe their children were taken away for very good reasons. But the interesting thing was some of the women didn't know *why*—and some of them were angry about it, but some of them didn't *know* why.

"So finally there was a hearing scheduled. This was the first hearing she'd ever had, and it was about whether Nikki should be remanded to foster care—as though she hadn't already been with us for several months. And we wanted to keep her. We would have allowed the father to visit her. If he wanted to stay interested, I thought that was nice. I just didn't think she should live with him.

"But I didn't know at that point that he had been charged with molesting a child."

Surprises. Always, in this world of foster care, there are these little surprises.

"The agency didn't tell us when family court hearings were scheduled, but we managed to find out. And we showed up. The New York State law was that the foster parent does not get to talk at such a hearing—unless you've been a foster parent for the child for a continuous twelve or eighteen months, something like that, and we hadn't been. There at the hearing was Nikki's mother, in handcuffs. The father. Each of them had lawyers. Lawyers for the city, and lawyers for the agency.

"The lawyers for the city and the agency objected to our presence at the hearing. The judge overruled that, but we could not speak.[2] What turned out to be the legal situation was that a petition of neglect had been filed against the mother. During the hearing we heard incredibly lurid descriptions of her neglect and abuse of this child—which we had never heard before—while the baby had been home for that brief time. And also about a scene at the hospital when the mother had been screaming about needing her drug. The city had filed a petition of neglect against the mother—on the basis of all these things.

"But they never filed a petition against the father—who, I would think, morally and in every other way, was as responsible as the mother for leaving Nikki in the hospital for so long. But the authorities didn't see it that way."

It is odd. At a time when much fuss is being made about fathers as equally the parent; when fathers are winning custody of children in divorce 70 percent of the time that they go for it,[3] it remains women who are charged with child neglect, with the failure to protect—even in cases where the male parent is the abuser of the child, or equally culpable. During the entire duration of my journey—among people, and in the literature—I virtually never heard of a father being charged with child neglect. If the present demand is for the father's equality as parent, with equal *rights,* why when it comes to accountability is he anything *but* equal?

"We had written to the judge beforehand," Molly says, "not about the mother because we didn't know anything—but describing the things we had observed during visits, and the things we had heard about his having no adequate home for Nikki at this point. And also the things he'd said to us about not wanting her.

"I overheard SSC's [the city's] lawyer ask the father—this is how I found out about it—'What about this arrest for child molestation? This is really hard to explain away. Can you tell me about it?' Then the lawyer noticed me—and he walked down the hall with the father, so I didn't hear the answer.

"It was the unanimous recommendation of the city and the agency—the agency almost always agrees with the city because it's the contractor—that Nikki be released immediately into her father's custody—with visits from the mother."

"How," I ask, "were you treated in court?"

"The SSC and agency lawyers were punitive. They knew who we were. They were angry. Whether that was because we had enough of a name to make noise, I don't know. Their language to each other—I heard them talking—was, 'This case will be too closely scrutinized. We've got to get that child out of that household.' "

"Why would they have thought you wouldn't make noise about that?"

"Because you're required to sign this agreement, one passage of which is, 'no media exposure of the children without explicit permission.' "

"You mean there's essentially a gag order on you no matter what happens?"

"Yes. There's a media clause in the contract with the agency. And the other foster parents I've talked to are also afraid to have their names used publicly. Because they're afraid of vindictiveness: that the agency will take the child away. And they have reason to be afraid. Because the agencies do.

"I think while Nikki was with us it was that. But I think there are other factors that came into play. One is, I did not and still don't want to publicize the baby and her family. Because she will be the target.

"Then there's the matter of not wanting to confront all that pain. And there's a fourth factor. When a child comes back into foster care, the agency is supposed to get in touch with the previous foster parents and see if they'd take the child back. They often don't. But I didn't want to close that door, because it's very likely that Nikki will be in foster care again in her life— if she is not now. I don't think they'd give her back to us, but I didn't want to do anything to hurt her."

"There's no legal way you can find out where she is now?"

"No. There is no way."

"Does that seem outrageous?"

"This is outrageous. And the other thing is—take the father and the child-molesting charge. It might be a comfort for us to know the story on that. Why was he arrested? Which they know. And they tell us not to worry about it. Well, why aren't we supposed to worry about it?

"The judge did express reservations. He was chiefly concerned with the mother's visitation because of all he'd heard. He had no legal reason to deny the baby's placement with her father, though. Because the city had never filed a petition charging that he'd neglected the baby. The upshot was, the father got Nikki. The mother was granted visits to be supervised by—the father."

As I listen to Molly, I find it uncanny. The system, in this instance, seems to have forgotten what all this was about: an infant abandoned by *both* mother and father in a hospital, left there for thirteen months, with *no* sign that either parent had any intentions of retrieving her. Why, in that instance, did the most important thing seem to be the reunification of the "family"? It is no wonder that, at minimum, one out of five children who enter the foster care system is, in fact, *re*entering it, after having been reunited with those from whom that child was removed.[4]

"What," I ask, "was the upshot?"

"She was released into his custody, but he didn't take her home. Because he didn't want her. Never had wanted her.

"And the judge got the city to say they were going to get him some child care training. The hearing ended at about four-thirty in the afternoon. And the agency insisted that she be delivered to their office at nine o'clock the following morning.

"It was horrible the next morning. We took her into the agency with many of her things. All the while I'm aware that her father has—nothing. And I want to give—her father—all the baby furniture, the stroller, all the stuff, so he'd have something for her. And we got there—and waited four hours. In that sense, it ended just like it began.

"He arrived with this woman who seemed to be like a fourth or fifth cousin, if she was in fact related. Who was going to take

Nikki for a while. The woman gave me her name and number. She'd never met beautiful little Nikki, who cried when the woman took her, and reached out to me.

"About a week later, we got a van and delivered all the stuff to the household where she was living.

"That was very sad for us. The woman was nice, and invited us in. And Nikki ran over to us. And by this time, Nikki had a pretty good vocabulary in English. But the woman, who was American born, and spoke excellent English, wouldn't talk to her in English. She was mad that Nikki didn't speak Spanish.

"And Nikki could feed herself—messily, as a toddler does. But the woman wouldn't allow her to feed herself. It was just sad that all of the kinds of social skills she had mastered were being squashed.

"I don't know what has happened since.

"We left our names and phone numbers—the agency was upset that we gave this information, by the way—and said, 'If you need anything, or help, or just want to know something about Nikki, call us.'

"I didn't hear from them. When her birthday came, I sent her some presents, and I didn't hear from them at all. When we called the number, it had been disconnected. We also sent letters there and they were—I just don't know what happened.

"Once the baby was given to her father she was no longer the agency's responsibility. And the city didn't take any responsibility for following up because the father was considered the perfectly adequate parent: he was never even accused of neglect or abuse. And what I think is that—Nikki is back with her mother. I assume that as soon as her mother got out of jail, she took Nikki back. I *assume*. Because the father never did change his mind. He agreed to take legal custody, and the myth was he was taking her home. But he didn't.

"It was not a happy period of time. It's not happy now. And I think the thing I failed, as a parent, to think through—is—I mean Nikki will always have a piece of my heart, and I'll never heal, but I'm a grown-up and I can live with that. But I failed to think out the consequences for my own children. They have pictures of her on their wall. They have her in their scrapbook. You can't tear her out and pretend she didn't exist. And they don't have the information. . . .

"We couldn't possibly tell them we thought she was going into an unsafe situation. But by pretending that hers was a normal family—our children had made the assumption that Nikki's parents had been sick and were now better; that was the only circumstance they could think of—they can't understand why her family doesn't stay in touch with us. And let them see Nikki.

"My daughter, who's going to have her birthday, she says, 'Can't we send an invitation to Nikki?' You see? It comes up in all these ways. And then we have to go through the whole thing. And I can say, 'Well, I can if you want. But you know I think her family moved. And they must have moved too far away.'

"So it's hard to deal with. You start—if not out and out lying to your own children—then you get pretty close to it. But it's never understandable because—we have friends who've moved. And we've written to them and gotten answers.

"I overheard my little girl tell a friend of hers who has a little sister, 'I used to have a sister too.' Her mother looked up at me. What is this? Has there been a death in this family?"

Catch what comes next, though:

"A couple of weeks after the hearing—somebody at the agency called—and asked if we would take another child."

"They really did? What did you say?"

"I said,"—Molly switches to a tone of flat, wry understate-ment—" 'I-don't-think-so. It-was-a-very-difficult-time-for-us-all.'

"I would never do it again. For two reasons. One is, it left scars on my family. The other is—even beyond the heartbreak—you do it to help. You do it to help the child. And if you can't help—I mean I saw punitive reactions toward Nikki. I feel we may even have done things that hurt her. We babyproofed the apartment when she came to live with us, which is not hard to do. And she was free to explore. To pick up things, and look at magazines, and experiment with her soft toys by dropping them on the floor. And these were the things she was being punished for—by the woman her father had stashed her with: because she was being messy, or however they interpret it. So in a way we set her up to be hurt."

The very last word anyone speaking with Molly would use to describe her is *sentimental*: the first words might well be *incisive* and *tough-minded*. Her tone of voice, in telling this story, is controlled; her language carefully chosen and precise. A few weeks after we spoke, she sent me this note:

"I can't bear to think of Nikki's future with a heroin addict for a mother and an aging, ailing man for a father who is—at best—uninterested in her. What can be in store for her but more rejection and neglect?

''My husband has told me he has had the same dark thoughts. We love Nikki and if she'd stayed with us, she would have had a bright life full of affection and promise.

''Where is she now, I wonder? Does someone hug her and tell her bedtime stories? Or is she crying in the dark?''

# COMPLICATIONS II

$A$gain settled in a chair in my hotel room, Pauli continues:

The morning after Laura's first weekend with her, Pauli called her office to explain that she would be a little late.

She then called the Department of Social Services and talked to the new social worker. "And I told them that I had enjoyed Laura very much and that I was considering keeping her since they had asked me to. But I had to talk to the Parker Institute first. I had a meeting at Parker that night—we had classes once a month. And I had to get everything straight with them first. So I asked them if it was all right for Laura to spend another night. And I would let them know Tuesday whether or not I could keep her."

Pauli also requested that someone come out anyway to tell her more about the child's problems so she would know what she would be dealing with. About 10:00 A.M., the social worker, Miss Jefferson, arrived to tell her a bit about Laura.

"Half the stuff turned out not to be true," Pauli says. "She did tell me that Laura was sexually active. And that she had been raped several times. But she also said her mother had had Laura selling her body to buy dope for the mother. Now in the first place, her mother's not on dope, even today. She admits she is an alcoholic, but she has never been on dope. And different things—that Laura was a thief, a liar—it sounded as though she was almost trying to turn me off. But it didn't do that. I felt the child needed help more than ever."

When Pauli got to Parker that night, however, she found everyone acting cool toward her.

During the break she talked to the assistant director about the new situation. She, in Pauli's words, seemed to "have an attitude"; was being nasty and snotty.

After the class was over, she asked the director if she could talk with her, and Pauli began by saying she didn't like the way the assistant director had spoken to her. "Did you feel she was calling you a liar?" the director asked. Pauli said, "Yes, I did." And that's when she learned that someone from the Department of Social Services had called Parker and suggested that Pauli was licensed by both the state and the city: that she was trying to gyp them both.

Pauli explained that this was untrue: that it had been the city Social Services that had called *her*—to get her, please, to keep this child for the weekend. And that, in these few days, she'd become fond of Laura.

"Well, Mrs. Mason," the director said, "you know if you do the city system, they're only going to pay you room and board."

"I know," Pauli said. "But what can I do? This child needs help."

The director agreed to look into whether Laura might qualify for the Parker program.

"What they came up with," Pauli says, "was they *could* take Laura into their counseling program, but they could not make her part of their placement program with me as long as I had Dana and Ali. They said the law allowed them to place two children in a home; they preferred to place only one. So if I were willing to give up Dana and Ali—then they could allow me to keep Laura through their program."

The carrot was attractive: truly adequate cost coverage for

Laura's care, plus all the services Laura needed. But the stick was not.

"I just couldn't do that. I don't see how I could choose the life of one over the lives of two. You know, that's just not an easy choice to make. Plus, these two kids I had known all their lives, and—well, it wasn't my fault, but I had started the negotiations that took those kids from their mother. And I didn't see how I could give them up into this system that, even in this short time, I had found so much out about. I just couldn't do it.

"So what they decided to do was leave Laura where she was—so I could keep all three of them. And they wrote me a letter telling me that Parker was terminating me from their program because of these things, and they wished me luck in what I was trying to do because I had a lot to offer."

The city then started the paperwork to change Pauli's license over from the state to the city. Since the training and qualifications for certification by Parker were far more rigorous than any requirements set by the city, one would think this would have been a simple matter. Rather, it dragged on for so many months that events overtook it.

Meanwhile, Pauli had to buy all three children clothes. (It turned out nothing was in all those boxes of Laura's but junk, rags, and dolls; one raincoat; two pairs of pants.)

"And the groceries," Pauli says. "There'd been just me, and I seldom ate at home. Fifty dollars a month for groceries and I was finished. But with three kids there—I was going to the market and spending $150, $160 a week. And that was my salary. My bring-home pay was $156 a week. So my bills were getting behind.

"And Laura's social worker, Miss Jefferson, told me that *she* worked overtime and *she* doesn't get paid for it, so I should be doing this for charity. Those were her words.

"And I said, 'Miss Jefferson, when I was working as a barmaid and my tips each night were more than my salary each week, I could afford to do things for children. And I did. My tips were $100 a night, or more. And with that money, I took care of other people's children—who had nothing to do with Social Services. I did this on my own. I don't make that kind of money now. I want to help children. But I cannot do it alone. I don't have it to give. You can only give what you have.

"And I showed her one of my paychecks."

Not long after Laura came to Pauli's home, Laura started menstruating. Pauli spoke to Miss Jefferson. "I said, 'Miss Jefferson, Laura has started menstruating and in view of everything you told me, I feel this child needs birth control pills.' She said, 'You're right. And I'll talk to the mother about it right away. And if she don't sign the papers, I'll take her to court.' She was giving me the impression that papers had to be signed before Laura could get birth control pills.''

"Not true?"

"No. It's not true. I talked to the social worker who was investigating my home—there were five or six of them in and out of my house from different departments. And she said, 'Mrs. Mason,' she said. 'I wouldn't want you to repeat this. But you don't need anybody's permission to get birth control pills for the child.' She said, 'They're giving birth control pills now and counseling—without even the parent's knowledge.' She said, 'Just to keep you clear, I'll check again to make sure.' The woman checked and she called me back. She told me that what she had said was the truth.''

As for Miss Jefferson's firm tack with Laura's mother: "The mother never knew that the child was menstruating until the child told her later on the telephone.''

For the next two weeks, Pauli's major problem was that the Department of Social Services, embodied by the social worker, Miss Jefferson, simply would not get around to putting Laura in school. This forced Pauli to keep hiring babysitters while she was at work, and to keep paying babysitters (for which she would not be reimbursed)—even when she was not yet receiving room and board for any of the three children. "See, *they* have to put her in school. They won't allow you to do it. They have to do it. Had they allowed me to put Laura in school, I would have.

"But then—um—Laura got raped."

Raped.

"Pauli," I say, "I think I've absorbed about all I can for the moment. Come on, let's get dinner.''

# THE PERMANENCY-PLANNING WORKER

It had been my original intention to stay away from New York City. Not only is everything in New York a hyphen crisis (transportation-crisis, crack-crisis, crime-crisis), but the city's system is unique in structure. New York has few foster care facilities of its own: it relies predominantly on independent contractors, many sectarian.

Something bothered me, though. It is possible to read a story like Molly and Nikki's on two levels (even on both levels at once). One is with total empathy for the obvious anguish, and a genuine disturbance at the events of the case.* Another is with uneasiness: children in privileged homes like that of Molly and her family have got an indisputable advantage, one that is in their

---

*In some states, after all, a child is considered abandoned if the parents have failed to visit for six months (Kadushin and Martin, p. 281). Nikki had been abandoned for twice that amount of time. Yet they called it *neglected*.

"best interests" in this society. Yet what are the implications of
that? There are those who can (and will) argue that the end of
that line of reasoning is stealing kids from the poor to give to the
rich.

My instinct, then, was to listen further, not to levitate to
shouldism. The world of foster care is a world of reality, not of
romantic abstraction. What, I wondered, was the reality, the
perspective, from inside the New York City system?

Not long after I spoke with Molly, I ran across Mark, who
works for one of the contracting agencies. Mark is not in the
frontline trenches: it is up to the protective service units of SSC
to respond to neglect and abuse reports, to investigate, and to
remove children. Once they have been placed with his agency,
though, Mark is responsible for seeing the kids, the parent, the
foster parent. His title is permanency-planning worker.

At the time we spoke, Mark had been with the agency a year
and a half. He considered the job an interim one, until he got his
master's degree and could move on: thus, his willingness to talk
with me. To begin with, he spoke a bit like a *Manual for Workers
on Foster Care*. . . .

"My job is to get these children out of foster care. Foster
care's a temporary situation. I have to provide a permanent
situation for these children. Whether it's back with their natural
mothers, or in adoptive placement—placement with other family
members is another option."

. . . but he quickly relaxed.

"How does your job work, Mark?"

"Okay. Here's a case. The mother lost her housing. She went
to, whatever, welfare, and requested for the children to be placed
in foster care. She didn't want to take the children to a shelter.
Because she didn't think the shelters were fit for children. I
completely understand her. So SSC refuses to place the children.
A voluntary placement will not be accepted just on the grounds
of having no housing. You have to say to SSC, 'Look, I'm ready
to pop and hit these children.' That's enough to get them placed.
But just saying, 'I lost my housing and I don't want to put them
in a shelter, so please take them into foster care until I can find
housing . . .' They won't take the children."

"They can refuse to take children?"

"They can. They did it in this case. And you know what this
woman ended up doing? She left her children. She abandoned
her children. In the SSC office. So their placement was consid-

ered forced—not voluntary. There are two kinds of placement—voluntary and forced placement. So in order to protect her children, she abandoned them.*

"This woman—she visits her children. She keeps in regular contact with me, always gives me her mailing address, but will not see me. She says to me, 'Why do I have to come to you? You don't have what I want. You can't offer me what I want. All I need is housing. And you don't have housing for me.' Which is true."

"So the child welfare apparatus in New York City cannot itself offer the things that are known as 'services' to the client? That's a different department, another place?"

"That is basically true. All I can do for my clients is to direct them to 5 Park Place, which is where you apply for public housing under Section 8, in New York. And what happens when they go there? They get on some amazingly long waiting list. And—okay. I can write them a letter saying, 'This woman's children are in foster care. Our aim is to return the children to the parent. Please give this woman preferential treatment on the waiting list.' But that means nothing. The waiting list is miles long."

"In what sense is a woman like this your 'client'? She's under the gun."

"Well, they're my clients because I have to serve them."

"But in what sense does the word 'client' apply?"

"Oh, I don't know. That's just what we call them."

Amazing, is it not, the way pastel words are adopted unquestioned, even by an obviously intelligent young man with very little vested, long-term, in the system?

"I've been told," I say, "that some of the time women don't understand why they've lost their kids. Is that possible?"

"Is it possible? It is possible. Because you know in some cases *I'm* still unclear about how the children ended up in foster care."

At this point I bring up a recent study, *Protecting Abused and Neglected Children*,[1] which examined two California counties. One was deemed an experimental county, and was permitted to remove children only in circumstances of drastic physical abuse or neglect. Instead, this county poured funds into real home-based services.

---

*Again, to try to square this with calling Nikki's abandonment in the hospital for thirteen months only "neglect" is to begin to understand that what is at work here is far more caprice than rational or consistent behavior.

The other county was doing business as usual, allowing placement of children based only on a finding that the home was
"detrimental" to the child. The upshot was that there was no
discernible developmental difference in the two groups of children over the next two years. "Doesn't this," I ask Mark, "raise
the question of what *is* the point of foster care?"

Mark pauses to think.

"It's almost like—let's make an analogy. To why society
pretends to be so concerned about drugs. And then some people
are calling for the legalization of drugs. And I almost see that
point in a way. But it's sort of like saying, 'Give away free
needles.' We say we're opposed to drugs because drugs are
immoral for A, B, and C reasons. Or they destroy people's lives.
Therefore, we have to be opposed to them and have this war on
drugs. So on the one hand, we're really not doing anything to
stop drug use, but we have to be opposed to it. And with foster
care—it's like we're not really doing anything to prevent child
abuse or child neglect. Yet when we see it, we have to pretend to
do something about it. Because if we don't do anything about it,
it's like saying drugs are all right."

"But following that track, you're suggesting that 'drugs' are
not all right primarily for the poor. Most of those you work with
are lower-class, right?"

"Mm-hmm."

"You've never been asked to go into a middle-class household?"

"Never. They're always in the worst neighborhoods. And
always in complete poverty situations."

"So basically you're going in on poverty, true?"

"Yes. They're so poor that by society's standards—just because they don't have enough—they're neglecting their children.
Only the poor wind up in the foster care system in New York
City. Overwhelmingly, it is black and Hispanic.* I have two
white children on my caseload and they're there because the
mother had them when she was sixteen. She herself was in the
system. But they were never neglected or abused."

"Then what are they doing there?"

"She didn't have a place to live."

"Are they in involuntarily?"

---

*Nationwide, whites still represent over 50 percent of those in foster care. But
minorities are increasingly overrepresented, given their proportion in the population.

"See, I'm not even sure about that. It's got to be a court placement after a while. Because if it were a voluntary placement, the girl could request her children back and we'd have to return them in ten days." Mark pauses. "Whether that happens or not is another story."

Indeed it is. The caseworker does a home visit and—bingo—your housing is inadequate; there is insufficient food in your refrigerator. Presto: voluntary becomes involuntary.

"There are cases," Mark says, "where the parent says, 'Okay. I want my kids back.' And they say, 'No.' They can do that. I don't know why they can, but they can. Because, 'We're the system.' And the mothers have to fight it."

It recurs and recurs, this point: that the system feels absolute complacency when intruding on the lives of women—especially poor women—and children.

Mark is clearly warming to his subject here. There are not too many people, he has told me, who want to hear about his job. "What we can do is completely go behind their backs. 'This child is thirteen, gonna be fourteen soon. Her mother, yes, says that she wants her back, but the current situation in the foster home is a very positive one. A strong bond has developed between the child and the foster mother, and we think, in the best interests of the child, the child might be better off staying in the foster home.' "

"And this can be true or false? In other words, SSC is never going to see this child?"

"No. They will never see it."

"So in essence a worker could write down anything they want to about a situation?"

"Exactly."

Not only is language in the world of foster care euphemistic and insincere, then, it can be used to lie.

Language is also used to label. And these labels remain unknown to the one labeled, and, in any case, would be irrefutable. The labeling, after all, has been done by a "professional": the one labeled has no credibility. This widespread random categorization of people within the system has itself been labeled: GLOP. *G*eneralized *L*abeling *O*f *P*eople—as "manipulative," "ineffectual," "passive," "aggressive."[2]

"And," as Mark says, "I'm beginning to think it might pay off to stretch the truth a little bit more. Because sometimes if you can't create a picture-perfect home that we're gonna discharge these children to, SSC will give us a real hard time."

The picture Mark is painting is this: Somewhere at 80 Lafayette Street, which is SSC headquarters, sits a caseworker, at the
foot of three or four supervisors (as Mark puts it, "three or four
soops"). Mark must report periodically to her, by form-filling-
out behavior, and she—who will never meet the children at issue,
the mother at issue, or the foster parents or proposed caretaking
adults—will decide whether Mark's "permanency plan" is correct, based entirely on what he puts on the paper. It is easy to
see why he would be interested in creative writing to achieve for
children what he—who is tapped into the real individuals involved—thinks best. It is also easy to see where that road leads.

"I'll give you an example," Mark says. "A different case
now. I'm trying to discharge these two children to two primary-
resource people. A paternal great-uncle and a paternal great-
grandmother.

"Great-grandmother is sixty-nine years old. Not young—but
a strong, capable woman. Spent thirty years working for various
rich people, taking care of their kids. So—taking care of children
has been her job. The uncle is forty-four years old, and then
there's another man in the home, who's about thirty-three.
Who's unemployed. The uncle's income is something like $35,000
a year. They own the home. All paid off. X number of bedrooms,
plenty of space. And SSC gave me a hard time about placing
these kids. They've refused already."

"Why?"

"They said first of all that the uncle is not in the home often
enough. He works. Under the 'Describe the family' part of the
form, I'd said he was very devoted to his career.

"And I'd said that he's not married. Then they ask me on the
phone, 'Well, why isn't he married?' I said, 'I don't know. He
just never got married.' They said, 'Well, if he's not married, is
he gay?' They asked me that. And then I didn't want to answer
that question right off because I wasn't sure what answer would
be the 'correct' one. I mean, if he were gay, that would explain
why he wasn't married, but . . . So I asked, 'Well, would it be
better if he was gay, or not?' She said, 'It would be better if he
were not gay.' So I told her, 'No, he's not gay.'

"And she's probably the third worker on the case. Everything
she knows now is second-, third-, fourthhand." Everything she
knows now is also as apt as not to have limited bearing on reality.

"The other reason they told me it wasn't a good idea to
discharge these kids to that uncle and great-grandmother: Great-
grandmother's too old. The children are a five-year-old and a

two-year-old. I described the five-year-old as precocious. Which she is. And the two-year-old as energetic, playful, and devilish. I kind of liked that word 'cause I thought that's the way he was: full of fun. And she said, 'How is a sixty-nine-year-old woman gonna handle a devilish two-year-old and a precocious five-year-old?'

"The kids are still in foster care."

"Why had these kids been removed from the mother?"

"That's another thing. It's so frustrating to try to find out *why* these children were removed. How. Under what circumstances. As soon as the children are removed, they do an investigation, something called an I & R, Investigation and Report. They present this to the judge and then the judge makes the decision whether the children should remain in foster care or not. And we never get a copy of the report, so we never really know what the finding was. We get a word: it was a finding of 'neglect,' a finding of 'abuse.' We don't actually find out the circumstances."

These things are *that* "confidential," then. They are so confidential that the information is not even available to the permanency-planning worker who is to help decide whether and when the kids should be returned.

"But if you don't know what the problem was," I say, "how can you know if it's gone?"

"We talk to the parents. 'Why are your kids in foster care?' "

"Do they know?"

"Sometimes they know."

"Do you believe they are telling the truth, telling you the situation as best they know it?"

"As best they *know*. But—I'm really, from the way my training is, the way my supervisor trained me, she gives me the idea that I always have to be on guard for picking up lies. My temptation—my real want—is to believe them. But then on the other side my supervisor always says, 'Children are not in foster care for *no reason*. She had to do *something*.' So that's always in the back of my mind.

"Every now and then I get real depressed about my job and I try to sit down and talk to my supervisor about it. 'This child shouldn't be in foster care! They should try to get this child home!' And she says, '*This* is foster care. And *there's* the door!' Meaning: this is the job, take it for what it's got, and you're welcome to leave. Other times, she says, 'Look. These children have to be in foster care. They wouldn't be if there weren't a reason.' "

Why, I am wondering as I listen to Mark, does this smack so of, "The Fuehrer makes *no mistakes!*" It is also a lot like arresting someone, putting them in jail, and then saying they must be a criminal because they're in jail.

"The mother whose two children I tried to place with the great-grandmother and the uncle, I'll tell you how she described it to me. 'I was in the hospital, for seizures, for an extended period of time.' Her children were staying with their grandmother—in the Bronx. During that time, the grandmother's boyfriend sexually abused the five-year-old. This was actually founded. The child talked about it. And nobody's denying that this took place. But it has nothing to do with the mother and the mother's care of the child.

"The mother comes out of the hospital. All this has happened when she wasn't there. Meanwhile, SSC had found out about it; it was under investigation. There's a home visit to the grandmother's apartment. They find out the apartment is a mess. The SSC worker tells the mother she's not to leave her children there. She says okay.

"It turns out one day the mother's visiting the grandmother. That same day a worker comes by to check up. I'm really shocked—that they actually had the resources to send someone. Coincidence. Mother said they were only visiting. And she lost her kids there and then.

"Eighteen months later they're still in foster care."

"I thought after eighteen months something 'permanent' was supposed to happen."

"No. Then you go to court and get an extension. It's almost automatic. After two years, if the kids are still in foster care, you have to request from the state a U.R.—I don't know why it's called that. Requesting an extension; saying why the kids have to be in foster care longer than two years."

So much for the meaning of the title permanency-planning worker.

"So," I say to Mark, "you're trained to have the feeling that you want to disbelieve the mothers?"

"And not only disbelieve, but hold everything against them. For instance. This mother—basically lost her housing. She was squatting—in a place without heat, hot water, or electricity. The children were staying at relatives' houses. These children, you look at the three girls I've met—there are other children who are with other agencies—these children are beautiful; not only beautiful-*looking,* but very well behaved, well mannered. It's obvious that these are well-bred children. Their ages range from five to twelve.

"Anyway, the mother, the first two or three times I saw her she was wearing dark sunglasses, even indoors. She didn't take them off. I didn't question it. I found her truthful, and we were communicating, discussing her situation.

"Then another caseworker asked me, 'Does she *ever* take her glasses off?' I said, 'No.' She said, 'Same with me. She never takes them off.' And just—the suspicion given to something as superficial as that. There are much more important things to talk to this woman about than whether she takes her sunglasses off inside or not.

"There's a lot of cases where I really don't believe that the mother was bad to the children. I believe maybe she had anger problems. Maybe every once in a while she had to hit them—to make them behave. But I'm very confused about why the children were removed."

"There seems to be no distinction: the woman who has no home; the woman who tries to kill her child; the woman whose husband tries to kill the child . . ."

"There *should* be a distinction."

"But there isn't?"

"No. There isn't. And we even try to blur the distinction by calling a homeless person an alcoholic. We try to make her have more than one problem. 'She can't just be homeless. She has to be on a drug too—or she wouldn't be homeless. Look! We have educational neglect on her also. Her children missed x number of days in school. Is *this* a responsible mother? She's not just homeless! Don't you *see?* She has lots of problems! She needs therapy! She needs parenting skills!' If you ask me what parenting skills are, I don't know."

How bizarre. What Mark is saying reminds me of all the testimony I have read in the transcripts of the hearings before Congressman Miller's Committee on Children, Youth, and Families, pleading that the reason things are so bad is that today there are *multiproblem families*. More GLOP.

"There are skills you can learn," Mark is saying, "like positive reinforcement. But that's another fantasy versus reality. 'Don't ever hit your children. Don't ever raise your voice. That's not necessary.' Yes. In the textbook it's not necessary. But we're human beings. We hit our children. And our foster parents hit the children. They do."

"They're allowed to?"

"No. They know they're not allowed to. And the kids find out they're not allowed to be hit. Then they tell their caseworker. Then it turns out a disaster. We report her. There's actually a special team that investigates foster parents. CIU is what it's called. Confidential Investigation Unit. Different from the state child abuse and neglect hotline."

"There's a Band-Aid for every boo-boo."

"Mm-hmm."

"What happens to the foster parents?"

"We just remove the children and they don't get new children. They get on a list, blacklisted forever."

I have this amazing thought: "Do they try to take the foster parents' own children away then, if they also hit them?"

Mark hesitates. "I don't *think* they do."

# THE
# "UNFIT"
# MOTHER

I am reading, for what seems like the five hundred thousandth time, in yet another place: "Children are our most precious resource." (Sometimes it says "most important resource." Sometimes, "most treasured resource.") Farther along in this same report, prepared by Attorney General Hubert H. Humphrey III's Task Force on Child Abuse Within the Family,[1]: "The issue in child protection is not guilt or innocence, but rather to determine if the child is in need of protection and the family in need of services." Why is the entire issue of child welfare so mined with cant? Of course it is about guilt or innocence if your purpose in going into the family is to determine whether Mommy or Daddy has been whacking Johnny over the head with a baseball bat. And if it is not about guilt or innocence, how explain the enormous power to punish (all the while calling it "help")? (How else, if not as punishment, is a mother meant to experience the removal of her child?)

67

More than in any other area of life, there seems to pervade here an abiding belief that saying something will make it so: that language can actually make something what it is not. They name the shape of a cloud, and then take the cloud to *be* what the shape suggests.*

"Child protection workers should not view their job as the rescue of abused children from families." But—if it is *serious* abuse—what else can be the point? And if it is not—if it is circumstantially related neglect—what are you doing there unless you can materially alter the circumstance?

At heart, the problem seems to remain what it always has been: the failure to correctly frame the question to which child protection/child welfare is the answer. Is it a police function? Is it meant to place serious sanctions against the parent who repeatedly assaults and batters a child—or rapes or sodomizes the child? (In which case, can you really forever avoid the demands of due process?) Or is it meant to tinker around with people's parenting skills, to fault those who are in no position to complain for their supposed insufficiencies, inadequacies, shortcomings, carelessness (or even uncaring)?

Kelly Josephs is fine featured, well spoken—and she lost her two kids to the system.

Raised by parents of the white working-class poor—her father works day shifts at a factory; her mother nights—Kelly did a stint in the air force right after high school. She married, but her husband left her when she was four months pregnant with her first child. He came back when the baby was four months old: "Okay, we'll try it again."

"That," says Kelly, "lasted until I was two months pregnant with my second baby." Husband left; they divorced; he has not been heard from since.

Living in a small midwestern town, Kelly then applied for government Aid to Families with Dependent Children, AFDC. "Everything was beautiful," she says. "We lived in a nice apartment. What AFDC didn't give me, my mother made up.

---

*An interesting sidelight to this is the tendency of agencies to respond to embattlement by changing their names, rather than their behavior. In New York, the agency went from being the Bureau of Child Welfare to Special Services for Children to the Child Welfare Administration. In Louisiana, the agency, under a series of sieges, went from Child Welfare to Office of Human Development to Office of Community Service.

Which was around fifty dollars a month. In the meantime, my mother and dad are buying clothes for the kids.

"I'm very independent. I don't like to be dependent on anybody. But my mother finally talked me into moving from my apartment back in with her so she could help me more."

Still, valuing her independence, Kelly soon looked for and found a nice place for her and the children to live. That lasted only a year, however, because the landlord kept coming into her house with his key.

"The only thing I could find then was a little one-room shack; a toilet off in one part of the house. Our beds were all in the living room. So when somebody came to visit you didn't offer a chair. You offered a seat on your bed. That was only fifty dollars a month. Welfare told me that was fine. They came out to check on the house and the kids—because I was on AFDC."

"And that automatically makes you a target?"

"Automatically. They can come at any time and check up on you because you are getting Aid for Dependent Children. So they came once in a while. Everything was going great. I mean my life was—good. I had no car. I had no job. I still had no money but what welfare gave me. But they did give me good food stamps. That's the only thing we did on welfare—we ate good. Benjy at this time was only a couple of months old. Danny was almost two.

"As I say, I never had any problem. My check came to the house on time. My medical card came to the house on time. Everything was beautiful. Then—the outfit that owned it decided to tear down this little one-room shack. So I had three months to get out of there.

"I moved to an upstairs apartment. My checks were delayed for a month. But they finally started coming in.

"Everything was fine. *Until* the day we were all taking a nap and the kitchen caught on fire. By the time we woke up, the house was on fire. It was due to faulty wiring—which the fire marshal stated. The fire marshal said there was no way I could live there. What did not burn in flames was smoke damaged or water damaged. So I went out of there with nothing but the clothes on our backs.

"After that, I went to welfare. Welfare told me to go to the Red Cross. The little money I did have had burned up. Everything was gone. So Red Cross put me in a motel for two weeks. They called the motel and gave the okay for two weeks to give my sons and me three meals a day—for nothing. They were excellent.

"Well, my two weeks ended. There was nothing else Red Cross could do.

"So we went and lived with a girlfriend of mine in a trailer park. And the trailer park manager did not like it. So I told the trailer park manager all my troubles. And he told me that he would give me a trailer for one month, free of rent. To get on my feet. This was beautiful, this was fine.

"I had no furniture, I had nothing. But people gave me mattresses, which I put on the floor in the trailer. We *did* have food because the neighbors were giving us food. My mother was buying us food."

> TO: Juvenile Court
> FROM: _____County Welfare Department
>     RE: Josephs Hearing
> The two initial referrals [note: not complaints or allegations] were received on April 29. These indicated that *Daniel and Benjamin had no beds* and little food. . . . *Also Mrs. Josephs . . . forced the baby to stay in his crib for the entire day* (emphasis mine).

"This was very nice," Kelly continues, "until I found out the trailer park manager wanted sex in return. So—we're not staying."

"You couldn't move back in with your mom?"

"We could have. But like I say, I am very bullheaded. And to run back to Mommy and Daddy with every problem degrades me. I was on my own. I was gonna make it.

"We wound up living with friends. We were going from one friend to the other. Finally, this friend says, 'Look, I can't do this. They want to raise my rent . . .' I said, 'Okay, I understand. Don't feel bad. This is how it's gotta be.' She said, 'I'll give you two weeks.' I said, 'That's great. Two weeks is fine. I can do something in two weeks.' "

Indeed, in that time, Kelly got a job. And she got Benjy and Danny enrolled in a church day-care center with welfare's assistance. What she hoped to do was save up enough for a down payment on a cheap-cheap car, and maybe a deposit for rent someplace.

"You had never, before this point, been contacted by Protective Services?"

"Never."

\* \* \*

From the County Welfare memo: "Mrs. Josephs had been contacted in regard to the first referrals prior to the June 1 complaint."

Toward the end of the two weeks came Memorial Day weekend. Kelly's friend and her husband invited Kelly and the kids to go camping with them for three days. Because Benjy was just starting to walk, they loaned Kelly a playpen to bring along.

"While we were there," Kelly says, "if I was not holding my son, or I was not beside my son—the baby—I would put him in the playpen. And keep him in there because of the campfire. The older one was three, he knew to stay away from the fire.

"Well, we're getting ready to leave, the last day. I waited till my girlfriend's husband had damped the fire. He takes the fire, he puts it out, he throws dirt on it, and he throws water on it. But he must not have gotten it all. I take my son out of the playpen—so we could put the playpen into the car. Sure enough, the baby decides to wander. He starts to toddle over—and he falls, straight smack on the hot ashes. And this is where the burned hand came in.

"The baby was screaming bloody murder. We threw ice on his hand. And I looked at my girlfriend and her husband, and said, 'I gotta take him to the hospital.' They said they wanted to drop their kids off first and then go in. So while they were unloading the car, I called the hospital. I said, 'I'm bringing my son in. *Should* I bring him in?' I was hysterical. This blister—by now it had raised to the size of a baseball. I told them, 'The blister is the size of a baseball. It is watery. It's bad. Should I bring him in now?' She said, 'No. There's nothing we can do that you can't do. We can't bust it, we can't do anything.' She says, 'Put a burn medicine on it. Wrap it in a cloth. Put a sock over his hand. Bring him in when the blister breaks. Because then there's a chance of infection.' I said, 'Okay.'

"Well, we knew a Boy Scout leader. That lived in the trailer park. So we went over to see him. And he gave me a burn medicine. We put that on. We wrapped it up in white gauze that he had in his first-aid kit. Then I put a white sock over it. And I gave him an aspirin—because my son was in pain. And I tried to keep his hand up as much as I could.

"The next day, I took the boys to the day-care center. I explained to the worker exactly what the hospital had told me to do. I said, 'Please. He does not have a fever. But please. If the

blister breaks, call me at work.' She said, 'Okay.' I leave there. I
go to work—which is twenty minutes away. I was borrowing my
girlfriend's car until I got my first paycheck and could put
something down on a used, even a fifty-dollar car.

"About noon, I got a call from the welfare department. They
had taken the boys and they wanted me to meet them at the
county hospital immediately because the baby's hand was
burned. 'Did the blister bust?' 'No. We have to talk to you. You
have to come to the hospital immediately.'

"So I went to the hospital. The hospital states that I had never
called. I said, 'I *did* call.' And she said, 'You *didn't* call.' So I
was there against the whole hospital stating I didn't call."

From the County Welfare report:
"When the complaint from the day-care center was received,
two workers went to the center to examine Benjy's hand. It was
immediately evident that the burn was a serious one, and had not
been adequately treated, if at all. One of the workers called Mrs.
Josephs at work to tell her of our concerns about her son's hand.
She responded by saying that she had taken her son to the
emergency room of Community Hospital the previous day and
that the doctor had treated Benjy's hand. [Kelly: "I *never* said I
*took* him. I said I *called*."] The worker stated that in any case, it
was obvious that his hand needed further treatment and that the
workers would like to take Mrs. Josephs and her son to the
emergency room so that his hand could be taken care of. Mrs.
Josephs agreed to this, and said that she would meet the workers
at the day-care center. In the meantime, the worker called the
hospital and found that Benjy Josephs had not been to the
hospital for treatment.

"The workers took Mrs. Josephs and her children to the
Community Hospital for treatment of the second-degree burn. At
this time Mrs. Josephs said that she had not actually brought
Benjy to the hospital for treatment, but had called the hospital to
find out what she could do for the burn and the hospital told her
not to bring him in. The nurse in the emergency room told the
worker that the hospital kept a record of all such calls, and that
the records indicate that Mrs. Josephs did not make such a call.
*The hospital phoned later on June 28, to say that Mrs. Josephs
had phoned, but that the call had not been recorded* (emphasis
mine)."

\* \* \*

Kelly says: "The welfare has the baby's hand checked and everything and they give me a prescription. And they insist that I get this medicine immediately because it's very, very important. Because of the infection. I said, 'Okay. I'll get it.'

"So I leave with the kids. I go to the drugstore and try to get the prescription filled. I can't do it. My medical card has expired. I go try and call welfare. There's nobody there. Closed. I'm stuck, I'm lost, I've got twenty dollars in my pocket. And I know I have to feed the kids until payday. I *can't* pay for this prescription.

"I go back to welfare the following day. I said, 'I can't get this filled.' She said, 'Why can't you?' I said, 'I had twenty dollars. I now have fifteen. I have no medical card. If I get this prescription, I have nothing to feed my children on for the next week.' She said, 'There's nothing we can do. We can open you a new medical card. It takes two weeks for the medical card to come in.' I said, 'But I've been *waiting* for the new medical card.' She said, 'But your house burned down. There was no place to send it.' I looked at her. I said, 'Well what the hell in the meantime do you want me to do about this prescription?' She says, 'I'll take you down there.' She took me to the drugstore and had the prescription filled."

The report: "After the child had been treated, the nurse explained that the bandage should be changed in three days, and gave Mrs. Josephs a prescription to be filled. The medicine was to prevent the infection of the hand and was to be started immediately. The worker discussed with Mrs. Josephs the importance of getting the prescription started, and she said she would have it filled that evening, and bring it, with the children, to the day-care center the following day. The worker checked with the day-care center the following day and Mrs. Josephs had not brought, nor mentioned, the prescription. . . . In view of the numerous complaints regarding this family, and in view of Mrs. Josephs's apparent refusal to provide adequate medical care for her son, a complaint was filed in Juvenile Court on June 3, charging that Benjamin and Daniel Josephs are neglected children."

Meanwhile, Kelly and the kids had nowhere to live. Unaware that a complaint had been filed by Protective Services with the court, she took the kids and went out house hunting the evening

of June 3. "I had nowhere to go. I started riding around looking
for a place to live. By total coincidence, I knock on a welfare
worker's door. How had I picked *this* house to knock on? 'Do
you know of anyplace to rent?' He says, 'No. What's your
problem?' I tell him my problem because I figure the truth will
break people down. He then tells me that he's a social worker
with the county welfare department. I almost fell. 'No!' I did
turn. I was almost ready to run. He says, 'Don't run. I want to
help you.' I said, 'You want to help me?' By this time I gave up
trusting welfare. He says, 'I want to help you.' I said, 'Okay. You
tell me what you can help me with.' He says, 'Well, I can take
you down to the office, and I can turn around, and I can get you
a place to live. We can set you up with AFDC. We can get you a
new medical card.' Beautiful.

"Then he turned around and told me that they had emergency
custody."

In the words of the report, however, "A placement was
averted at this time as Mrs. Josephs made arrangements to live
with her mother."

The caseworkers appeared regularly to express their distrust
of this situation and to file critical reports. The scrutiny and the
pressure began to get to everyone.

"My mother talked to me," Kelly says. " 'Now maybe this is
better. Try a foster home. Just till you get on your feet. This way
you won't have to pay for day care. You won't have to buy
medicine. You won't have to buy clothes. You can save the
money and get a decent place.' " Kelly waffled. She was ex-
hausted from struggling, but—what was foster care about? How
long did it last? How did it work? Could you count on getting
your kids back when you were ready for them? Could she trust
it? She called to find answers. "They used this against me in
court," Kelly says. "Because they said that I wanted my children
in a foster home. I only called to find out what it was like, how
long it would be before I could get them back. Information."

A hearing was held on July 2. The kids were remanded to
temporary foster care. They were placed separately. It was
ordered that Kelly could not see them for thirty days so they
could "adjust to foster care." *She was also ordered to pay ten
dollars a week child support.*

I have begun, as one will, to develop a level of—if not
immunity, then at least tolerance for—the short sharp shocks of
travel on the bumpy roads of foster care. But when Kelly tells me

that she, of whom it is now to be asked that she prove she can "stabilize" her finances, is commanded to fork over forty dollars a month so her kids can be placed elsewhere by the state against her will—I am flabbergasted.

I pick up the phone and check with the American Bar Association: Is this possible? Yes, I am told. A number of states have specific provisions for that. They don't always do it. But they can.

And this money is demanded *despite* the fact that the federal government pays 53 percent of cost for children like Danny and Benjy, who are AFDC eligible, and the state the rest.

Kelly may not have been a perfect mother. (Is any woman perceived to be a perfect mother? Is any *poor* woman, alone, perceived to be an adequate mother?) But it is clear, both from talking with Kelly and from the records (despite the agency's efforts to make it seem to the contrary), that she is a passionately caring, kind, protective mother—who needed a leg up, not a boot down.

Kelly continues: "After thirty days, I can go see my child. By this time, I had no car again. It wasn't running. I almost got hit by a train because the car stopped in the middle of the tracks. These guys jump out, push my car out of the way.

"I called my son. I said, 'Danny, it's Mommy.' He started crying. I said, 'Honey, Mommy can't come today.' 'Why? Please come!' 'Okay. Calm down. I'll be there.' I hang up. I hitchhiked and walked fifteen miles. I got there. And my son comes running out and grabs me, and, I swear, he puts marks on my arms he was so happy to see me.

"I sat down with him, and when I went to leave, he said, 'Don't go! Don't go!' And he started screaming. I looked at the foster mother and I said, 'What the hell is going on here?' She said, 'This boy is terrible. He has nightmares in the middle of the night. He drinks out of the toilet.' I said, 'Why does he drink out of the toilet?' 'You ask him that. When we bathe him, he shies away and he cries through the whole bath.' I looked at Danny and I said, 'Honey, why do you cry at bath?'' He said, 'Mommy, they make me bathe with those girls.' She had two daughters. I said, 'Well, what happens?' 'They laugh at me.' His body parts were being explained to two little girls while he was bathing.

"I said, 'Why do you drink out of the toilet? You know that's not nice.' He said, 'They won't give me anything to drink.'

"When I went to leave, he was still screaming. The foster father actually pulled him out of my arms, and the mother stopped me from going into the house after him. He takes Danny into the living room and he says, 'If you don't shut up, I am going to spank you.'

"I left. I ran half the way and got a ride the other half the way back to the county courthouse. I walked into that office, and I looked at the woman that was behind the desk and said, 'I want to speak to the goddamned head, and I want to speak to him *now*.' They're writing all this down.

"A girl comes out. I say, 'You've got exactly twenty-four hours to get my son out of that home. And if you don't, and if something happens—you'd better write *this* down—I will sue you and everybody for everything.' "

Coming from a mother (most especially an on-and-off-welfare mother), this was not perceived as a threat with which they could not cope: They wrote down that she was crazy. "Mrs. Josephs was found to be hostile, defensive, dependent, and uncooperative." More GLOP.

"She denied that she had any problems," the report states, "and has persisted in believing that the children were wrongfully taken from her in the first place." Well. Imagine that high offense. "She is very apt to blame others for her troubles," writes the social worker who had engineered the children's removal: *the same worker with whom Kelly is now meant to be in "counseling."* "I quickly attempted to work with Mrs. Josephs to come up with specific areas we could agree upon. We felt that housing, financial support, transportation, visitation, day-care plans, and counseling were needed before the children could be returned. In addition I felt that some sort of child management training and budgeting training were needed. Mrs. Josephs did not really agree that these were problems."

More specifically, Kelly did not feel that these were problems that affected her ability to be a good mother to her children. Housing, of course, was a problem. And finances (which would take care of the housing). But "child management training"? (To agree to it is to agree that you *need* it; that you are guilty of poor child management. Just as to agree to "counseling" is to "confess" to emotional "problems.") And "budget training"? Go budget—what?

What this caseworker saw in Danny, a child who had been summarily yanked from his mother and denied her presence for thirty days, was "a child with many problems. He was a frightened and nervous little boy and exhibited a lot of anxiety." This is meant to be damning. It is meant to say that this is the way he was *before* he was taken away. It is meant to demonstrate how Kelly had failed.

Benjy, on the other hand, "adjusted very easily to foster care, almost failing to distinguish between acquaintances and strangers." What can this mean? If the child does not "adjust" to being yanked from his mother, that just goes to show . . . And if the child *does* make an adjustment—well, that just goes to show . . .

Even as the two boys were being moved, and placed together with new foster parents, the Holstroms, a "goal plan" was drawn up for Kelly: a contract.

As the report describes it: "The agreement specified financial responsibility, meaning a budget, support of children and some means of income, adequate transportation, suitable housing and documentation of efforts to locate housing, child care plans, child management training, counseling and regular and good visitation. This program was supported and regularly evaluated by the worker. Additional services, including Mental Health, General Relief and Legal Aid were offered. Mrs. Josephs made use of Legal Aid briefly, but was not interested in any other services."

A year later, under the "Evaluation and Current Functioning" part of her report, this worker would write: "No one from this agency has yet seen any housing which Mrs. Josephs intends to present as suitable. She has had three jobs within the last month according to her [sic]. She has paid no support [sic], has not had any counseling, and we have not begun child care training as she has not performed in any other areas. Mrs. Josephs has no day-care plans at this time [she had no *children* at this time]. She has not presented any sort of budget and has not provided any documentation of attempts to find housing. She has visited regularly although visits have had to be cut back from the original court-ordered three times per week to three and one half hours once a week. At this time there appear to be few problems around visitation."

This is followed by a "Request for Permanent Custody."

Kelly says: "Because I talked to the welfare department about Danny being in that home, they have, 'Mrs. Josephs was hostile, defensive, dependent, and uncooperative. We felt that housing, financial support, transportation, visitation, day-care plans, and counseling were needed before the children could be returned.' I'm supposed to go through all these counselings and everything.

In the meantime, looking for a job, getting a car, getting a house.
I'm supposed to go through psychiatric treatment.

"Yes, I could not hold a job. Because every time I got a job,
it was not enough money for welfare—to get my kids back. Or it
was not making enough to pay day care and rent. Or it was
because they ordered me to be in the court. They *ordered* me to
come to these meetings with the social worker—during work
time. How am I going to hold a job?

"How can you make somebody do all that if you have nothing
to start with? Have nobody's help?

"The court ordered me visitation rights three days a week.
That started out fine. But there were times I could not get there
because—my mother worked evenings, my father worked days. I
had no car. I had to rely on friends. All through this case: 'The
mother has failed miserably to provide any financial support for
the children, due in part to a poor employment record, a lack of
real marketable skills. All this would indicate that the financial
strain of raising two boys would be more than Mrs. Josephs could
ever handle alone.' "

The report goes on: "It was mentioned at the October 12
hearing that [Kelly's mother] would be able to provide care for
the children while Mrs. Josephs works during the day at her
present job. Evidence was presented to indicate, however, that
this setup would be unreliable, especially in view of the fact
[Kelly's mother] is employed herself and works the night shift."

Kelly says, "Not thinking that she could get a sitter now."

The report: "Also, her age, at 48 years old, would be a factor
in considering whether or not she [Kelly's mother] would be able
to care for the two boys until they are old enough to care for
themselves."

"Forty-eight?" I say.

"My mother was forty-eight. That's exactly what's in this
file. Then it has, 'Mrs. Josephs cannot be deprived of the custody
of her children just because someone else could better rear her
children. Obviously, no parent is perfect and there is always a
problem when it could be said that someone else could do a
better job.' "

"But that's exactly what they *do* say!" I exclaim in the face
of this fatuous moral disclaimer.

"That's what they *did*. Instead of giving me the hand, they
stripped me of everything. They took my kids because these
other people could raise them better. This whole file does nothing
but counter what they've done."

Evidence of the truth of this does, indeed, pervade the file. "According to the social workers and foster mothers, Mrs. Josephs has at times shown an inability to properly feed the children, keep them clean, or show a lasting affection for them." (This last—meaning what?) "Whether or not the children are always kept clean by itself is of little significance—" (Then why mention it?) "—but there appear to be grounds to believe that the children have received poor care and are likely to be so treated in the future.

"An inescapable conclusion, therefore, is that the Josephs children would be better off in a new home where the parents can provide the care and affection that Mrs. Josephs cannot provide."

Kelly's attorney sought discovery and inspection of all the materials and records related to her "neglect." The prosecuting attorney denied his request.

Her attorney petitioned them to show cause why they had summarily cut Kelly's visitation, and why the social worker who was also assigned to be Kelly's counselor would not restore her full visitation rights—despite those rights' having been granted by court order. Nothing happened.

And, Kelly says, "I had to pay them $10 a week. At the end of all this, I still owed them $1,389.30. And I was not even allowed to see my children. I had to pay child support payments to welfare for not letting me see my kids. And I *refused* to pay. That's why the judge did not like me. He said I was a fighter. And he would not stand for a fighter against him in his own court. That's why we had him thrown off the case. That was on a tape recording."

"What did they accuse you of in order to terminate your parental rights?" I ask Kelly.

"Financial status."

In effect, she is entirely correct. In the Memorandum of Ruling, Kelly is accused of—and in effect convicted of—having "failed or refused to provide housing for the children; . . . failed to provide adequate nourishment and clothing"; failed "to provide medical care. . . ." But her real offense seems to have been her refusal to knuckle under and confess to sins she had not committed; her refusal to repent of them.

A litany of the workers' "reasonable efforts" to "bring some stability to her manner of living" and "improve her parenting capabilities" is recited. "Appointments were made by the case-worker in order to discuss and discover the cause of Respondent's situation and to correct the inadequacies. For the most part these appointments, when kept, were met with resentment, hostility and a refusal to accept that there were any deficiencies in her manner of conduct as a person and parent." Dickens, hell—this is Kafka. There is no indication that anyone involved in all this perceives even dimly that *poverty* was her "insufficiency"; and that poverty may not be due to a defect in her psyche. Nor is there even a modicum of comprehension that a person might be somewhat miffed and resentful toward those who have exercised their unfettered power to enforce their dislike of her by removing her two children, threatening to terminate her parental rights—and eventually terminating her parental rights.

"Some six months after Respondent's children were removed, she perhaps realized that her children would not be returned to her without some positive demonstration of cooperation on her part." Thus, she "entered into an agreement with the Welfare Department for the purpose of making certain modifications in her behavior and situation as prerequisites for return of her children." (Yes. But where was her right to refuse to do that and still have a shot at regaining her children?) And in that agreement was a final date by which, if she had not achieved "financial responsibility," a car, a house, child care plans, child management, visitation, and counseling—her kids could be taken permanently.

The document recites all her shortcomings, her failures to achieve the "goals" which only the authors of the agreement understood. (Only *they* could determine "adequate" income, "suitable" housing . . .) "Testimony presented clearly established that Respondent, although apparently capable of finding work, has not achieved financial responsibility and further has paid token support for her children although able to support." (Kelly: "They took my children away because I had no money. Now they want me to support them in their care!") "Respondent showed little or no interest in child management training in order to learn acceptable child care habits. Respondent has not arranged for counseling to aid her in understanding her problems and coping with them as well as recognizing the emotional needs of her children and satisfying these. She has further refused to be evaluated by a psychologist." Nonetheless—the lack of psychological evaluation notwithstanding—"Respondent is an emotionally unstable person, unable, unwilling to provide adequate subsistence, medical care, guidance, or other care necessary for the health, welfare and morals of her children."

(Notice how morals crept in here?)

Summarily: "Daniel and Benjamin Josephs have been the victims of physical *or* emotional neglect (emphasis mine)."

Parental rights terminated. Judgment affirmed.

Kelly decided to appeal. She was told by the social worker that her visitation was ended during appeal (although there had been no court ruling to that effect). It preyed on her mind that, now that the county had permanent custody of the children, the agency workers could do anything they wanted with them. They could move them from home to home: they could separate them. Kelly knew that the foster parents wanted to adopt Benjy and Danny: she hated it—but part of her hoped they would; at least the kids would stay together. The court continued to hound her for the back support payments she "owed."

Nearly three years had now gone by since Benjy's accident. Danny was seven. Benjy was five.

Finally, the appeal hearing was held—before a different judge.

Kelly says: "After lunch we went back into court. The judge turned around and he said, 'Stop this case. I want to see Kelly in my chambers now.' My attorney got up to go in with me, but he says, 'I want to see her alone.'

"I went into the chambers.

"He said, 'Kelly, you're gonna have to sign the adoption papers and waive the hearing.' I said, *'Why?* Are you crazy? I have fought this for three years—and you want me to sign papers?' He said, 'Let me tell you something. You may not have another chance at appeal. And, if you don't sign papers, I am going to have to give the custody to the Welfare Department, which would mean that they can be separated. Adopted separately.' I fell off the chair. I didn't want this to happen to my children. They'd lost their dad—early, early on. They'd lost me. They'd lost their grandparents. Everybody they knew. I did not want them to lose each other.

"I said, 'So in other words, what you're telling me is if I sign the papers, the foster parents can adopt them because they want to.' He said, 'Yes, they can have them. I will make sure of that.' I said, 'Okay.' I was threatened into signing those papers."

I am thinking: "This is the moment, is it not, when King Solomon would have said, *'This woman is the real mother! Give those children back!'* "

* * *

"Who are these people—the foster/adoptive parents, the Hol-stroms?" I ask. "Are they major middle-class citizens?"

"They're upper-class. They have money."

"Golf club, country club—that kind of money?"

"That's right."

"They have kids of their own?"

"They can never have kids. But they have money. I don't. At the appeal, the judge told me my kids would have to be taken because of my financial status."

Kelly is now remarried. "Now we own our own home. He's driving a 1986 car. I'm driving a 1988. Everything welfare wanted me to have then—I have now. But it takes time. It does not take three months' time, six months' time—when you start with nothing."

Kelly and her new husband have a son. Despite the stability of her life and her marriage, the fear, the sense of vulnerability to the system, continues to pervade her life:

" 'I'm not gonna be a good mother. I'm gonna lose this baby.' My husband had a hell of a time—in fact it was three years after my son was born that—they tried to take him, Billy. I got a letter from the welfare department stating that they wanted to make an appointment with me the next day—and stating that they had a complaint against me.

"When I got this letter and it said 'Social Services'—I opened it and I literally let out one hell of a big scream, and I said, 'Oh, my God! It's happening again!' My husband had already gone to bed because he works nights. But he came running out of that bedroom: 'What's the matter?' I said, 'They're gonna take my baby. I told you I'm not a good mother. I told you I wouldn't be a good mother. Welfare told me that.' My husband says, 'Oh, bullshit, you're the best mother he's got.'

"So I called them. I said, 'What the hell is this? You have a complaint against me?' The worker says, 'Well, we have a complaint that you and your husband fight and you throw things and your child's life is in danger.' I said, '*What?*'

"My husband is so easygoing. When we get in an argument—and you can ask my son, we very seldom argue—but when we get in an argument, he goes in to bed. He says, 'Write it down. I'll read it in the morning.'

"And I let them come to my house. But first I called my attorney and I told him I wanted him here. Now. Because of what happened with Benjy and Danny. So he came and he sat on the couch. This big idiotic caseworker walked into my house like she's God and she says, 'Who are *you?*' And he says, 'I am this family's attorney.' She says, 'Well, I'm not allowed to speak to you. I'm here to speak to Kelly.' And he says, 'Well, you're gonna have to speak to her with me present.'

"She looks at me and she says, 'Well, if you have nothing to hide, why is your attorney here?' And my attorney said, 'I will call your superior tomorrow morning because I don't like what you're insinuating about my client.'

"They came in. They talked to my husband. They talked to me. They talked to Billy. They went to his preschool. They questioned them there. They questioned my husband's work. They questioned where I worked. They did a thorough, complete investigation. Then they called me and said they were gonna leave the file open; they had found no evidence of anything. They questioned every neighbor in this neighborhood. That was embarrassing. To find out if there was fighting.

"Every neighbor came over to me and said, 'Kelly, what's this about?' And I said, 'I don't know. What did they ask you? What did you say?' They all told welfare, 'We don't hear *anything* over there except her husband out in the yard playing with their son.' They said, 'We hear *no* fighting, *no* anything—not even a loud TV.'

"Welfare was satisfied. But they said, 'We're gonna leave this file open for six months.' No more reports, they will close the file. I did get a notice from them that the file was closed. But somewhere, someplace, somehow, we have an enemy out there. I think if this enemy had known that if there were any more calls they would have taken Billy away—they would have continued to call.

"You know what the social worker said to me after the appeal hearing? She said, 'Time will ease the pain, honey.' Well, it doesn't. It just doesn't."

As she has, off and on throughout our talks, Kelly weeps.

# HE WHO
# "MAKES
# TROUBLE"

The woman on the telephone is thirty-six years old, and telling me a truly gruesome story: "Forgive me," she says, "if I'm not perfectly coherent. I just got out of a mental hospital and I'm on medication." This hospitalization she attributes to a flood of memories of her childhood victimization. She was in nine different foster homes, spent three years in a girls' home, starting at the age of eight. There, she received no schooling (and thus has only a second-grade education). She was released to the custody of a man who was not her father, and who raped her. Only recently, through tracing prison records, was she able to locate her real father, now seventy-six.

The system's response to this? "They don't deny it," she says. "It happened. But 'what's done is done' they say. They say they don't do things that way anymore." Perhaps they do not. However, that was only twenty-some years ago. And given the ongoing reportage of disaster after disaster, it would be unwise to treat their assurance as a sign that all is now well.

The newspaper clipping on my desk is headed, "A Mother Kills and the Blame Must Be Shared".[1] It tells of Tracey Maye, who killed her young daughter, Tess, by "striking her repeatedly with an electrical wire." It tells us how Pam Miller, a nurse and a highly regarded foster mother, cared for the child for nine months and tried to plead that it was too soon to release the baby to her mother. She was not listened to because foster mothers have no voice in court if they have not had the child for over a year.[2] It tells of the failure of social workers to visit after the baby was returned home. The system's response to that? To the fact that there was only one caseworker visit after the baby was returned home? John Allen, Westchester's social service commissioner, says, "One social worker left and one didn't pick up."

In yet another news story, two former workers with the Illinois Department of Children and Family Services were charged with official misconduct and falsifying records. According to Patrick Murphy, Cook County public guardian, "They lie, and they do it all the time. They can do this because there is nobody to scrutinize them. They are above the law."

When, on top of all this, Murphy challenged the right of the social services attorney to represent the estate of an eleven-year-old girl killed by her foster parents, the county's attorney replied that, after all, Murphy had agreed to the girl's placement.

Murphy then pointed out that his staff had agreed with the decision based on faulty information. What was the system's response to that?[3]

That Murphy should have known the information was unreliable, "that the information the DCFS provides is not always reliable."

That surely has to be one of the weirder defenses in legal history: Effectively: "We're not guilty because you should have known we were crooks." The very absurdity of it is symptomatic of a hysteria that signals a loss of grip.

The system's response, overall, to the stories of the extreme abuses that occur under its aegis is that these are just "horror" stories. The clear implication is that they are atypical, the exception, aberrant; and that the real abuse is in the press's blowing them up. The suggestion is that they are somehow fiction, "stories"; they lack the imprimatur of scientism.

"I do hope," officials in one agency or another would say to me, "that you are not going to just print horror stories." The problem with this is that we are talking about children, not apples. If you were responsible for a shipment of apples, and some got demolished in the shipping, that could probably be factored into the cost of doing business with apples. However, when it comes to state intervention in the lives of children, the clear idea is that the state, in removing children from homes they deem detrimental, is prepared to guarantee a higher level of care and safety for *each* child it removes.

The voices in this book are not telling the horror stories, the kind that make the press. The events they describe can be taken for fairly routine examples, not of what always happens, but of what easily can happen. None of these stories, however, bears any resemblance to the shoulds of the rhetoric and pieties about protecting children; or to the public's image of what a protective service is.

A good deal of the literature attempts to measure the "positive" impact of foster care. But even the measures of this are a little peculiar. The measures are often school performance, the presence or absence of behavioral problems, likability, social skills, the presence or absence of entanglement with the juvenile justice system. But I know lots of middle-class-raised adults who, for one reason or another, got kicked out of schools as kids, who were viewed (without necessarily the labeling) as having behavioral problems, who would not necessarily have been seen as likable by adults (or professionals), or as having the correct social skills. And "delinquency" in children, much as it conjures up gangs run amok, as often as not has to do with a child's attempt to save his or her own life: running away from abuse, then doing— what?—to survive.

Each time I descended from the stratosphere of theory to the literal reality, it was with a thud. Whatever the federal policy, as it filters down to the state, the city, the county level, whatever intelligence and reason may have informed the studies that dictated the policy seem to get lost. All that remains of the meaning behind the theoretical shoulds are the tiny little should-shards of conforming to guidelines that will appease your mandate, and match the guidelines that get you your portion of federal funding.

The impression at the research and policy level is of judicious

consideration of the best interests of children (and, more mut-
edly, of the state's interests). At ground level, the impression is
often of a willful, punitive, arbitrary parent: a being whose many
cells add up to something that explodes in a tantrum on inquiry;
that demands, above all, pleasing and unquestioning conformity.

This "parent" targets the most powerless members of society—largely poor women, mothers; other women, foster mothers; and children. Even where there is a male of life-threatening
brutality in the picture, the system tries resolutely to keep its
focus on the mother, the foster mother, and to a lesser extent, on
the behavior of the child.

I have referred to the extensive testimony that women fight
long and often fruitlessly to get their children back from foster
care.

When the father decides to fight, however, the system seems
to accord his case considerably more respect, out of fear that the
father, the male, can "make trouble."

I had not known that Marsha would be bringing her mother,
Rowena, with her when she came to talk about her now-adopted
daughter, Mandy.

"My mother has taken a lot of abuse about Mandy," Marsha
explains. "I thought you'd want to hear about that."

Marsha chooses a chair; her mother, the far end of the couch.
Barely seated, Marsha is off.

"We have one child, Alison, a nice house. We thought we
could help. The training they offered was—maybe two meetings.
So we qualified. Seven, eight months went by. They call up. They
have this two-and-a-half-year-old girl who has 'no problems.'
'Sure, bring her out right now.'

"When she got there she was sick, so sick she could not
breathe. Her father abandoned her three months before. He left
her with this couple. He was supposed to send money. He was
supposed to take care of her. And he disappeared. And the
people said they had not heard anything from him. They knew
nothing about this child other than her first name, her approxi-
mate age. Mother was gone because he threatened to kill
mother."

"Whoa," I say. "Slow down."

"See, the mother," Marsha enunciates, a little bit as though
I'm just learning English, "took the opportunity when he left
with the child to go to her parents for medical help. And when

she got there, she reported him to the police—that he was violent, that he was not taking proper care of the child.

"Meantime, he was living with some woman—who was supposed to be taking care of the child. And he came home one day and another boyfriend had moved into the house. So he got angry and took the child and left. The next thing we were able to trace about the child, Mandy, was he left her with this couple. He was supposed to be working and sending money to take care of the child. Well, they said after three months of not hearing from him they had to do something. Because they could not care for this child.

"All Mandy did was sit in a corner and beat her head against the wall. And she used to pick her legs and arms until they just bled. They said this child sat on the floor and beat her head against the wall. And they turned her in.

"We apparently got her the same day. She had no medical checkups, nothing. They brought her to us. She had eyes that were crossed so bad that she could not go from our den—which was paneled—into a white hallway without careening into the wall. It took her a couple of weeks to learn that when she hit that doorway she should stick out her hand so her hand would hit the wall. She also was so choked up that mucus was pouring out her eyes. The nose was absolutely disgusting. Her ears were closed up; you could not see the ear canal.

"She had shoes that were half a size too short. When we took them off, the imprint of the shoe was in her foot. That's how small and tight the shoes were. Her legs—her feet were crossed. The left foot was crossed facing right. The right foot went this way behind it. And her knees were against each other. She would try to run and she would maybe make three or four steps and fall flat on her face. Her arms—I don't even know how you would describe them—they just hung funny.

"This is the child they tell us has no problems.

"And the clothes—I have never seen anything like it in my life. So as soon as the worker left we took her to the store and bought clothes. We tried some on her and she wouldn't take them off. We had to check her out with the clothes on. She threw herself to the floor and was kicking and screaming. So we just told the salesladies the situation, and they clipped the tags off.

"We had a time getting those clothes off her that night."

"I will never forget the picture," Rowena says. "She just came in and she flopped right down on the floor. I don't know how to describe it. 'What's *happened* to her?' I didn't know what had happened.''

"She's sitting there," Marsha says, "against this wall in the foyer, and there's not a sound. And tears are running down her face. And one of the things they did tell us to do—is have some of my nieces and nephews there, my daughter, have toys thrown all around. That would look friendly. And my little girl says, 'How about some cookies and milk?' Now the minute she said 'cookies,' the smile got this wide.

"But that night we thought the child was gonna die. She could hardly breathe. We couldn't get anybody on the phone. We had no authority to get anything done. Nothing. I called their office the next day, but I got a recording. I said they can go jump in the lake. And I took her to my doctor. I told him we had just gotten her and we didn't know anything about her. But that as far as I could tell this child was just about to choke to death. And he checked her out and said the best we could do was give her some mild medicine, since we didn't know anything about her. And watch her and see—if it got any worse, he could just take her to the hospital.

"At this point we didn't know what had happened to this child. We found out later that the day after she was born, her father went up there and told them he wanted his child, and told the mother, 'If you want to come, get your ass out and come.' And took her out of the hospital. So the mother went too. She was thirty-one. These people were not teenagers.

"But the mother did not get the follow-up care she needed. She had a very bad time having the child. And apparently, soon after, she got pregnant again—and he made her have an abortion. She got an infection which went all through her body. And he took her to the hospital and left her there. She was in bed for most of the child's first year of life.

"He went to work at six o'clock in the morning, and that child probably was changed at six in the morning. If he didn't get home to lunch, that child probably did not get fed. If he came home at six in the evening, she probably got changed and fed then—assuming he wasn't drinking. But the mother has told me he was drinking up all the money he made. So you can picture what the first year of this child's life was like.

"Her mother, Sandra, did not get well enough to start caring for her until Mandy was maybe eight or nine months old. Then after that, she told me the daddy used to beat this child—

unmercifully. She was less than two years old still. Still—no-body's done anything.''

It was only after the child had been dumped with that couple that Mandy was brought to the attention of the system and the placement made with Marsha and her husband, Larry.

"It took us eight weeks to get them to give her glasses. It took us seven months—to get braces on her legs. Seven months—to get the approval. Because they had to give us the approval. I could pay for it, but we couldn't do it. Certain things they won't let you do. When I took her to the doctor, I sent them a copy of the manual page. I said, 'This child is sick, I'm supposed to have her treated. There was no one available at your office. I called. So I had her treated because I felt her life was in danger.' I guess they figured me for a troublemaker right from the start. I don't know.''

*Uncooperative* is the word I often heard used, about mothers and foster mothers alike. It signifies "uppity." Foster mothers themselves liken their role to that of a mother. The act of mothering, after all, does not depend on biology. But in this mothering you are engaged in a second marriage—to Super-pop, the state. Super-pop comes across a bit like the Victorian father: absolute ruler, unwilling to acknowledge his own transgressions but holding those in his charge to a rigid standard of morality, behavior, and the following of his dictated procedure.

"I can't think how long it took them to evaluate Mandy," Marsha says. "They did that kind of faster—three or four months. We got this strange person and she evaluated her, and said she was functioning at the level of an eighteen-month-old. And she was two and a half. I watched the child take the different little tests. And this child had no idea what half the things were. But some of the things on there were things that my child at her age would not have known.

"I saw this evaluation about five or six years later. I finally got my hands on a copy of it. And she put in there that the child's coordination level was not properly developed.''

A gift, obviously, for understatement.

"The worker was so far off on some of the other stuff—she described the wrong child. I saw the physical description. And I remember saying, 'That's not her. That's not her.' She was never a blond. She's got auburn hair. The woman's *physical* description of the child was wrong.

"She put down that she heard this child talk. This child didn't talk. She said 'mama,' 'daddy,' that was it.

"So about five or six months after we'd got the braces for her legs the parents showed up again.

"Let me see if I can think. He was in jail from the October after we got her until February. And then they showed up in March or April. And disappeared again until September. In October they showed up and started monthly visits. And at Christmas we arranged to bring her to her aunt's house for a family visit. And then we gave them tickets and they took her to the circus. Mandy made sure to tell me she hated it. I said, 'Okay.'

"And in March the workers told us they were giving her back. By now she's turned into a halfway normal child. She was almost four years old."

But it was not simple getting Mandy to that point.

"We went through having curtains ripped off the windows. We got kicked. She threw temper tantrums. She couldn't talk. She'd scream and scream. She'd be on the floor and we had the special shoes on her feet for her legs and all. And when she'd start, we got to the point where we'd take her by the foot, grab her foot if we could, pull her out to the middle of the floor where she couldn't hurt herself. And just let her kick and scream. Because I was scared to death the child was gonna throw herself around and hit her head on a piece of furniture. And kill herself.

"At that point we didn't know what had happened to her. Later on we found out through the psychiatrist that in her opinion the child was probably sexually abused as an infant. Then the fact that she was totally neglected the whole first nine months of her life. She had none of the handling or anything that she was supposed to have. She was already trained to kick and scream. That's what she did for nine months."

"And she never called for her mother," Rowena says. "She was callin' *him*. When we finally found out what she was sayin', she was callin' her father, not her mother."

"Because he taught her from little that her mother was nothing," Marsha says. "She was dirt. All women—were nothing. He told me this himself. How he sat in a barroom and told this child—a two-year-old child—how her mother went off and left him. He forgot to tell her—she went off because he threatened to kill her. And he was extremely capable of killing. He was dangerous. He kept guns in the house. At one point in time he put a gun in this child's face. And told her he was gonna kill her mother and her."

Violent husbands, violent fathers do just that, of course. And for the reader who is thinking, "Why didn't Sandra, clearly a battered woman, take this child and leave him?" it will be useful to know that leaving does not at all ensure an end to the violence. In fact, it may be the step that provokes the batterer to murder.[4]

"Why weren't you afraid he'd kill you?" I ask.

"I didn't have enough sense to be afraid. And he knew my husband stood right behind me. The first day we were to meet him at the Social Services offices, we were walking—and we came to a four-way crossing. To cross there was to take your life in your hands. So there we are—this child cannot walk more than three steps without falling. Common sense to me tells me you pick this child up and carry her across this four-way maniac zone. Well, he was watching us from inside. I carried the child across the street and I didn't put her down.

"We go in, we look and find out where you're supposed to go, and we tell them we're there and we go sit down. The child sees nobody she knows. She's lookin' all around. We see a kind of sad-looking lady movin' at her and callin' her by her name. And we see this really immaculately dressed person, immaculately clean—sitting next to her. With his newspaper. He's just glued to the paper.

"This is the loving father who hasn't seen his child in six months. And she's waving at the child. The little girl finally went over to her. And so—they call us at about this time. And we all go up at one time. And the worker's introducing us. His first words to me were, *'She . . . can . . . walk.'*

"And my words were, *'I . . . know . . . that.'* In the same tone.

"But the first thing we had to do—the orthopedic doctor had us teach her to ride a bike. We had to build up the pedals on the bike with blocks. Then we had to pick up the bike so the wheels would just spin. And you had to sit in front of the bike and actually hold her feet and turn the wheels with her feet on the pedals till she finally learned the motion. She had to be taught to crawl, because they assured us she'd missed that stage. One person in front, one in back. The one in front had the arms, and the one in the back had the legs. And we had to crawl her across the floor, moving arms and legs till she finally learned that motion."

Rowena says, "Listen, listen. You don't know what it was like. When we put them braces on her. Well, you put 'em on at night and you have to leave them on a couple hours. Well, about three o'clock in the morning—I was wakin' at that time . . ."

"Her room was next to Mandy's . . ."

". . . about three o'clock in the morning she would start screaming. She had enough of the braces. She couldn't tell you no kinda way. Everybody in the house was woke up. Everybody up, because you had to take the braces off her legs."

"She had a bar across here," Marsha says, "and one that came all the way up to here—so she could not move her legs. And she'd try to move. She couldn't even turn herself over. Finally she couldn't stand the pain anymore. And the doctor said, 'The first time she cries, try to get her to keep them on a *little* bit longer. The second time take the things off.' That went on for six months—until they gave her back to them.

"But luckily, between that and the dancing—my daughter went to dance class so we wanted Mandy to go. We were looking for any kind of coordination therapy that would work. This nice dancing teacher, every week he would make her do this extra exercise, little ballet exercises with her legs, turning her legs.

"At the end of the year, though, she walked out on that stage when he called out her name in the auditorium and she walked up there and she did her little steps and you would have thought it was his own child, he was so proud. We were all thrilled to death. She did it."

Rowena says, "Not only that, there are so many good things you get out of it. When she came home one night from the dancin' after she was goin' about a year and she could turn her feet this way? '*Mi*-ma, come and see what I can do! *Mi*-ma! Come and see what I can do!' The first time she could ever turn her feet out. That's the kind of thing that makes you feel good, you know?"

"The last thing I can accurately tell you the day we brought her back to them," Marsha says, "she told me, 'Mama, you come back and get me and my furniture Sunday. Don't you leave me here. You come back and get me.' And I kept tellin' her, 'I can't come back. You're goin' home to live with your parents. You know they're your parents, and you're goin' back to live with them. They love you.' It was a horrible time. I was cryin' all the way there.

"She had a bedroom. They had a sofa in their room because they only had two rooms, a kitchen, and a bath. They had painted it and cleaned it all up when she went home. It was deplorable— but it was clean and neat. I didn't think they were good enough for her."

"Well," I say, "but you don't want to start deciding whom

children should be with depending on who has the better home, do you? How did you feel, Rowena?"

"I mean, I hated to see her go home. But I was glad. I thought the people would be better, would try and make a home for her. And I didn't see it like Marsha. I saw it like you say, you know. I came out of a family with nine children. And we never had a whole lot. We had our own home, cows, chickens, all that kind of thing. Enough food. But we never had no extras. So as far as I was concerned—her family was poor, it didn't make no difference to me—if they loved her and treated her right."

Marsha says, "They agreed to let me continue to see her—because she was in dancing school and she was gonna be in dance revue. And in the meantime he was sick with stomach problems. So he was in and out of the hospital. And the mama would sneak the child to me to watch her. She'd lie and tell him the neighbors were watching her. So I had the child with me on a weekend or whatever."

Rowena says, "The child kept crying to come home, meaning wanting to come back to us. What did I think? I told Marsha—'Marsha, take her back.' But you know what that child would do to me? I'd sit down in the rocking chair and I have a little shawl that I put around me, and I'd rock and I'd rock and I'd rock, and I'd pick her up and try to take her to bed. And she kicked me in my face one day. She kicked me in my stomach. She kicked me in my leg. Me and Mandy never really got off at all—from tiny, up. Until a few years ago. Three years ago, I got cancer and I went to the hospital. When I came out of the hospital, Mandy was a different child entirely. I was shocked myself. But all those other years, me and Mandy didn't get along at all. It was hard, very hard."

Marsha says, "Mandy never did say her father hurt her or anything. But one day I was drivin' her back home and she said, 'You know, there's secrets I can't tell you.' And by this stage of the game I was watchin'. I said, 'What kind of secrets, Mandy?' 'I can't tell you, Mama. They're secrets.' I said, 'You mean that he drinks?' She says, 'Yeah. That's one of them.' I said, 'I know that. I'm not stupid. I've seen him drinking.' She said, 'That's not it, Mama. But I can't tell you.'

"And then—he was in the hospital again—I was drivin' Sandra down to visit him one day and she says, 'You're gonna have to help me raise that child. If anythin' happens to him, you're gonna have to help me raise that child.' I said, 'Oh, all right, Sandra.'

"And then my daughter, Alison, had a birthday party and they were comin' and they didn't show up. And for some reason—that was another warning bell.

"The next week we got a phone call—it's Mandy. 'My mama wants to know if you could come and get me. I'm at Aunt Lollie's. Can you come and get me?' I say, 'Is Aunt Lollie there?' So Lollie gets on the phone. I said, 'What is goin' on?' She said, 'I don't know. They just came here, clothes in a bag, and Sandra said he's beatin' her up again. And they left him.' I said, 'Well, does she want me to come and get Mandy?' She said, 'Yes, she does.' So I said, 'Well, let me talk to her.' I asked Sandra, 'Do you want me to come tonight?' She said, 'No, but come tomorrow.' I said, 'Are you sure?' She said yes.

"So the next morning I went down there and Sandra's talking to me and asking me what can be done to protect the child. And telling me how she's seriously not ever going back there. And she tells me, 'No matter what I say or do, don't let him get this child back. She can't ever go back there to live again.' I said, 'Are you sure?' She said, 'No matter what I say or do.' I said, 'All right.' I said, 'But you know it's gonna be a fight. And Monday we have to go to the social worker and we have to make a report. If we're gonna do this, we have to do it right.' She said, 'Okay.'

"So I called the supervisor that I knew and I told her what was goin' on the way I suspected it. And she told me, 'This is what you do.' Then I called Sandra at Lollie's and I told her we were going to the country for the weekend. 'That's fine. He doesn't even know we're gone yet. It'll be two weeks before he sobers up and finds out we're gone.' "

Unfortunately, it was not two weeks.

"Monday morning, I called Protective Services and told 'em I wanted to file a complaint. You don't have to give your name in this state if you don't want to. But I give 'em my name and address. They said, 'Well, can you come in tomorrow?' I said, 'Can't we come in today?' 'No. Come in tomorrow. Bring the mother with you, and the child.' So. 'All right.'

"The next morning we go to get the mother at the aunt's house and bring her to Protective Services. We get there and she's on the phone with somebody. She comes to the door and she tells me she changed her mind. She can't go. So I got mad. Temper went. The entire hurricane. Tried to get her to go. She would not go. She wouldn't budge. I got so mad I couldn't see straight.

"I took Mandy by the hand and I said, 'Let's go. We're goin'.'

And when I got there, I told them everything that had gone on. This child was in foster care before. The mother told me to take this child and get help and don't let him get her back—no matter what. 'And,' I said, 'now she won't come.'

"Luckily, this was a really good protective service worker. Got on the phone and tried to get Sandra. The first couple of times she wouldn't talk to her, but finally she did.

"Then the social worker took Mandy in the other room and she talked to her privately. She did not tell me anything that Mandy said. She said, 'Better for you not to know anything. . . .' "

Whipping out my Captain Foster Care Decoder Ring, I take this to mean that if Marsha knew what Mandy had told the social worker, it might be made to look as if she had put Mandy up to saying it. In any case:

"When she came out, the woman put her arms around me and hugged me. I mean, I never had a social worker do that.

"So I didn't know what Mandy told her. We get back home, goin' on four o'clock, and there's a message there from Sandra that she has to have Mandy back in her custody by such and such a time. Six o'clock, or whatever. And that they were comin' to get her.

"Well, at this stage, Mandy is runnin' around screamin', 'Don't let him get me. He's gonna hurt me. Don't let him get me! *Don't let him get me!* Keep me with you!' And ran into her room and literally got under the bed and would not come out. And at this time I'm having a heart attack, screamin', 'Over my dead body he's gonna get her back! Over my dead *body!*'

"Then I calmed down. I said wait a minute. He's comin' here—and he's probably comin' with a gun. So I called the social worker and I said, 'Look, this man's dangerous. He might have a gun in his hands. And he's not gettin' this kid. That's it. I'm not givin' her to him.' Well, she called Sandra back and now she had the judge on the other phone.

"See, what happened was he got to Sandra on Monday and started threatenin' her—which was why she wouldn't go with me Tuesday mornin'. He told her he was gonna kill her if she didn't get Mandy back. And I didn't have the sense to call the police. I mean, I have more latitude in what I can do than Sandra does. He puts a foot on my property I can get the police out here and have him arrested. She can't do these things.

"So the social worker already had the judge on the other line, and he issued a . . . what-do-you-call-it? 'You put her back in foster care right now'?

"I said, 'Well, what am I gonna do? He's on the way here.'
She said, 'Well, I was gonna stop and get somethin' to eat. Then
I'll come.' I said, 'I'll give you food here. Come.' She said, 'All
right. I'm gonna call the police and have them get there.' Because
Mandy was now officially in state custody.

"So she got here and she ate—I couldn't eat, I was too upset
to eat. Mandy is hidin' under the bed; won't come out. My
husband had gone outside to get somethin' in the garage and he
was comin' around the side of the house and—here they come in
the yard.

"So—thank God—my husband said, 'Hi, come on in and
have a cup of coffee. And let's talk.' It defused everything.

"The father came in—immaculate. You would never know he
had been drinkin' for two weeks. We gave 'em coffee. And the
worker's very calm and cool. And she told him that Mandy was
in the custody of the state. And that he could not remove her.
And that there would be a hearing within seventy-two hours.

"He said, 'You mean I fought for two years to get her back,
and she's back in the custody of the state?' And something to the
effect, 'If you don't give her back, I'm gonna *get* her back.'

"In the meantime, the police show up. Thank God my husband went to the door. And he told them, 'It's all right. Don't
worry about it. Just go ahead and go.' Rather than have *him* see
the police out there.

"So it was this thrillin' day where you have the police car,
you have the state car—in my neighborhood, where you never
see a police car."

The mind boggles. I think, "And this is a situation in which
things are going *well:* The protective service worker is effective;
the judge is responsive. . . . This is what happens on a *good*
day."

"At the hearing, they're up front and I'm sittin' in the back—
because I made the complaint. And they had put Mandy in my
custody. She was in an approved home. Why take her and
separate her from us and cause more stress on the child? And the
judge and the district attorney are askin' questions. And I notice
they are watchin' my reactions to the father's answers. And I'm
sittin' there holding the chair like this. I was about to kill. I was
goin' to explode. He was lyin'. Through his teeth. Under oath.

"And Sandra was too afraid to say anythin'. I had been
warned, 'Do not say anything about Sandra talkin' to the social
worker!' Because nobody'd let him know Sandra told the social
worker that everything I said was true. And that he was gonna

kill her if she didn't get the child back. And she told the social worker, 'My death will be on your head.' ''

It took six months for them to get an adjudication. And during those six months, Mandy was ordered to go for regular visitation with her parents.

"Mandy did not tell us till then—what he had done to her," Marsha says. "One night it just started spillin' out. She was havin' horrible nightmares; she was screamin' all night; kickin' the walls every night.

"The games he played were really perverted. One game she described—she says he dressed her up in her mother's underwear, and then climbed up on her. That's how she described it. When she started tellin' me how he raped her—she told me exactly what he did. And she said, 'Mama, I cried for you and I called you and I called you and I called you, and you didn't come. And he hurted me, Mama. He *hurted* me. And he made me go in the bathroom and he poured that red stuff all over me.' I thought it was Mercurochrome. She said, 'No, Mama, the one that burns.' Merthiolate. 'Then he made me get out of the tub and he made me change clothes and he told me if I told Marsha or Sandra he'd kill me. He'd beat me and he'd kill me.'

"You never knew when the stories were gonna come. And I had my book. I knew I was supposed to write it down. So that I could tell the social workers what she told me. They did not want to believe it. The doctor that I took her to would not examine her. And they kept makin' her visit. One time she had a hundred-and-one fever and they made me bring her down there. And this was our good social worker. But she said we had to bring her— *or he would make trouble."*

Immaculately groomed, presenting himself well ("a real charmer when he wanted to be," in Marsha's words), the father is perceived by the system as able to "make trouble." In all of the stories I have listened to, read about, never have I heard concern expressed about a mother's or *single* foster mother's ability to "make trouble."

"He would sit there in the office with Mandy on his lap," Marsha says. "He would brush her hair. And it would look like he was just bein' the most lovin' father. He was threatening in her ear the whole time. She'd come out and tell me what he said to her.

"Well, by February that kid was just fractions away from a complete nervous breakdown. Her first year in school was just totally destroyed. He forced the mother to call up and tell Mandy he was comin' to get her. That they were gonna get her. The child locked every door in the house for nearly a year after that. I had to call the school and tell them that under no circumstances was anybody except myself or my husband to take her out of that school. And they were not to allow my husband to have her unless he showed his driver's license.

"But he totally destroyed her first year of school—because he kept draggin' us to court. And forcin' her to go for the visits.

"So finally we got to see a child psychiatrist. And Mandy walked in the door and she just told her everythin'. And then when I went to see her, she didn't tell me anythin' Mandy had said. She asked what Mandy had told me. And after I finished talkin', she took out Mandy's papers and said, 'There it is in black and white. The same thing you just told me.' Mandy drew her a picture of what the monster did to her. She made it all red and said the monster hurted her. He put his whole self in her and hurted her."

The psychiatrist was able to get the visits stopped. Nevertheless, the court case dragged on for three more years, with continual hearings, as the father fought and tried to get the venue changed.

"At one hearing we went to, they made us bring Mandy. And the parents come in—'Come see this little purse we have for you.' And they took her out and bought her candy. And the worker was sitting there. I said, 'He's doin' one of his numbers again. He's pullin' somethin'—I'm tellin' you.' So after a little while, he's fillin' her up with candy, and he knows the kid's so hyper it's not funny. And he takes her out for soda, and all of a sudden Mandy comes back and I was sittin' with the worker, and I said, 'Well—I don't know what he told her—but he found the key.' She said, 'How do you know?' I said, 'Look at her. He found the key. He's done somethin'.' Mandy comes back and she said, 'I've decided I want to go home with my mom and daddy.' *'What?'* 'Yeah. I have to go home.'

"Well, the social worker and the attorney convinced the judge that what she meant was us, our home. So he said she stays with us.

"Well. Child threw tantrums for a week and a half. And then when she wasn't wild, she was all withdrawn. She came home and she started in on me. And she threw one of her throwin'-herself-around-the-room things.

"And I would sit on the floor and hold her so she couldn't hurt herself, so she was throwin' both of us all over the place.

And all of a sudden I started hearing, 'You just go ahead and take my life. You take my life. I'm going to Jesus with my mom. You take my life.' And I looked at her, and I said, '*What'd* you say?' 'You just take my life.'

"I said, 'I'm not gonna take your life. What's wrong with you? What is the matter?' I said, 'What are you talkin' about?' He told her that if she didn't go home with them that day, her mother was goin' home and take her life and go to Jesus. And that's what this little not-even-six-year-old kid was carryin' around.

"She thought her mother was dead."

For an instant, just a split second, I drift: Is *that* child abuse?

Marsha continues: "I said, 'First of all, your mother wouldn't kill herself. She's not the type.' I say, 'He might kill her. But she's not gonna kill herself. I guarantee you that.' 'Are you sure, Mama?' I said, 'Yeah. She wouldn't do that. She would never do that.' But Mandy was convinced that her mother went home and killed herself because she didn't go home with her. I mean, unbelievable things like this. Just unbelievable.

"And at the final hearing—we'd always fought to keep Mandy out of the courtroom. But this time Mandy said, '*I* want to go there and tell the judge what he did to me. *I* want to do it.' 'You sure?' 'Yes, Mama. *I'm* gonna do it.' So I called the psychiatrist and I told her. She said, 'Okay. If she feels this way, this may be the beginning of the healing process. This is something she has to do to show that she is in control of her life. We have beaten him. We have proven that we are stronger than he is. He doesn't own the world.'

"When it came time for the termination hearing, the judge did everything he could to put her at ease. The social worker did everything to put her at ease. There's a lot they could have done to shorten the process. There's a lot they could have done better. We have been luckier than a lot of people with things that we got done. The stress has been un-be-liev-able. The burnout is still around three years later. Hopefully, a lot of Mandy's damage will go away. But they claim—Mandy was a throwaway kid to start out with. Just stick her in the institution and forget her. Zero.

"It's been a struggle. But she's in the sixth grade; she is not retarded. She is bright. She can be very compassionate. She can also be mean as the devil. She can be truly aggravating when she

wants to be. All the statistics and everything said this kid will
never accomplish anything.

"And she's done a lot."

"You've done a lot," I say as Marsha and Rowena gather
their things to leave. And I think, "Well, there you are. Not a
'horror story' at all—is it? In fact, a happy ending."

# COMPLICATIONS III

**P**auli and I are having a glass of wine. "About Laura's rape?" I say.

"It was about April twentieth," Pauli says. "I had come home from work and I'd paid the babysitter, and the kids went out to play. I was washing the dishes. I think Dana had asked could she go out and right around the corner to play with her girlfriends, and Laura stayed on the block with her friends.

"And the next thing I know, this lady was at my door—a lady that lived on the block, and Laura played with her children. All of these kids were coming down the block, and the lady was holding Laura.

"And she said, 'Keep calm. But Laura has just been raped.' And she had Laura in her arms, and Laura is crying, and in view of all these things Miss Jefferson had told me—

"Like, the other time Laura had gotten raped in the other foster parents' home—this was *in* the parents' home; some of the family did it—she say that Laura had provoked it. And had sex willingly with the people. And then had accused the people of rape. This is what the social worker, Miss Jefferson, told me. So they made their own summations and let it go at that.

"I looked at the lady and I looked at the children. I said— 'You say Laura was raped?' They said, 'Yes.' I say, 'Who saw it? Did someone see this?' And all of the kids told me that they saw it happen.

"And I said, 'Come on, let's go down the street. We'll meet the boy that did it.' The lady says, 'His sister is right down the street.' So all of us went down there—'cause I didn't want to hurt a child's life if Laura was saying something that wasn't really true. As Miss Jefferson had told me she did.

"So we went down the street together and the girl was coming up our way, and they say, 'That's the sister. That's Wayne's sister. Ask her where he is.' So I asked her what was her brother's name. And she was hesitant. But she told me. And I asked her what was his address, and she told me. And I said, 'Well, where is he?' And she said, 'I don't know.'

"And all of the kids were telling me that they saw it. So the only thing I could do was have witnesses. I'm a foster parent. Had I not told it . . . Which I wanted to tell it anyway, because the way I feel about it, no matter what Laura's problems are nobody has a right to take her body if she doesn't want them to have it. . . .

"So I had no choice. The police station is right in front of my house. I took her across the street to the police station, and I told them what had happened, and they called a policewoman. They were all upset because this was a little young girl. And they know the neighborhood, and they know some of the kids in the block. This officer was very nice. She investigated. And she talked to all of the kids in question, because they'd given me their names and I had written them all down.

"Then—the Department of Social Services was closed. I wanted to take Laura to the doctor. And I asked the policewoman did I have to get in touch with Social Services to do that. She told me that she had an emergency number and she would get in touch with them. But—um—she never could. Because no one ever answers that number. So she told me that I would have to call them the next day.

"The doctor told me that he could see where Laura had been penetrated, or they had tried to penetrate her—but her hymen was still intact.

"And Wayne—he was fifteen or sixteen—he was the only one who really put his penis in Laura. And they tried him in adult criminal court.

"The other boys held her down.

"She does get fresh with boys, she does. But see, the doctor told me that her hymen had never been completely broken—Miss Jefferson told me her hymen was broken before she came to me."

"What other problems did you have with Laura?" I ask (although I am thinking that getting raped was "Laura's problem" only in a very specialized sense).

"She didn't want to obey. She didn't want to follow orders. She'd go into fits and tantrums. And one day—they had a fight outside. But I had told them not to go off the front porch. So I heard all this noise, I went outside, to find out what was happening. She was yelling and screaming.

"I said, 'Laura, did you go off the front porch?' Because I had told her not to. And she started yelling and screaming that I was taking their side against her, that I say she did this and she did that. I said, 'Laura, come in the house.'

"And I took her in the house—to talk about it. And I was trying to explain to her that I'm not accusing her of anything. I just want to know what's happening and why it's happening.

"She went crazy. You couldn't talk to her. This was when she first came. She just went into hysterics. She wanted to go back outside—how she was going to kill everybody—and how her whole family had a reputation for beating people with bats and boards and busting heads and stuff. And so I said, 'Laura, you're not going back outside.' And she's telling me I like Dana better than her, and I'm taking sides against her.

"I said, 'Now, Laura, you know that's not true.' I was just trying to talk to her privately, you know. But I wouldn't let her go out the door. And she sat down—and she rolled her eyes at me. Then she jumped up and I followed her. And she went upstairs. I went upstairs behind her. And she got a pair of scissors.

"And then she came back downstairs. And she sat in the chair. And I just sat in the chair across from her. I didn't say anything. I didn't touch her. And she held the scissors and she looked at me and her mouth puffed out and she rolled her eyes and—well, I'd never really confronted anything like this—before.

"I didn't say anything. I just sat there watching her. I didn't know if she was going to try to do something to me with the scissors or what she would do. I just waited.

"And then she picked up the scissors and reached up to start cutting her hair off.

"I don't know where I got this knowledge from; I don't know how I knew what to do at that moment—I really don't. I just got up and I went over to her and I said, 'No, baby, you don't want to do that. . . .' I said, 'Come on, now, give Nana the scissors.' And she held on to them for a little while. I said, 'No, you don't want to *do* that. Because your hair all cut off, you're gonna laugh at it tomorrow.' And she said, 'No, I'm not.' I said, 'Yes, you are. Give me the scissors.'

"And she turned to me and I just took her in my arms and held her. I guess that's what—it must have worked. It must have been what she needed.

"When I took the scissors from her, she got up and then she went back upstairs. And I just followed her up. I didn't say anything to her. And Ali was in his room. She went in, she sat on the side of his bed, and she just sat there watching him for a few minutes. He was playing with one of his things. And then she started playing a game with him. Like nothing had happened."

All this while, Laura was not in school. (Mind, children can be removed from *mothers* for educational neglect. And only the system, the system said, was allowed to put Laura in school.) After Easter vacation, Dana and Ali would go back to school. But Pauli would still have to find care for Laura. Miss Jefferson had promised she would pick Laura up and put her in school the day after Easter. The day arrived. Miss Jefferson did not.

So Pauli trucked Laura over to the babysitter's. No one was home except an aunt, who had a job interview later in the day. The aunt said she would keep Laura if someone would pick her up in time for the job interview. Pauli called Miss Jefferson, who said she would certainly be there in time for the woman to get to her job interview. She didn't show up. The woman didn't get the job.

Now Pauli didn't have a babysitter for the following day. In the afternoon, Miss Jefferson was supposed to take Laura for a family reunion with her mother, Maria, and her six sisters and brothers—who were also in foster care. But what about the earlier part of the day? The woman who'd kept her (the aunt) had another job interview scheduled for that afternoon. Still, she said, "Miss Pauli, I'll keep her until Miss Jefferson comes. I could have taken her with me today if I'd had carfare. So I do need carfare so that in case she don't come I can take Laura with me to my interview. I cannot miss another one."

"So," Pauli says, "I gave the woman carfare for Laura. Miss Jefferson was two hours late—and she didn't call, she didn't come. So the lady took Laura with her. And Laura missed her family visit.

"And that's how I met her mother."

Complications.

# "YOU
ARE
TROUBLED"

I began to notice: some of the stories that were not the worst—in the sense of parental brutality, multiple rape, deliberate rejection—seemed the saddest. At the core of some of these stories, I would hear an almost unbearable ambivalence, which seemed to keep the tormented child-self undead, restlessly wandering the landscape of the adult's life as though in search of some ultimate stake through the heart.

One would think, for example, that the child whose mother was terminally ill, or psychotic, would have a much better shot at understanding that circumstance, not his or her existence or personality, was to blame; a better shot, then, at laying the demons to rest. But that was not always so.

And that stands as one of the more sobering things about playing Solomon Says: You can operate according to the best psychological principles; you can think you know what you are doing; but you cannot know how what you are doing will affect any particular child.

It is one of the most vigorous arguments, I think, for what the system most blatantly lacks: humility.

Bob is thirty-six. A teacher for thirteen years, he switched careers and is now a successful sales executive, married, with two children, a house, a dog. . . . He comes in carrying a briefcase. In that briefcase is a one-inch-thick stack of papers, the reward for years of troubled and troublesome search: the records of his life; the reports that seem to confirm his existence. Though he occasionally will read from the documents to me, he will not let them out of his hands, or out of his sight. Nor will he agree to Xerox them and send me a copy. "I cannot bear to think of these in someone else's hands," he says. It is as though I have asked for a photograph of him naked, in some awkward or compromising position.

In recent years, Bob has involved himself with foster care as an issue, been on a foster care review board, done what he terms the "foster care circuit"—the conferences, the conventions. . . . It is getting too much, this obsession. His wife, understandably, feels that his intense focus on his own past is stealing from her, and from their children's, present.

"It's not like I want to talk about this," he says, "but I need to do it. Because if I don't talk about it, who will? I went through seven years of therapy uncovering things, and primal therapy of going back—so far back in my life that I uncovered things that lots of times I wished I had never uncovered. And I didn't do all that for nothing. So if I'm gonna do all that, then I owe it to myself and anybody else who may have gone through similar experiences to talk about it."

Bob is amiable as we talk, articulate and present. But there is, nonetheless, that atmosphere of dense pain—that seems, over all this time, to show no sign of having a half-life.

"My parents separated somewhere around the time I was six. They were having marital problems. My mother had muscular dystrophy—though it wasn't diagnosed as muscular dystrophy at the time. She was limping as early as I can remember. She eventually went into a wheelchair. I think my father had a lot of difficulty with that. He expected her to do more than she was able to do.

"And there was some violence in the home. My father would get upset with my mother, and there were at least two occasions

I can remember that he became seriously abusive. I remember
my grandparents were in the house. My brother and I were in the
house. And my father was throwing my mother against the wall.

"I was huddled in a corner. The only thing I remember is my
grandmother asked my father if he was gonna hurt her. And he
said, 'I'm not gonna hurt her, I'm gonna kill her.' And those
words have rung in my ears for many years.

"He was—management level in a store. We lived in a row
house. In the middle. On one end, farther along, were my
grandparents—and my father's brother, his wife, and their three
children. When it became difficult for my mother to take care of
my brother and me, we ended up at my grandparents' house. It
was convenient.

"I think the straw that broke the camel's back was probably
another night when my father beat my mother up. Threw her
against the wall. I remember her screaming and banging on the
wall. The police came. He was held in jail overnight. And my
aunt, her fiancé, and my grandparents bailed him out the next
day. My parents were not together after that."

"What," I ask, "do you remember of that scene?"

"My mother was on the floor. And my father standing in front
of my mother. And my grandmother going over and pulling the
blind down on the window. I remember being huddled in the
corner. I remember the kitchen and the dining room were an
arm's length away, and my brother and I both went to the door,
but the door was locked and we couldn't get out. The back door.
And the screaming. My mother was doing the screaming. My
mother had a particular scream. It was the same scream she
would scream years later when she needed help. When she had
fallen. When she was trying to walk out of the wheelchair
someplace. A particular pitch.

"I went to school the next day like everything was normal. I
remember coming home from school and being sad. It was just
an aura of change that was going to take place. And I was afraid."

Bob remembers that he and his brother moved into an apartment with his mother. He remembers, in the second grade,
coming home from school and seeing a big box, the one the
wheelchair had come in. He remembers playing with the box,
and with the wheelchair. "I remember it was new. I remember
when it was new. Because I remember later, when it wasn't new
anymore, and it was kind of beaten up. And it was fun. To move
around the house. It was a toy. We didn't have a lot of toys. So
that made it even more special."

Bob's parents separated when he was six. He went into foster care when he was eight. During that period his mother got worse and worse. They got evicted. Their things were put out on the street. They moved.

"We lived in a one-bedroom apartment. My brother and I slept in the bedroom. My mother slept on the sofa. She was more demanding. She required that we do more for her. She would call in the middle of the night, sometimes, to have a bedpan emptied. I was eight by this time. My brother was nine. She required having her shoes put on. When she wanted to get up out of the wheelchair, we'd have to actually physically pick her up. And as she stayed in the wheelchair longer, she got heavier.

"We cooked. I can remember, eight years old, ironing my own clothes. Cooking my own food. Washing clothes. Washing dishes. I don't think that's a horrible outrage. The difference was—there was no choice."

"Yes—but," I am thinking, "yes—but." For thousands and thousands of children it has been this way throughout history: children of immigrants when tuberculosis was rampant; children of the unemployed or meagerly employed poor, whose labor was needed to keep everyone alive. . . .

"But," I say, "in history so many kids have survived that kind of 'need' circumstance. Is it sufficient reason to put kids in foster care? Isn't that an argument for providing some help in the home? Some real services, instead of removing the kid?"

Bob is ambivalent. "Eventually, my mother went into a nursing home. But that was several years later. I'm not sure that it— I needed to be someplace else. I did. It was not a healthy environment. Living with a sick, demanding woman. It was her nature that she was a demanding person. But her illness caused her to be more and more demanding. Because as you get more and more uncomfortable, you look for ways to find comfort. And—in terms of her being cut off from the world—she placed more and more demands on my brother and me. So we became means to fulfill her needs. And didn't really have lives of our own. I didn't have the life of a kid. I wanted one, and it would always cause me conflict. I'd throw temper tantrums—because I just felt so frustrated all the time. And then I felt guilty because I threw temper tantrums. There were times when I'd get so angry at my mother that I ended up being abusive to her. I guess it was like I had no control over it. My life around me, I had no control over.

"I mean, I'd get mad at my mother and dump the wheelchair over. That's how angry, how frustrated I was. I'm not proud of that, but that's the way it was."

If Bob felt no control then, in his mother's home, he was to experience even less once removed by the state. In speaking with children who wind up in state care, the issue of control arose again and again, in various guises. The whole business of raising kids, after all, is meant to be about allowing them to experience ever-greater degrees of autonomy as their abilities increase: from feeding themselves, to walking alone to the school bus, to managing limited amounts of money. . . . Kids in state care have had a fundamental sense of control wrested from them. They are wherever they are "on spec"; on consignment. They have no idea what will happen next, or when it will happen: and no idea, later, of *why* it happened. This blank as to causality leads the kids into unwitting complicity with the system. Because, once they are in its care, the minions of the state scrutinize the kids relentlessly for their faults and for their "problems." And they are all too ready to collude: to make up reasons for events that have to do with the children *themselves,* their actions, their personalities—as though it is either inconceivable or intolerable to them that what is happening often has, in fact, far less to do with the children than with state workers' whims, or with expediency.

"How," I ask Bob, "did Social Services get involved?"

Like most foster kids and former foster kids, Bob has little information about why the adult world behaved as it did. He refers to the only history he has, his meager stack of papers—compiled by social service workers.

"It says here: 'Reason for Referral'—and it says the matter was referred by the school personnel and the visiting teacher, who requested the courts and the caseworker. Oh! This was the reason for psychological testing . . ."

"But in your own memory . . . ?"

"In my memory? I don't remember why. I only remember that my mother told me something about my brother and I threw eggs—that the neighbors were complaining that we threw eggs in the basement stairway. And there was something about pouring gasoline in the hall. I remember being with my brother, pouring gasoline. And I think—it's like things had gotten out of hand. Something strange was happening.

"I only remember being in the courthouse. I can remember the image of a judge. The next thing—we were going into foster care. I can remember going home crying. I remember my mother telling me that we were going into another home, a foster home.''

"Did you know what the words *foster home* meant?''

"A foster home meant a home that wasn't yours. And I just kinda went along. I was going to another home. I was going to another home. I didn't like it. I cried. I went on nerve medicine.

"I remember the first time my foster parents told me that my mother was coming to visit me—I was a mess. I can still remember the smell of the blue mint anxiety medicine. It was some liquid blue mint that was supposed to calm my nerves. I remember being in the bedroom and not wanting to come out. Just wanting to hide. I have a mental picture of what my mother looked like on the day that she came to visit. She was teary, she was puffy. Her face was bloated—like she'd been crying.

"That turned out to be a temporary foster home, although I didn't know it was supposed to be.

"My brother and I were in the same house. They had three or four of their own children—the Bensons. My brother got letters from them years later. My brother always seemed to cultivate the relationships with people. Where I was just kind of shy, timid. I went along with things. I didn't want to get close to them. I didn't want to trust them. I didn't really want to stay too long. I wanted to be home.''

"For all that you said about hating having to push your mother in the wheelchair . . . ?''

"For whatever reason. It was my home—good, bad, or indifferent. I wanted to be there. I wished that home would have been different—but I still wanted to be home. I wanted the closeness of somebody who is your parent. And your home. I never felt the freedom in somebody else's home to do what I wanted to do. I always felt like in a straitjacket.''

In a few months, Bob and his brother were moved.

"I don't remember packing or anything. I suppose it's too painful to remember. I can remember the room. It seemed very big. It also seemed empty. I remember the curtains blowing in the wind. The high ceilings. The bed—it seemed like a lonely bed, with a chintz spread. I don't remember any pictures on the wall. Lonely. I think that's the primary word.

"Before I knew it, summer came. The Elks put me in a summer camp, paid for it. My brother and I were together. We slept in the same bunk. I remember liking camp.

"Then we moved to another home. I was not yet at the point where I knew that that's how the system worked.''

The next home was the Allens'. They had a daughter a year younger than Bob. Mr. Allen worked as a guard at a penitentiary. Mrs. Allen stayed home. The family was Catholic, so Bob and his brother were rebaptized Catholic. At first, Mrs. Allen seemed stoic, cold. And Mr. Allen seemed warm. The physical circumstances were agreeable enough. Materially, Bob had more. Still:

"I was in the house. As a person, I wasn't there. I was very shy, very lonely.

"I remember one particular time I didn't want to undress in front of anybody. And I was more or less thrown into their daughter's bedroom until I took my clothes off. Because Mr. Allen wanted me to take my clothes off. I didn't want to take them off. That was his method of my getting over shyness. If you're talking now-rational, no, it doesn't make sense. But my thinking back then was such that he just wanted me to do it. And he wanted me to do it because I didn't want to do it."

Things got worse.

"He would make fun of my brother a lot. And they did things like—you had to have a bowel movement every night. And it was humiliating because every night he had to check it. He had to check to make sure it was a sufficient bowel movement. I remember just the humiliation of having to squeeze on the toilet to have a bowel movement, and then having to come out in the living room when everybody was sitting around watching TV—and announce that I was finished and having him follow me up to look."

"Didn't that seem awfully strange?"

"It is strange. I know it sounds strange—as a thirty-six-year-old. But as a kid—that's the remarkable thing about children. It's the thing I miss about children, not being in the classroom anymore. The thing I loved about children the thirteen years I was teaching was they are so damned accepting. Whatever their circumstances are. I see it in my daughter—and it's wonderful to see it. And it's horrible to see it when it's misused.

"I also had to work an awful lot in that home. Meaning—clean up the yard. I don't know if you know anything about primal therapy. It's based on a primal scream. They call it doing a piece of mat work because you do scream until a particular part of your life comes into view. And the very first time I ever did primal therapy I recalled the time I lived at the Allens and our task was to rake all the fucking leaves out of the woods. Out of the *woods*. Like here's a tree, there's a tree, there's a tree. We did that. It was Mr. Allen's way of making men of us."

During this time, Bob continued to see his mother.

"The Allens would pick her up and bring her to visit. Sometimes we would go and spend the weekend with her. I liked the weekends, but the ending, leaving, was always incredibly sad. I was happy to see her, and happy to be there. And then—when we had to go back to the foster home—I was sad. I hated those mood shifts. Being happy and then being sad. It almost would be to the point where—eventually I started to not want to see my mother because I hated that feeling happy and then feeling sad. I hated feeling.

"I always had people tell me, 'Stop looking so forlorn.' Or, 'Stop looking so sad.' I did not smile. I did not laugh a lot. Those years that I was in Catholic school, I was afraid to go to the bathroom. I never went to the bathroom. I was afraid that somebody would see me. I didn't want anybody to look at me. See my organ."

What precipitated the move from that home? One Saturday the Allens wanted to do something alone with their daughter. They gave Bob and his brother money to go to the movies. Told them to take the bus home.

The boys didn't go to the movies. The film turned out to be a horror movie, and Bob was afraid to see it. They walked around all afternoon, bought things with the movie money, and then, after dark, they went back. At dinner, they did not tell the Allens they had not gone to the movies.

"Somehow," Bob says, "they found out. Mr. Allen had gone upstairs with my brother. All of a sudden my brother came down and he said, 'We're leaving.' He'd had this argument with Mr. Allen about our not going to the movies and Mr. Allen must've said, 'Go on. Get out.'

"It was dark. It was raining. We walked to my mother's apartment. Got there at one o'clock in the morning. A good twenty miles I'm sure it must have been. I remember walking over the railroad tracks. I was a follower. I was not a leader. I didn't have to be. I just followed my brother and we got there. And my mother was livid.

"Monday morning she called the social worker. My mother was a fighter, you know. She was spunky. When she had something to say, she would say it. And she'd fight for her two boys. And that's what she did. She said we were not going back there."

Bob and his brother were placed in another temporary home near the Allens' so they could finish the school year. All along they had been together. At the end of that year it was decided that Bob's brother would go to the children's home. And Bob would be placed in another foster home, in another community.

"I was real scared. But I liked it at the same time—because I had to do for myself. I had no other choice. I didn't have him to lean on anymore."

It is almost axiomatic in child welfare: siblings should not be separated (if possible). Yet even that should does not seem to be universal.

Bob went to the new school. He made friends for the first time. He started to feel that kids liked him. He developed a sense of humor. He went bike riding for the first time, did puppet shows in the basement, camped out with kids in the backyard, did all the regular-kid things.

"At the same time, I was living in a foster home with a woman who was going wacko.

"She'd stay up late at night, turn off all the lights, and sing old songs from when she was a child. She'd take out these old photos of where her father would take her to sing—like she was going to be the next Shirley Temple. And she would sing these songs from when she was a kid. All night long.

"She had this other foster child, Hank, who must have been in first or second grade. Crew cut, big brown eyes, a cute little guy. But he used to wet the bed. She would get so violent with him. She would throw him on the floor, or take diaper pins and just poke them in him.

"By this time, I was developing a keen sense for the crazies. I knew when she was going to go into one of her moods. I knew enough to work around it. But Hank didn't. He was younger and didn't have the skills. And I didn't know how to help.

"I can remember just standing there, staring at her while she was poking him with pins, or grabbing him by his penis and throwing him down on the ground. She'd turn and she'd look at me—and I would know that she knew what she'd done was wrong.

"That's when she would get remorseful. That's when she would rock in the chair and she'd sing the songs. That kind of thing went on all the time. In fact, she also took Hank and she beat him on the head with a butcher knife. He was six, seven.

"I came home from school and Hank had a patch on his head. I asked him what had happened. He was just sitting there like this when I got home, on the chair against the wall. 'Hank, what's the matter?' He said, 'I cut myself.' I said, 'Oh, come on. I saw Aunt Rita on the way in and she told me what happened.' To this day I don't— I guess I must have just known. And he told me that she had done it. That she had taken a butcher knife and cut his head.

"And I panicked. I was in seventh grade. I went and I called my mother. She said she would take care of it. That night, we were all sitting at the table and the social worker called, and Rita answered the phone. I don't know what the social worker told her, but she just went into a rage. She just started screaming. She threw the Bible at me. 'I swear on the Bible I didn't do that.' "

Once again, Bob refers to his folder of papers. "I have it in the record here. The worker said I was accusing Rita of doing something. How could I have made up such stories? 'This child has always had a vivid imagination.' "

Neither Hank nor Bob was moved at that point.

Shortly afterward, though, Rita's marriage exploded. Rita left. The social workers found another home for Hank. Bob was returned to his mother. At this point a young worker offered him a "choice": he was told he could stay with his mother, he could go to another foster home, he could go with his father, or he could go to the children's home where his brother was. Bob turns again to the Documents of His Life and, referring to his interview at the children's home, reads:

"Bob was accompanied by a worker from the welfare board. They arrived at two-fifteen. The worker explained that they got lost. Bob did not have any idea why he was here. He was not surprised when told. My guess is that he did not want to know. He knows he has to take a test to get in here. He does not know what sort of test.

"He is now living in a foster home where he was placed two years ago. His foster parents are separating and he has to leave. He does not want to go to another foster home. He does not want to come here either. He does not know what he wants to do. He appeared to be close to tears.

"Before entering his present foster home, he was placed in a temporary foster home and prior to that a third foster home for about three years. He does not know why he was moved. He thinks it might be because the foster parents did not want him anymore.

"Before entering foster care, he lived with his mother. He had to leave because she is crippled and cannot take care of him. His parents are separated but his father has continued to see him, visiting him at the foster home about once a month. He also sees his mother. He would like to return home to live with his mother.

He thinks he can look after himself because he is older. He quoted the worker as having told him he had a choice of four things. He could come to the children's home. He could go to a foster home. He could live with his mother. Or could live with his father. His worker told him it was up to him to decide. He wants to go and live with his mother. But he has not told the worker this because he thought the worker, the welfare people, wanted him to come here. He would do what welfare says because he figures it is best for him. . . .

"Later, I spoke with the worker at the welfare board and in essence he confirmed Bob's statements. He remarked he does not believe in forcing a child to do anything and gave him the four choices. I expressed that placement at the children's home at this time was not indicated in view of Bob's reluctance to accept placement here, when as an alternative he has a choice of returning home. He might return here for another interview next week."

By the time of the next interview, the worker had told Bob that he had no choice but to go to the children's home. Because: His father did not want to take him. Because there was no foster home. "And because I never really had a choice in the matter."

"But why did they give you a choice if you had no choice?"

"Because this worker was young and felt it was best for children to make up their own minds. And probably had planned on how to manipulate me into making the only choice that I had.

"It's also possible that the social worker believed I could go to live with my mother and then, when he talked with his supervisor, the supervisor said, 'Out of the question, he can't do that.' If they don't have any more foster homes available, the children's home is the only place.

"What it really boils down to in the end is you really don't have any say-so. 'We'll give you some examples and make you feel like you have some control, but then we're gonna take it away from you. You're not gonna get what you want anyway.' That's the screwiness of it all. The system plays with your head. It makes you believe things, and then it takes your beliefs away from you. And strips you of all that. You're lucky if you have any belief."

"You've worked with the system in recent years. Do you see a significant difference now from when you were in care?"

"I don't know. I want to believe that. See, I think that social workers start out being social workers because they're idealists.

There's some that are kind of mean and malicious people. But there are a lot of them that really have good intentions that when you tell kids these idealistic things they think that they're gonna do it. And they don't necessarily think about the implications of reality.

"I have to believe that things are different. I mean, to think about the things that might be happening in a home right now that happened to me when I was in a home and that system, I can't deal with that. I have to believe that things are different. And I know, in reality, that they're not.

"I guess I wish that I could bury my head, that I could find the way people do that they turn away and they don't look at it. I envy those people because they can run away in their BMW and stick their nose up and say, 'Fuck you, world. I'm living my life.' "

"What was the children's home like?"

"It was an old mansion—that had belonged to a wealthy merchant and philanthropist—in what they had then called the suburbs. And when he died, he donated all his money to form a library. Somehow it got into the hands of the children's home of the city. It was a three-story old mansion. A big winding staircase. Big, thick banister that wound up three floors. You could look down from the top and drop a marble or something all the way down to the floor. And hear it echo.

"I liken it a lot to the home that Oliver Twist was in. There were dormitories. Each floor had eight boys on it. On the floor I was on, there were two dormitories—three boys in one, five in the other.

"The first week I was there I had someone approach me—at my bed. I'm thirteen years old, and that kind of shocked me. I learned that you had to actually physically fight—in order not to be fought. That you had to establish yourself.

"I hated it. I always hated it. I was the type of person that I would just let things build—so much that no one could control me. I would let the rage bottle up—and then somebody would say the wrong thing and I would just let off steam and go wild. And they'd say, 'Boy, nobody'd better mess with him.'

"I remember one particular time: I was just taking stuff, trying not to let it bother me, and not saying anything to anybody. And I had to actually physically beat a kid up. I just kept pulverizing him. And then everybody said, 'Oooh!' you know?"

"Who was in charge?"

"There were two houseparents, a director of the home, and

an assistant director. There were two houseparents in my building, a married couple, Mr. and Mrs. Ives. Mrs. Ives had the
second floor, and Mr. Ives had the third floor. He was kind of
dignified, always wore wing tips and suits. They had a bedroom,
bathroom, living room apartment. Mr. Ives would think nothing
of smacking somebody. The rumor was Mrs. Ives was an alcoholic. She wouldn't come out of her rooms very often.

"I remember—I had to go to public school, and walking
home, and having some kids that I recognized as having been in
one of the classes with me. And I did not want anybody to know
that I lived in 'the home.' So I turned a corner and ducked down
in the woods behind the home and came up that way. I did that
for some time. So nobody would know that I lived there. Eventually, it had to be found out. You can only go on hiding things
like that for so long."

"What was the worst part?"

"The worst part? There are lots of worst parts. There were
parts that I would have adjusted to and I would have accepted. I
think the worst part was after being abused."

What happened to Bob in the children's home has, for many
kids, a kind of weary, dreary inevitability. Kids like Bob are
sitting ducks for adult sexual exploitation. In Bob's case, he was
abused by his male social worker. It's an old story, but no less
poignant in each case for that. Needy child preyed upon by
greedy adult disguised as a benefactor.

It began with walks in the woods, progressed.

"The first time that I actually remember very clearly was a
time when my mother was in the hospital. And I had not corre-
sponded with her. I had gotten angry with her about something
and hadn't talked to her in a month or two. I got word that she
was in the hospital and she was dying.

"She was in intensive care. And I ended up being molested
on that particular day. And my pants were wet from the molestation. And then he took me to buy flowers—for my mother. In the
hospital. And I remember trying to hide myself while I'm buying
flowers for my mother who's dying in the hospital. I felt like it
was a price that I paid. Kind of like a whore."

It went on for a while. For a while, the worker left to travel.
But then he came back. What Bob was being bought with was
more than warmth, more than money: the worker dangled before
him a sense of *possibility* that simply had not appeared in his
universe before.

"Nobody at the home was even talking to me about going to

college. There are aspects of social work today that do that—and they tell me there were then, too. But nobody was doing it for me. The social worker I had at the home was saying, 'What are you doing about college?' What am I doing about college? It seems to me that person should have said, 'Let's sit down and look at some different things that you can do.' It's almost like that circumstance forced me to seek out other ways. This man, the social worker, he told me that I could go to college on the tuition waiver. That I could come to live with him. That I could just leave the home, and that I wouldn't have to tell anybody I was leaving. I mean, he was scheming me. He schemed everything.

"He told me the social workers in the home were my enemies. So I perceived them as my enemies. And him as my friend. And that was what made me mad—the mental game that had been played on me. To disbelieve and distrust all others. And to believe and to trust only him.

"And then when I discovered that the one I was trusting was the least trustworthy—I wouldn't believe it for a long time. Then when it finally hit, it was like, 'My God!' I was having fits of rage. It was too much to deal with, and I'd go on and deal with something else. And forget about it for a while.

"For a good-good-good portion of my life I thought I had made these things happen, and I had wanted it—you know he told me that I wanted it. And there were times later on as things got more and more bizarre when he would say, 'Tell me how much you want it.' And I would say, 'I want it, I want it, I want it.' Till somewhere along the line I had convinced myself that I wanted this to happen. And I didn't want it to happen."

Later along, Bob would sue the social worker, and there would be a settlement. It was a suit he planned and worked on for years. "I just worked so hard toward that goal. To make him suffer. And when I reached the goal I expected to be happy. But—I wasn't happy. I wasn't any happier than when I started. Because I always end up being who I am. And I'm not happy about that.

"I'm one of the lucky ones. Most people that go through foster care or institutions don't go to college, don't come out with a master's degree. Don't come out and become part of society. Don't have a home in the suburbs. I wanted the house with the white picket fence, the two dogs and the cat, and the wife and the children. I have that now. I have the two cars. I don't have the white picket fence and I don't have two dogs. I have one dog and a lot of fish. I have all those things that I thought—I would be happy if I had those things. And I'm still unhappy.

"Because I'm always left with my life."

Why, I ask Bob, have I encountered so many former foster children who don't choose to talk about it, who can't bear to talk about it?

"Because you're nobody's child. You're never quite the same. You don't have the same rights. You mesh into the background so that you don't get rejected. But you get rejected anyway. That's the way it was for me. You do everything to make yourself acceptable—when you're not acceptable. And you never meet the standard.

"Why is nobody talking about it? I could pick anybody out there and you would find maybe one or two that's had a somewhat okay experience. And then the other three would have unpleasant, jerked-around experiences.

"And then there's—a lot of people say, 'Well, foster kids come with their share of problems anyway.' Meaning they're not right to begin with. They have to be reshaped and remolded. And changed. They're not up to par with anybody else to begin with. And that's a stigma. And you have to live with that.

"If I tell you you're an emotionally troubled person, and I keep telling you that you're an emotionally troubled person— 'You're emotionally troubled, you're emotionally troubled, you have problems, that's why I'm talking to you'—pretty soon it starts to groove into your thinking. And it narrows your vision. It narrows your capabilities. Because 'troubled' people can only do so much. They can only go so far. You're a cripple."

"So you thought it was you? That if—with all that therapy— you fixed *you,* everything would be all right? Only to discover it's part of a larger problem? Is that what you mean?"

"I think that's a good way of saying it. That I thought once I got all put together—then the world would be together. And of course I was in an elementary-school classroom environment. I felt like I'd been in a monastery, or a tunnel, for all those years. And finally this awakening came to me: that it wasn't me that made these things happen in my life. That the world had a rhythm and a control of its own. I wasn't the one that was controlling the world. If that makes sense."

As Bob repacks his precious papers in his briefcase, I think: In dramatic terms, if you rail against the gods, you have the stuff of high drama (but little hope of being effective). If you rail against the system, the form is agitprop (but with the possibility, however slim, for incitement to action). If, as the system—which constantly touts therapy for kids, counseling for the kids; harps on the kids' "emotional problems"—encourages its wards to do, you rail against your own "role" in your life, what you get is dead-end psychodrama.

# FLAMBOYANT

The place where I am to meet Lawrence is a New York City walk-in storefront facility for homeless kids called Streetwork. These are the truly down-and-out. They are kids who've been kicked out of other youth shelters; runaways who choose to stay out of the system; some kids who—having hooked to survive—now have AIDS. The facility offers counseling, it offers help in locating jobs, it offers food and an opportunity to do laundry and somewhere, during the day and evening, at least, to safely sit down.

When I arrive, the place is in what I presume to be its usual state of controlled chaos: kids coming, kids slumped in chairs, kids going; kids vying for counselors' attention, for particular items, particular needs. One girl is seventeen and seven months pregnant. With her is her "fiancé"—they mean to get married; at the moment, however, that's the least of their concerns. They have been sleeping in the Port Authority bus terminal.

\* \* \*

Tall, rangy, Lawrence slinks in. He's black, nineteen, and a self-described queen: in his word, "flamboyant." We find ourselves a small, glass-partitioned office in which to talk—only barely removed from the ongoing clamor of phones and kids' talk.

Lawrence is an "okay-'kay?" talker, gesturing continuously with his long-fingered, slim hands. He reminds me, to begin with, of a character who might be portrayed to you by Whoopi Goldberg. Here is Lawrence, censored for only some of the liberally sprinkled "likes" and "whole bits."

"My mother was fourteen years old when she had her first child [Lawrence] and then she was fifteen when she had the second child. When I'd see her, I'd say, 'I can't believe you're my mom.' She looked so young, you know. She's real hyperactive; she drinks, she does drugs and the whole bit like that.

"My sister—she's still in a foster home. But me—my life has been from one scandalous part to another.

"I don't remember all the foster homes because there's been so many. The first real influential foster home was when I was six. That had the greatest impact on me. Me and my sister were there together. They used to play roles against us: 'I like the little girl so much more. She's so cute. Who wants that big-lipped black guy?' And I was only six, and so—bed-wetting and things like that were a problem. And I literally received beatings that were unbearable. That left like a ton of bruises all around my body. I was really scared.

"The lady, she was a reverend, her name was Sister Porter. I remember we used to go to church all the time—and little things really hurt me. Riding with her it would take us like forty minutes to get to church, which was five blocks away. All of us crampacked in a car and she would drive ten miles per hour and if I speak up like, 'Can't we go any faster?' I would get a backhand across the lip: 'Why don't you shut up?' And my lip is bleeding and I'm sitting in church with a big bloody lip and little kids, like, 'What happened to you?' 'Oh. I fell down.'

And I remember she used to make me sleep on the floor beside her bed, which I used to hate. Because my sister and the other foster kids slept upstairs. She had me sleep downstairs because, 'Oh, you stole this.' Or, 'Oh, you stole that.' She's like, 'I left this chicken in the refrigerator and now it's gone.' And the kids would be like, 'Oh, Lawrence took it.' Because I was a 'problem' child: it was very easy to say I had done it.

"There were four other foster kids. And she had like four kids of her own. And the kids would say, 'Oh, Lawrence done it.' And she would beat me senseless. And make me sleep on the floor: 'I'm gonna watch you and make sure you don't get up and go steal any of my food.' 'It wasn't me that took it.' 'You're lying. Yes you did. My kids aren't liars. I sent them to church.' And, 'They were here first and I know my kids more than I know your crummy little ass.' "

Lawrence remembers the move to the next foster home (but not the reason for it).

"Miss Spanner. Now she was really fab. We stayed with her about four years. Now at this point I was so jealous of my sister because everybody said she was so much better and because of me being accused of everything.

"But at this home we were treated differently. Like, 'No one gets more than the other.' And then I started school first, so I learned to read. I had always been a very smart child. That has helped to my advantage."

At this point, Lawrence's stutter begins to appear. It starts almost imperceptibly, and since he is talking so rapidly, for a moment or two I think it to be my inability to hear and register as quickly.

"Let's s-see. I guess I'm about ten now. I was becoming aware of my sexuality. I knew I was gay. Little kids at school were calling me, 'He acts like a sissy. He acts like a girl.' The foster parents, they denied it. 'He's not gay. He just acts like a little girl because of he feels like little girls got more attention than little boys. So the way to get attention is to act like a little girl.' So I guess becoming feminine, the way I am now, with my feminine characteristics, was wanting to get the things that my sister has.

"Because I was a little boy—just got me in trouble. Play outside, play in the dirt. 'Oh, look at you! You're absolutely filthy! I just washed your clothes. . . .' And, 'We're gonna wash you down in bleach.' And they literally poured bleach and tried to wash me. I remember that. When I had a scratch or a sore— from playing in the dirt? With the bleach it just made it burn— beyond belief.

"So when I got to Margaret Spanner's house—she took us in—she'd bathe us. She really did us good."

Margaret Spanner, however, decided to take on an infant

whose mother didn't want her. It turned out to be a child with
enormous medical problems, and, with Lawrence and his sister
at each other's throats all the time, a choice between the sick
child and the older children was forced. At that point, Lawrence
and his sister were placed separately. As Lawrence says, 'Because this problem of fighting was out in public, out in school. It
came down to an actual denial of relationship: 'Oh, that's not my
brother, that little faggot.' And I was saying, 'Oh, that's not my
sister, that little baldhead girl.' Because my foster mother, you
know, she had to cut my sister's hair because the previous home
had permed my sister's hair and the perm had made her hair fall
out in patches. So she had to cut it all off. And I was, 'Ha-ha,
you have no hair. You're not a little girl.' And she was real
insecure about that. Because in foster homes, each family has
their idea of how they want their little girl to look: 'I want my
little girl to have a perm, curls in her hair.' And then the other
foster mother: 'I want my child to look natural.' 'I want my child
to have dreadlocks.' Then another foster home: 'Well, I want my
child to be bald.' ''

Kids who come into state care at infancy, and are then
bumped around, are forced—almost heroically—to invent themselves. If any further evidence were necessary that sexuality does
not come in a package marked ''optional,'' Lawrence's story
should clinch it: Is there anyone in this whole universe who
would *choose,* growing up as Lawrence did in the South, to
invent himself as a black effeminate foster child?

Lawrence's sister went to a foster home he describes as
''fab.'' ''I went to a nastier foster home than the one I came
from—another churchgoing people. And they had their kids. And
I'm alone. S-s-s-so it's no good. So—me being jealous of my
sister again—I got myself in trouble.''

Lawrence was moved again.

''With a reverend and his wife. They were an older couple.
They had no kids. It was fab. But he used to make like sexual
advances at me. And I'm, 'Oh no you don't.' Like, 'Come and
lie on top of me.' Like, 'Here's a quarter, your ice cream money.'
And if I didn't do anything with him, you know, I had no ice
cream money.

''Because I was in f-f-f-f-f-foster care, I got the f-f-f-free lunch,
you know. School was my only release. From my body. I could
study. I could learn things. I could read. When I'm in a book, it
was my state. I would read-read-read-read-read. Then, 'Why you
always got your face in a book?' I would hold the book up t-t-t-to

ignore her and she'd snatch the book: 'Don't you hear me talking to you? Don't ignore me that way!' And slap me. 'You've always got your face in a book. You're really dumb. You never talk to me. You're stupid, you're really stupid. You don't know shit. You're never gonna be nothin' in your life.' It used to really hurt my feelings. 'That's right, look at the little sissy cry, now, look at him cry.' It's like, 'Well, if you're gonna cry, I'll give you something to cry for.' She'd spank me. I'm like, 'For what? For reading a book? That's how it all started?' ''

By this time, Lawrence's sister had moved again (into the foster home where she currently lives): her fourth home. Lawrence is then on his fifth (that he can remember)—and about to move again.

"The neighbors started complaining. I'd be in the backyard and they'd see my foster mother slap me hard, knock me across the yard. So they reported."

The next home, Lawrence says, was a better one. They were, by his standards, people of means, childless. In short order, however, the couple decided they preferred being childless, and became part of whatever statistic presently speaks to foster parent churn and turnover. It is easy enough, given Molly's story, and Pauli's, to see why people would drop out. It is also possible for them to simply drop out because . . . they feel like it (or don't feel like it). Being a foster child, then, is this knowledge: There is not even the illusion of a place where, when you go there, they have to take you in. And certainly no place where, once you're in, they have to keep you.

From there, Lawrence moved in with a woman whom he describes as "a real fruitcake." The social worker discovered serious negligence and—Lawrence went to his first group home.

To begin with, everything was "fab."

"I was given appreciation for the good things I did. Which I had never received. I became a little snobbish, a little snottyish: 'I'm so fab now because I did good in school.' My good grades, you know. 'Oh, he's a wonderful child!' 'Thank you.' I'd go into school and get one of these little certificates for my report card: if you get A, you go shopping for free.

"But then I was starting to go through puberty and being aware of myself and, 'No, I don't like girls.' So I was kind of flamboyant—because I was out, and I could be myself.

"But now schools were another issue altogether. I would get in fights. They'd throw things at me. 'Look at the faggot.' That was down south—where homosexuality is not accepted in no way, shape, or form. When cars drove by, they'd throw bottles at you. And then I was going to therapy. The therapist said, 'Just ignore them. As long as you're comfortable with yourself that's all that matters.' That's what I was led to believe. That's what I did. But it wasn't true at all.

"I found that out the hard way. 'I'm gonna be myself.' That just caused the kids to go off."

"What," friends keep asking me as I am writing this book, "is the answer? You're going to have to come up with an answer." (I don't know why. No one else has.) I think glimmers are becoming apparent, including a need for change in the public's attitude—and forced change in the attitude of the minions of the state—to one of almost holy humility when playing Solomon Says. But what would the answer have been for Lawrence? Let me fly this: placement with a gay male couple. Do I hear the crowd roar: "But then he would have been molested!" Do I really? Lawrence was molested by an apparently heterosexual foster father.

It is mysterious. Over the past decade we have heard the testimony of tens of thousands of men and women who were molested as children by fathers and stepfathers within the apparently heterosexual nuclear family. And certainly, as one travels around the world of foster care, reports of children molested by foster fathers—again, men part of a standard nuclear unit—are entirely common. Yet there continues to be this ferocious bias against placing children with same-sex couples. Why? It would seem to be based on nothing more than a groundless, retrograde stereotype which would equate even stable same-sex love relationships with licentiousness, deviance, and perversion. Even more disturbing, and less remarked on, is that this prevailing bias operates against the gay children themselves. If gay couples are most prevalently perceived as unfit parents, it is as though gay kids are perceived to be unfit children.

Joyce Hunter is director of social work services for the Hetrick-Martin Institute, which serves lesbian, gay and bisexual youth in New York City. She says, "What happens to the kids who are openly gay or effeminate is that they wind up in diagnostic centers where they're supposed to be evaluated and processed. What happens is they wind up *staying* in diagnostic centers in lieu of foster care. So what you find is that kids are living in diagnostic centers—for years. These are the kids that wind up getting lost through the cracks. They're in one center,

they go to another one, and eventually they drop out of the
system—with no employable skills or independent living skills.
This happens in a lot of cities around the country, and I don't
think it's just the major cities. I've been a consultant on a case in
the midwest where this kind of problem exists as well.

"I think this is homophobia at its core. The kids are perceived
as a quote unquote problem because they're perceived only in
sexual terms. And they are seen as 'not being able to fit in.'
These foster care placers will say, 'Well, this kid will pose a
problem for all the other kids.'

"The *kid* becomes the problem, not the attitude of the staff,
not the attitude of the other kids in the group home. This is
discrimination. So not knowing what to do with these young
people, and not really having programs for them, these kids are
denied access to quality care, and the right to a stable living
situation. I am having such trouble finding homes for these kids.
It is so hard. And it doesn't help if they are black or Hispanic
either because—then, the racism. It's a double whammy for these
youngsters. But the homophobia is the overriding theme.

"If you get a gay couple who is a family willing to go through
a foster care screening and they come out really good, you're
gonna have two people who really want to be parents. And I
think that lesbian and gay people should be able to take children
in."

"Particularly," I say, "when your alternative is placing them
in what are effectively detention centers."

"Exactly. Can you imagine growing up in a diagnostic center?
I have kids who spend two or three years in those places. It is
not conducive to getting any sense of who you are, your sense of
self; developing any kind of interpersonal skills. No sense of
family or anything. Because kids are coming and going at a
diagnostic center—and the gay kid sits there."

It is a poignant image: the child, effectively permanently
sidelined, watching as other kids are selected for placement. To
this child—whatever the reality of those placements may be—the
fact that others are placed and he or she is not is what signifies.
The child takes it as evidence that he is an unfit child. Even were
he to understand that it is not himself but what he *represents* that
is being rejected, what effect would this have except to impress
on him that his primary identity is his sexual orientation?

"And for girls, it's even more difficult," Joyce Hunter says.
"I have a difficult time with boys, but sometimes I can get them
placed. But with girls, it's very, very hard.

"So these kids wind up being homeless, turning to the streets, living in the subways and at risk for antisocial behavior, also at risk for prostitution and drugs. And AIDS. These kids on the street are very knowledgeable about that issue. Some of them can even personalize their knowledge and their vulnerability. But they don't care. Their sense of self is so low. 'Well, I don't care. I'm going to hell anyway. I'm gonna die anyway. Who cares?' If you've talked to these kids, you know that a lot of them are really, really neat kids—and just had a lousy break. I think the society has failed them. Social services have failed them."

As you listen to Lawrence, then, know that his story is not only far from unusual—it is not even close to worst-case.

"It was," Lawrence says, "like I started dreading school. I really started s-s-s-slipping. I was gonna turn into a total fuckup now. They put me in special ed. And I pictured myself as, 'Hey, honey, I am *smart*. I'm not retarded.' It's just that I hated school, to be taunted and tantalized just because of my sexual preference."

By tenth grade, Lawrence had been moved again, to a family group home. Once again, he was "taunted and tantalized." By eleventh grade, things were so "scandalous" that he was moved to another group home—and then another.

"School was still hell. No one wanted to sit near me in the cafeteria. No one wanted to talk to me. I was treated like I had leprosy or AIDS. I was the freak kid. Kids would say, 'Oh, hi, Lawrence.' And I would speak back. And, 'Oh my God, you sound just like a girl.' Guys wanted to pick fights. People would say just a whole bunch of v-v-v-vulgar things to me. Every day I'd come home from school cryin'. Kids would yell from the school bus, 'Faggot!' Throw stuff out the window. Made me hate kids, hate school, hate life."

Lawrence discovered his first gay bar. He discovered drag. He'd leave the home in his regular clothes and change in a men's room somewhere. Then, if he was drunk, he'd say the hell with it, not change back; go back to the home as he was. He didn't care. " 'Cause I was ready to give up on life anyway."

He left the group home, moved in with some queens he had met. Lawrence figured that with the part-time job he had he could make out. His housemates then involved him in some kind of check-forging scheme with the fantasy that "we could quit our jobs, quit society, just have fun." They all went to jail for thirty days.

When he got out of jail, he tried going to live with his mother, whom he had been in touch with off and on. When she told him, 'I wish you were never born. You're a little faggot,' Lawrence suspected it was not going to work out. When she said, 'I don't want you here. Get out,' it was clear.

Lawrence was working. But now he had nowhere to live. "And my boss would complain, 'You're dirty. You're smelly. You're wrinkled. Where are you staying?' I'm like, 'I'm stayin' nowhere. My mom kicked me out.' In Virginia they have no men's shelters. So if you're out there on the streets, you're just out there on the streets. So that's where I was. I was an eighteen-year-old bum."

With his last paycheck he bought a bus ticket to Atlanta, hoping to stay with some friends. "The friends I *thought* I had— 'I'm sorry, honey, we have no room. You've burnt your bridge here with your smart mouth and your little flaming ways.' " He stayed awhile at the Salvation Army. Then he was out on the mall. "And people ridiculing me. So here I am cryin'. Hungry. Nothin' to eat. No motivation to do anything because—who wants to hire someone that's smelly and dirty? Hasn't had a bath in weeks. And gay. Who desperately needs a haircut, a shave. No one's gonna hire that person. And no one did."

Some guy appeared who had been given a round-trip ticket at a place in New York called The Mission, and was willing to trade Lawrence his ticket back to New York for Lawrence's last seven dollars. "That was about seven o'clock. Nine o'clock I was on that bus to New York. No money. No clothes. Nothing to my name. Didn't have a thought of where I was goin' or nothing."

Some guys on the bus who'd just been released from prison gave him a change of clothes. In the bathroom at Port Authority he washed up, changed; found a comb, combed his hair. The guys on the bus had told Lawrence he could get help in Greenwich Village.

"I'm nineteen now, no place to go, no food. All I had was just, 'Go to the Village.' I went to the Village—no luck. I didn't know what to do. Just walk the streets. In case someone would pick you up and say, 'Hey, come home with me. You look like you need to be fed.' I'd heard about prostitution. But I thought you stand on the corner with-a-with-a-with-a miniskirt on and flash your leg, and they get out of a car, 'Hey, babe, stop.' That was my idea of prostitution. How wrong I was!

"New York then—it was snowing, it was cold. I did not have
a coat. But I found a coat in a garbage can, shook it out. It was
four sizes too big, but—wonderful, I'll use it as a blanket and a
coat. And I went looking for jobs and all, filled out applications.
I was so surprised at how friendly the people were. 'Sure, you
can have an application. No problem.' I'm like, 'Well, I'm gay.'
'So what? Who isn't?' Oh fab! That was when I really came out
of the closet. *I'm gay!* I don't care. I was starting to feel good—
still hungry.''

Lawrence found a gay bar. "I thought they'd go, 'Oh, he
stinks, he needs a shave, he needs to cut his hair.' But there was
one guy there, he said, 'I'm staying at Covenant House. Why
don't you come stay there? You're not from New York. Someone's gonna grab you and kill you. New York is dangerous.' I
went with him. It was fab. They fed me. I hadn't eaten in three
days. All I'd had was—sh-shit I could find. They fed me, took me
to the doctor for my asthma medication. They gave me plain
clothes. They took me for a haircut. They gave me classified ads.
Some tokens. Everything was fabulous. I found a job and the
whole bit.

"So now I have money. A place to stay. Now I want to go see
the sights of New York. I've never seen the Statue of Liberty.
I've never seen Twin Towers, Rockefeller Center. Now's the
chance to do it. That's the way I felt. I was doin' all that, I got
kicked out. 'Lawrence, you violated the rules. You can't do this.
You gotta be in at seven-thirty. To sign in. And then you gotta be
in by nine-thirty.'

"I'm like, 'Well, wait a minute. Clubs don't open until ten
o'clock. I'd have to be *in* before they open. I don't want that. I
have my money. I'm makin' money on a job. I'll go out and get
an apartment. So I went out and got a hotel—which cost me
twenty-one bucks a night. Fab. I'd party, stayed out all night.
Doing drugs. Had a bad time. I was workin' as a messenger.''

Wait, wait. "You could afford twenty-one dollars a night?''

"Yeah. I got a two-hundred-dollar paycheck. The first time I
paid off a hundred—and the other hundred I could blow. Fab.
But the money ran out. I started to get hungry again. I moved to
this place on Saint Marks. Where I got hooked into the wrong
crowd. Doing drugs. Having fun. Because I was doing good again.

"How fab. I'm gay. I'm in the Village. What more could I ask
for? The piers were right there. And kids were teaching me how
to trick. That you just go t-t-t-to the piers and snatch someone's
glasses away. And tell 'em, 'You can get your glasses back if you

give me twenty bucks.' The man wants his glasses. So he'll cough
up the money. So five people for twenty or fifty bucks—you got
a large sum of money. So I was able to go out and buy drugs, go
out and drink. Go dance the night away and have a really fab
time.

"And then the kids started teaching me how to mop clothes."

"Mop?"

"That's like—pull a girdle over the top of your pants—you
gotta wear a long coat. Put a girdle on. You stand at the rack.
You wear the girdle around your knees. You rip the tags off the
stuff and put the stuff in your girdle. Then you pull the girdle up
as high as it will go, and you walk out of the store fab. Then you
go to Forty-second Street, and you sell them to the girls that be
strippin' and stuff. 'Honey, *look* at these stockings. These are
twenty-five-dollar stockings. They're yours for only three dollars.
'God, these are the stockings I've been *dying* for! I'll give you
fifty dollars for everything you've got in that bag.' I had two
hundred dollars' worth of clothes and I sold them for fifty. No
problem. 'Cause tomorrow I could get more. And more, more,
more. A lot of kids now—that's the only way to survive—is doin'
that. Goin' out and moppin' clothes.

"At this point, I got kicked out of Saint Marks—drinkin' and
drug issues and shit like that. So I went back to Covenant House.
And they were like, 'Well, we're sorry. You had your chance.
We tried to help you. Now you have to prove yourself. You don't
hang out. You don't go moppin'. You don't do this. You don't do
that. You don't go bum and borrow and beg.' "

By this point, however, Lawrence had "got involved with this
child" who had forged a check. "Another check-forgery thing I
didn't need, right?" Whatever the complications involved (and I
found them hard to follow), Lawrence now owed money. "Now
I owe a hundred twenty-five and the only thing I can do is mop
clothes. And two of my friends—they got caught stealing and
they're in jail. So what can I do? You don't want to go mopping
alone. 'Cause you want someone to cover you.

"So I went to the men's shelter in Brooklyn. And it's really
horrible. Most of the guys there just got out of jail, where they
were facing twenty years. They haven't seen their girlfriend in
ages. There's rapes there. Just yesterday this guy was stabbed in
the bathroom. Six buildings. And in Building One there was two
murders there. Within a year. All these constant fights and
beating-ups, and death threats.

"And I've been beaten up on the train. So many times it isn't funny, you know. 'He's a fag. Look at those faggots. Get 'em.' I got socked around pretty bad. I don't mind trains at night, b-b-b-b-b-but I was told . . .''

Suddenly, Lawrence looks alarmed: "What time is it?"

I tell him it's 7:35. We both look through the partition toward the storefront window. Since it's spring, it's still light, but getting on. Lawrence clearly is terrified of going back to the men's shelter after dark. And so, the wrap:

"Basically, what I'm doin' is tryin' to get my life together. Tryin' to get out of the shelter. I called my sister and I told her—we've had like casual contact—and she's like, 'Well, I'm sorry. I wish you the best of luck. Hang in there.' She's still in the foster home after I've been through jail, and through foster homes, and through beatings on trains. And she's in a little mommy-daddy foster home and having fun.

"Now I'm basically surviving day to day. And I risk going to jail by hopping trains. Because I don't have any money. That's why the Streetwork project—they don't provide housing—but they feed you, do your laundry, counsel you, help you find jobs.''

Lawrence tells me he's just started school today, taking "cashier technology." ("They teach you travel agent, banking, ticket sales.")

"I just don't have any training in any specific field. Plus, it's kind of hard when they ask you, 'Well, where do you live? Where can we call you?' 'Well, I stay in a shelter, you know. The shelters don't have phones.' 'Well, we're sorry. We want somebody who's gonna be dependable. Who can come in when we need them.'

"The only thing I see facing me now is going back to the shelter and having to get back and forth every day to Manhattan—hopping the turnstile and risking going to jail. Hopefully, if I can just do that for the next three months I will be able to keep skimping and scraping and sliding by. Until I graduate. And get a job, and can afford to live near my job.''

I had thought, to begin with, to buy Lawrence dinner. Now I feel badly. He clearly is frightened of traveling after dark. For all his "tricking" and "mopping," in this town (in this country?), Lawrence is less predator than prey.

I pull out twenty bucks. "Listen," I say, "I really meant to buy you dinner. You buy yourself something to eat. And the rest," I say sternly, "is to be doled out in small increments to the Transit Authority.''

# TO CUT
# AND
# TO RUN

It was a blizzard and not at all clear to me that I would make the appointment with Carol and her foster daughter, Dani. However, in this northern region blizzards are far from uncommon and natives appear to know how to drive—or at least steer a perpetual skid on the highway—in these conditions.

Me? As a passenger, I just closed my eyes.

Carol is thin, light haired. She offers me a seat on the couch, and chooses the floor for herself. Her back gives her trouble, and so she alternately sits and lies flat. A former nurse, she went into foster parenting when a back injury made nursing impossible. Dani is not yet home from work, so for a while Carol tells me about some of the other kids she has had—before she said good-bye to the system last year.

She talks about Lila.

"Lila was taken from her family because of an incestuous relationship with her dad. Her dad was not penalized by the

137

system, and was referred into treatment." Lila kept asking, "Does the judge rape his daughter?" And, "Why was something not done with my dad? Why was I the one that was taken out of the home and placed?"

Carol says, "The system put her in foster care for six months. And said, 'You're going to be in foster care for six months.' There was no reference to, 'This is what you need to do to go back home.' No reference to, 'There will be therapy for the family members.' Lila fought the system literally for six months. 'I wanna go home, I wanna go home.' She was fourteen. Very suicidal. Constantly asking for help. Wanting answers. And immediate relief for her pain—which there was none. She requested many, many times to speak to her attorney. It was just a real systems mess. She couldn't understand why she had to be placed. That didn't make any sense to this kid. She saw it as a punitive action. Which, indeed, for this child it was."

Carol used to leave a pad for each kid in her home to write their feelings in when they didn't feel they could talk about their problems—but wanted to communicate them to her nonetheless. She shows me some of the pages Lila left for her to read:

"Today was fine. Could have been a hell of a lot better. People tell me that I have something to live for. Well you tell me what it is and then we will both know. It seems the only thing that I have or love that means anything at all to me is my mom and I can't even be with her. . . . Yes, I had another dream last night and I am going to kill the sucker. You always want me to go to bed on time and stuff. I know that I have to. But it's not something to look forward to—getting raped by that son of a bitch all the time."

"Today was fine. Roller skating was really fun last night. And today has been really fun too, thanks for everything. . . . I feel like shit. The way things have been going lately and the way I am feeling about different things and people, as far as I am concerned things are just going to keep getting worse. I am seriously beginning to think nothing or nobody can help me and am beginning to lose all hope. So please find something or someone who can help. I want to be straightened up."

"I have dreams about that crap all the time. What can I do? Just sit back and bear it all (bull!). I can't handle all this shit. Can't you see that? I don't want to fall apart at 14 years old, but it looks like that is what is happening. And people just sit around and watch it happen. They say you should pray. Why? I always prayed to God for my dad to leave me alone and the sucker turned around and raped me. Look where I am now. I think he's just up there for a name and that's it. You seem to have answers for everything. Well please answer this. Why did my dad rape me? I've done bad things in my time, but nothing bad enough to get raped. Why did he do it? When I asked him, he says it was my fault. Maybe I am just a worthless piece of shit like he always told me. He told me I was only good for one thing. I hope he's happy. Everyone else is. Especially the judge. The judge must have raped his daughter too, that's why he let my dad off so easy. Right? Well, he's not going to get away with raping me. No damn way."

"You guys can't keep me here just because you are afraid of me getting raped again. Who gives a shit if I get raped again? No one cared before. Why do they care so damn much now? Is it because if I am sad or get raped again the world is going to come to an end? Well, I wish it was. Then I wouldn't be here right now because I would get out in the street and beg someone to rape me."

"How come you are trying to help me anyhow? I am not worth it. All I am is exactly what other people have said I am—a bitch, a slut, a whore, a brat, and a worthless piece of shit, just a victim."

"From the cases that I worked with in the foster care system," Carol says, "these children continually acted out to be suicidal. That was a way of saying they hurt and for people to listen—and when the pain got so bad, that was the only way to make people listen. And these are also the kids that are oftentimes referred to institutions and things; or residential treatment centers. Dani was in quote unquote residential treatment—a group home. And had some real problems with that."

As we are talking, the door opens, and Dani comes in. She's a large young woman who, with her stocky, brawny build, her short hair, her deep, definite voice, could easily be taken for a young man. After we are introduced, she asks, "How'd you make it? It's not nice out there." As she goes toward the back of the house, Carol and I keep talking. Dani passes by us again, heading for the front door.

"How long you gonna be out, hon?" Carol asks. (Since the expectation has been that Dani will join us, I later realize this is instead of asking Dani, more intrusively, where she is going.)

"I'm just gonna shovel the steps." As she opens the door, I notice the mounds of snow on the steps are considerably higher than when I arrived (and I wonder whether this is the couch I will sleep on tonight).

"Dani was fourteen when she first came to me. Did a lot of running away, was very promiscuous. Did a lot of body mutilation. Cutting on her wrists. Cutting on her breasts. Trying to get pills to overdose on. She'd been sexually abused by her dad, and by her brothers. She went into a group home because her behavior was—she needed the care of somebody who was—up—around the clock. And while she was in there—I was visiting another foster child of mine who was now in there—I became real uncomfortable with the programming that was going on. There was such a thumbs-down on her. To make her behave. And that's what she was responding to. There were so many people policing these children. She was labeled by the system as a lesbian. And was policed. And was shamed. And was told, 'You're nothing but a lesbian.'

"They didn't have any resources for this kid at all. And the first Christmas that our foster daughter was in there, Dani was walking around the group home with a sign on her back saying, in effect, 'Does anybody want me?' Because she was going to be the only child left in this facility for the holiday. She didn't have anywhere to go. So I asked the staff if I could take her home. And they agreed to that.

"There was no place for this child. Everybody was saying, 'Her behaviors are so antisocial. There's nothing we can do. Just give up on this one.' The churches told me that. The staff told me that. And I didn't believe that."

Dani comes back in, takes off her outdoor gear, gets a Coke, and sits down on the floor. There's a brief silence. It always wants to be awkward—beginning.

"I don't know how to start," she says. "Where do you want me to start?"

"Try the beginning?"

"I was born in Florida, and we lived in a shitty home. There were seven kids—four brothers, and two other sisters. I was about six when we moved up north. I remember we lived on this farm. My dad was a handyman. We went to school. I can remember us always walking over to this babysitter's house.

Then we'd come home and listen to my dad yell. To him and my mom fight.''

"Was he physically violent to your mom?''

"Mm-hmm. I would just take off and go someplace else. He would make us go to our rooms, or make us go outside. He would tell us to get out of the house: 'Get the fuck out of here!'

"One time when somebody had stolen some prunes out of the basement and nobody would admit to it—we all got blamed for it. It was night. He would make some of us go upstairs, and some of us had to stay in the cellar. I can remember standing out on the porch—until he decided to let us back in. It was a long time—dark out, cold. I got to stand out there and stand out there and stand out there.

"He didn't talk to us. He didn't know how to talk. He'd just yell or beat the shit out of us. He'd come home and bitch about anything—if the house was dirty, just anything would set him off.

"I can remember one time when he beat up my mom and we were there. And one time he beat the hell out of me—for stealing some homemade bread. I didn't steal it. We had a babysitter, and me and my oldest brother—we were hungry so we were gonna sneak a piece. And they told us before they left that if we ate it we'd be in a lot of trouble. And he came home and told us to take our clothes off, and took us outside and beat the shit out of us.''

Evidently, he was a lot hotter under the collar about bread than prunes.

"When we were moving back to Florida, he fell off a train and got killed. Broke his neck. Passing through cars, somehow, to go from car to car—he fell off.''

Dani was now seven. "We ended up at my grandma's house. We stayed with my grandma for a while. And my mom went nuts, and my family went nuts, and I went nuts. From then on, life was hell. My brothers beat the shit out of me. I had to fight to survive. My mom was real physical.

"Grandma was good.''

Carol says, "You talked about running to your grandma over the years to be safe. She was the safe person.''

"She was the only one you could go to and not get slapped or cussed at or something.''

"When,'' Carol asks, "did the older boys start getting you sexually?''

"I wasn't very old. Because my mom used to make me go see my brother when he was locked up. He was sixteen. He's eleven years older than I am. He was in prison for raping a woman. He'd always say, 'You gotta have sex with me because it gets so lonely around,' and all this, and I'd say, 'No, I don't want to.' And then he'd make me. And my mom would make me go all the time.

"He could get a pass from the prison, and we'd always go down to this one place where we'd go fishing. My mom would stay in the car. I told her I didn't want to go, I didn't want to go. She'd make me go anyway. He just said he had to have sex. They always talked about it. I remember one time when my brother came in—my brother that I like—and beat the shit out of one of my brothers because he wouldn't leave me alone."

"How many of the four boys made you have sex?"

"Two of them."

"When did you start running away?"

"About nine. I started playing softball. And my one friend, my softball coach, Alice, I used to always go over to her house, go someplace with her. And stay with her. And when I had to go home, I'd go home, and then start all over again. My mom would always get mad and tell me I can't go over there. I can't go over there with her, I can't go here with her. But I'd run away and go. I stayed with her a lot. I'd talk to Alice and she'd come over and pick me up sometimes, and my brothers would be fighting with me and beating the hell out of me. And then Alice tried talking to my mom one time. And my mom told her she couldn't see me anymore. All this good shit. I'd still take off and go over there though."

Not only was Dani raped regularly by two of her brothers, she was raped by her uncles on visits to her grandmother. Those rapes, she says, went on only "two years at the most.

"But my family was sayin' that Alice was a lesbian. That was the only reason we were together. I'd just come home and get clothes—and then I'd leave again."

When Dani was thirteen, her mom fell in love with a guy she had known before her first marriage. He was from these parts—the northern Middle West—so she decided the family would follow her heart.

"I said, 'No. I ain't gonna move. I'm gonna stay with Alice.' And that's when the big spill started. So I went out with a couple of my softball friends, and then we went over to this other town where one lived and we stayed there. I ran away from there to Alice's house. So they had to come back over there and pick me up. By then, I was getting high all the time. So—'No big deal. I can always get high and not worry about it.' I thought.

"We fought all the way up here. I made a big scene because I wasn't gonna go. And the guy my mom lives with was always hittin' us. And I would call my friend Alice and tell her all the time. I would have to come into town to do that because we didn't have a phone.

"Then they would start saying, 'Well, you're lesbian,' and all this. So I said, 'Oh, big deal.' Finally, I got to the point where I didn't care and was always gettin' high. Partying all the time.

"And then I left home. I went to this concert and they threw out this tear-gas bomb. We didn't get home till real late, after I was supposed to. It was an Alice Cooper concert. I don't know why they threw tear gas off. But you had to be checked when you got out of the concert.

"Next morning I came downstairs and I tried to tell them this, and tell them I wasn't lying. And [my father] slapped me, and then I went to hit him back. And then I left home—for good. I stayed with a friend I used to get high with. And my little sister would bring me clothes and stuff into town.

"I hung around, partied all the time. Stayed wherever I possibly could find a place to stay. Then my mom went and talked to this one social worker. And they were gonna try counseling. We started on that and that didn't work out. My mom was always sayin' I was like my dad, and I was gonna be no good like my dad, and that nothing worked out with the guy she was living with 'cause it was all my fault. I ran away from that meeting.

"Then I got picked up and taken to a foster home. For a while. It was okay. They were nice people. They were pretty laid-back. They lived on the lake. They had a pontoon, they had a little boy. But I was still gettin' high all the time. They couldn't deal with that because I wouldn't go to school.

"By this time I didn't feel anything. I didn't care. When you're high all the time, you don't have to care about anything. From there, I had to go see another social worker. And then I ended up in the group home.

"They tried to fix it up with more contact with my mom, and going home for visits. I couldn't have dealt with it if I hadn't been constantly stoned. I wanted to die—because I couldn't stand the way my family had treated me. The physical and sexual abuse. And I still have a hard time dealing with it.

"My buddy and I would get high on whatever we could find to get high on. This included sniffing glue and smoking dope and popping different kinds of pills—it's easy to get things in the group home. Whatever I could find to get high off, I'd get high. Go out in the garage and sniff gas. I did a lot of cutting on myself.

'Cause I had anger and I just hated myself and I just wanted to die. So I'd just cut on myself, put tattoos on myself—as a good way to take away pain.''

''Whom would you really like to have hurt?''

''My family. I always said if I could go and have a shotgun, I'd probably go and kill them all. Not even think twice about it. I could see myself sitting there and shooting them all and it wouldn't even bother me. I know it wouldn't. Just 'cause of all this shit they did to me.''

''How were you treated by the staff in the group home?''

''One counselor, Don, he grabbed me one time, lifting me up off the floor. Told me he was gonna send me to a reformatory or an institution or wherever—'cause I wasn't no good, and I'd never make anything out of my life. I'd never accomplish anything. He used to get really mad at me. I remember that one time in the kitchen he picked me up. That's when I told him to keep his fucking hands off me.''

Carol says, ''Wasn't there stuff about you being a lesbian?''

''Oh, yeah. 'Checking out the women.' That was a big thing there. I don't even know what that was about. I can remember being called into this meeting because I'm looking at this woman all the time—the only woman I'd associate with. Until this happened, sometimes I'd break loose and talk to her—if something was bothering me. After that, though, I just kind of got real angry.''

''She was your friend,'' Carol says, and to me: ''One of the staff was her friend. She finally felt she trusted someone to talk to.''

''And then—then—then—they tell me I'm a lesbian because I talked to her.''

''Why,'' I ask, ''do you suppose they wanted to do that?''

''Probably because I wasn't the friendliest girl, like most girls are, you know. I was more of a tomboy type.''

Carol says, ''You still get called 'boy,' 'sir,' when you go in places. But it was real threatening to the staff.''

''Is it possible,'' I ask Dani, ''you don't want to appear 'girl' because you don't want to be raped anymore?'' (That seems to me an eminently sensible idea.)

''Yeah. Yeah. I always figure people aren't going to know if I'm a boy or a girl, so that's one less thing I have to worry about. I don't know what they were thinking. 'Cause we'd get high all the time, upstairs in the group home. And we were only caught one time out of the two years I lived there. We'd sneak booze in.

One girl would go out with her big old coat and come in with a bottle of booze. We'd sit upstairs and party. They were pretty good kids, the ones I got along with. They ran away from home, and they used drugs. They were abused: it was their way of coping with things."

"What sort of help, or counseling, or what have you did you get?" I ask.

"Just talking to this one guy, Fred. It was real hard for me to talk to him because he was male. But I'd be high all the time. That made it easier. I would shit around the bush with him. Tell him what I wanted to tell him and let the rest go until he figures it out himself. In the group home, you had to do that to make it look good. Go talk to him. They'd just think I'm cruising along the ropes there—no problem at all.

"See, if I didn't reach these certain goals, or do these certain things, I could never get any privileges.

"There'd be these few girls there and we'd have all these jobs. And there was one girl that was the job checker. She'd go down and make sure all your jobs were done. If they weren't done, then she would report you to the staff. And the staff would get on your ass, or restrict you, or whatever they decided to do with you.

"And we had intern staff come there sometimes. This one intern—to go through school she had to do an internship?—she was neat. I always talked to her. I was able to kind of trust her. But there was the same old thing again. I could get high and talk to her; we really got close; we were really good friends. But she left. And it just seemed like every time I started trusting somebody or got close to them, they would leave, or something would come up that would cause some kind of problem. Every time you opened up to somebody, they would take off. And you'd have to start all over again. And I wasn't too gung ho on starting in the first place."

"How many times does it take, do you think, before you start to lose the will to trust?"

"Not too many times. I know that. See, Alice—it took me a long time to trust her. Carol. My counselor in these past two years. There's been just those three people I've been able to talk to, really trust. Everybody else, I don't trust them. They either leave, or you fuck up a couple of times and they don't even want to deal with you."

Carol asks, "Then what did you do when it became time to leave the group home?"

I ask, *"How* did it become time for you to leave the group home?"

" 'Cause. They couldn't deal with me." She smiles. "No. See, I have always been this hotshot softball player. My softball coach, he kind of knew who I was, and that I got high, and that I smoked. He didn't want me to get kicked off the softball team.

"So he and his wife wanted me to come live with them. To get out of the group home. They wanted to try being foster parents. I kind of considered that. I'm sure in the back of my head all this time I'm thinking, 'No rules.' Well, rules, but things I *could* do. So we trucked off. I went and lived with them for a while. I liked being with him because he'd never hurt me or anything. He was always really nice. But his wife expected so much out of me. She tried to make me something I wasn't."

"They bought her all kinds of expensive clothes," Carol says. "Real feminine clothes. Tried to have her fit this model. Frilly dresses? Didn't work. She acted out, ran away. . . ."

"I was still getting high," Dani says. "He knew I still got high. But one time she caught me. I was smoking hash and I passed out in the basement, and she goes—I can still hear it, because I was listening to this hard-rock music, and I can still hear her saying, 'She's stoned again.' And he says, 'No, she's not. She's just really tired.' He had all these big plans of sending me to college if I could get a scholarship in softball—which sounded good to me.

"But after I got caught, she was like, 'Well, you've got to move out.' And I was like, 'Well, where am I gonna go?' "

"Dani was living in a trailer house," Carol says. "With some other kids. And was so active in the drug culture that she almost died."

Dani had known Carol from the visits Carol had made to her other foster daughter in the group home. Dani says, "And when Carol would come to the group home, I was real jealous 'cause I thought—that'd be neat to have a family like that. So I used to hang a sign around my neck: 'Kid for Sale'; 'Kid for Rent.' When she would come. I wouldn't ever talk to her. I'd just kind of sit back and watch her the whole time. Then I got to know her a little better. Then she asked me to come home on passes once in a while, on the weekends. Or like Christmas? So I'd have a place to go. Because I wouldn't go home."

While she was living at the trailer house, a friend had a car. Dani used to cruise over to Carol's house, stop by, chat awhile. "It wasn't me to say, 'Oh God,' or, 'I need help,' or something."

"Did you have any sense at this point of what 'help' would be?"

"Nobody wanted to help me at this point. They just wanted to kill me, I think."

"She'd come down here and ask to stay," Carol says, "she'd ask if we could keep her. 'No, no, no, this wouldn't work.' Finally, I needed surgery; I'd been hospitalized. She was trying to see me, causing all kinds of chaos. And I just—simply—said—'What else can I do? She's asking for it, she's connected, she's got no other resources. I don't understand why she can't become a part of this.' I put her in drug treatment for an evaluation—mainly because I had younger kids in the house—and I was very concerned about drugs in the home. They did an assessment. The psychologist brought her back and said, 'She needs to be with people who care about her. Sure, she is chemically abusive. We don't see her as chemically dependent at this time. But she definitely is abusive. And somebody's gotta listen to what that's saying.' She did get put in with us."

Three years have now gone by.

"How are things now?" I ask Dani. "Do you have an idea of who you are?"

"Yeah. I know who I am. I'm pretty happy with myself right now. If I accomplish nothing else in life, I'm pretty content where I'm at right now. The most important thing that I accomplished is—I'm the only one that graduated, out of my older brothers and sisters. My younger brother and my younger sister did. I was the first one that graduated. I think that's a pretty good accomplishment. High school, and a year of vo-tech. And I've worked—all my born days, it seems like—to support myself.

"And I'm not cutting on myself. I'm not getting high anymore. I do drink occasionally. I still get pretty angry. Still don't understand how to deal with a lot of things. I mean I do, but I don't. I don't understand why I feel the way I feel when I think I shouldn't feel that way—and I do feel that way.

"When I find a friend I'm really close to, it feels like—if I don't see them for a while—and be with them for a while—it's like—things are gonna change."

"How much of that," I suggest, "is, if you grow up under great emotional extremes, turmoil, perception of extreme danger—you don't know how to be without that stuff?"

"Crisis. I can relate to that. I always—when things are going slick, I always think, 'Something's missing here.' It's like, this isn't possible for things to be going so well for me for so long. It just doesn't seem right. 'Cause it seems like something's got to go wrong in my life to—to be my life.''

The doorbell rings. It's my friend, who is also my ride back to where I am staying. It is still snowing heavily but—harness the dogs and let's go.

"How'd it go?" she asks in the car.

"Extraordinary. This whole thing is just ex-fucking-traordi-nary.''

# COMPLICATIONS IV

"**W**hy," I ask Pauli, "was that how you met Laura's mother?" (Complications make for complicated-sounding questions.)

"Because. You should not promise a child—especially a child like that—things that you don't intend to keep. I mean there are always extenuating circumstances. But if you feel something might stop you from keeping your promise to the child, then you don't promise it. You tell her, 'I'll do this if I can.'

"So the woman brought Laura home that afternoon. And Laura looked all sad and the tears was in her eyes 'cause she had wanted to see her family; she had *expected* to see her family. So I told her, I said, 'Well, Laura, don't cry. I promise you—I don't know about your sisters and brothers because I don't know how to get to them—but I promise you that you will have your visit with your mother. I'll see to it that you do.' And I did.

"I called her mother. They say the mother was not to come

149

to my house. The only visitation rights she had was when they set up visits in the Department of Social Services. (I think that's wrong anyway. That's no way to get children and family back together.) I asked her if it was all right if I brought Laura to see her. Because she had missed her visit.

"She said, 'Would *you* do *that?*' I said, 'I certainly would.' I said, 'Is it all right with you and when can we come?' And she told me. And she told me where she lived. And I took Laura to see her. And I was scared to death.

"Why? It wasn't in a nice area. And all these people that were sitting outside looked like they were high on something. And she was sitting on the steps waiting for us. Dana and Ali were with me, and she took all three kids into the house. I didn't want to stay in the car—I mean I didn't want to get *out* of the car, but I didn't want to let the kids go in the house by themselves.

"So we went inside and the house looked nice and it looked clean. But they didn't have any lights. It was light outside. Then her boyfriend started to close the door. And I said, 'Please, mister, don't do that.' My excuse was that I didn't lock my car. 'I left my windows down. And if you close the door, I can't see out there.' This is what I told him, but I was just scared 'cause when you closed the door it was really dark in there. He say that, 'Everybody around here know me. Nobody's gonna bother your car.' 'I know. I believe you,' I said. 'But I'd really rather be able to *see* it.' "

We both laugh.

"They lighted candles. Then—she took the kids upstairs. 'Cause she had told Laura all these things about she had her a bedroom, and all these toys and things she had bought her. Which, she might have had a bedroom up there, but she didn't have all these clothes and things for her that she said. I guess she was tryin' to look good for her kid. They came down with a few of her clothes that she had loaned Laura.

"And we went home. But I *took* her. And that started the change in Laura. She didn't get perfect—then. She's not perfect now. But she started improving. Because she knew if I promised her something I was gonna do it."

Good things did, indeed, seem to be happening. Laura was reported as making progress in the Parker Institute counseling program. Her ability to accept Pauli as the adult-in-charge seemed to be coming along. On one occasion, when Laura had gone off with some kids to do something she'd expressly been told not to do, Pauli went chasing all over town looking for her. Finally, Laura walked into the house. After some initial rancor, she tolerated being sent up to her room: she even *cleaned* her room on her own initiative. And she eventually ran to Pauli, threw her arms around her, and said, 'I'm sorry, Nana.'

Pauli had, however, already planted the seeds of full-blooming disaster. During the month before the caseworker, Miss Jefferson, finally got Laura in school, Pauli went over Miss Jefferson's head.

"I didn't know where to go, what to do, who to turn to. But a girl I work with has a friend who's a social worker. And I burst out in tears one day at work, so she said, 'Well, Pauli, I'm gonna call my girlfriend and she'll tell you what to do.' And what the girlfriend did was she went to her supervisor—they both called the chief of foster care, and they wrote a memo, and they both signed it. The chief called Miss Jefferson and *her* supervisor. And they promised they would have the girl in school the next day. And they did.

"Then—over a month went by and I hadn't received any check. So I called the chief of foster care myself—because the girl had given me the name and telephone number and told me if anything wasn't right again to call. She called Miss Jefferson again. And Miss Jefferson hand-delivered a check the next day— but she was angry.

"That was when Miss Jefferson started trying to remove Laura from my home and put her in residential treatment centers outside the state." This could only be done with the mother, Maria's, permission—or by court order.

At this point, the feisty Pauli turned to Mr. James of Legal Services, who became Laura's attorney.

On at least one occasion, Miss Jefferson commanded Pauli to take Laura and her mother, Maria, to an interview for an out-of-state placement for Laura. (What Pauli said was, "Miss Jefferson, *slavery* has been *abolished.*" But she complied nonetheless.) By this time, Pauli and Maria had become quite close. Ever since that first meeting, Maria had come to visit occasionally; had come over to babysit. As Pauli said, she did not think the rule that put the mother's visitation at the discretion and infrequent convenience of Social Services was any way to keep a family together.

In fact, Maria had come to view Pauli as though she were her own mother. Like Laura, she called Pauli Nana. On the drive to the meeting with the official from the out-of-state placement, Maria said to Pauli, "Nana, I don't know why this woman keeps makin' me go all these places. I told her I am not goin' to sign these papers for Laura to be put in any of these places. And she tells me I have to go anyway.''

Pauli says, ''Maria told me she wanted her daughter to stay with me. She said it was the best home Laura had ever had in her life. It was better than the one she had provided. It was better than anything she had ever had. And she wanted her to stay there. And Miss Jefferson told her that she would have to go anyway. That she was supposed to cooperate. And if she didn't sign the papers, that she would take it to court and the judge would sign the papers.

''So I told her, 'This is your daughter, and cooperating does not mean that you have to do something you don't believe in. If you don't want to sign the papers, don't sign them. And you talk to Mr. James, the Legal Services lawyer, and he'll tell you what to do.'

''So we went to this meeting. And when the gentleman who had flown down to interview children for his school called us into the office, he didn't ask a lot of questions. He tried to get acquainted with Laura and started telling about the school and what nice things it offered—and Maria just cut him off in the middle of it. She said, 'I don't mean any harm to you, but I do not want my daughter to go. And I'm not gonna sign the papers.'

''Laura was just sitting there. And he looked at me. And I told him, 'I don't have anything to say about it. I'm just a foster mother.' And then he was really shocked. He was upset, angry. He said, 'I'm sorry. If you don't want your child to go, that's the end of it. We are not trying to force kids that their parents don't want them there.' He say, 'But this has really put me at an imposition because a social worker is supposed to be here with the child and the child's parent. And since this is the child's parent, I assumed that you were the social worker.' So I told him, 'No, I am not the social worker.' He said, 'Well, she should have been here, or someone representing her.'

''So he thanked us for coming and we left.''

Next, Miss Jefferson drove Laura and Maria up to be interviewed at a school in another state. Pauli says:

''She brought Laura home that evening and she looked at me and she said, 'Mrs. Mason'—real stern—and she threw Laura in the door. 'Here's Laura. And they accepted her.' 'They *di-id? That's* nice.' She said, 'And Laura slept all the way back and I'm going to have to get her medical attention.'

"And all the while she was trying to threaten Maria, to force her into signing these papers—which Maria refused to do. 'Well, Maria, if you don't sign them, I'm gonna take it before the judge and he will sign them and that will make it bad for you.' Maria told her, 'Well, you just gotta do that.' "

Meanwhile, there were more Complications, which would quickly lead to the end. A neighbor, Ruby, called Miss Jefferson to report that Pauli was allowing Maria in her house. Pauli had, in the past, shared with Ruby some of the difficulties she'd had with Miss Jefferson—so Ruby knew who she was and how to find her.

"See, after Laura got raped—the family of the little boy were friends of Ruby's. That's when she got angry and started treating the kids differently. She just nagged and picked at them all the time. So I started just trying to keep the kids out of the block. When I got off work, I'd pick them up every day at the sitter's and we'd go someplace. Sometimes I'd bring 'em home and feed 'em before. I just didn't want them in the neighborhood. My house was—dishes would pile up in the sink—it was a mess—because I didn't stay in there long enough to do anything. We didn't get home until after nine o'clock at night. Long enough for them to take a bath and get in bed—and be ready for school the next day.

"But the first time Ruby called Miss Jefferson she told her that I had Laura's mother visiting the house and taking the kids out. The way I found out about this was Mr. James called me. And told me he had talked to Miss Jefferson. Mr. James's reason for calling was he didn't want me to be upset and to fly off the handle or whatever. Because he didn't feel there was anything that they could do about it. Really, it was his suggestion that I *let* Maria come and visit. He had told me it might be a good idea to allow Maria to babysit—if I didn't mind her being in my house. He said he felt it might be good for her and Laura. If there was a way for Laura to be with her mother—and it was a way for Maria to learn something about parenting—from me. I thought it was a good idea, so I did it."

Then one night Ruby called Pauli to complain that the kids were outside making noise. Pauli said the kids were right there in the house, and they were playing, but not making noise. Ruby said, "Well, fuck it, then, goddammit. Next time I'll call the police." "Well, Ruby," Pauli said, "you do what you feel you have to do. After all, you called Miss Jefferson. So I guess calling the police isn't that much different."

"And then," Pauli says, "she started cursing and telling me she resent that. And why would you do this and why would you do that. And I said, 'Well, Ruby, that's what I believe. I believe you called 'em and that's the end of it.' So she slammed the phone down in my ear.

"And then she called right back. She said, 'Why don't you ask *Maria* who's telling Miss Jefferson things—that's who you *had* over there.' I said, 'I know. That's what the "anonymous" caller told Miss Jefferson. That's why I know it was you.' And she started cursing and yelling and screaming and telling me to kiss her ass. And she told me I was going to regret the day I ever heard the name Laura.

"That's when Ruby called Protective Services and said Laura was hooking school. She was stealing from 7-Eleven. That Laura was sexually active. That she was riding downtown alone.

"So then—it was a Friday, and summers I get off work at noon on Fridays. The lady from Protective Services called me and she told me that she had had a complaint of neglect. It was supposed to have been anonymous. And I told her who it was. She said, 'Well, we're not allowed to tell you who it was.' I say, 'I don't expect you to—I *know* who it is. But if it's anonymous and you *don't* know who it is, then it doesn't matter whether or not you're allowed.' "

The protective services worker said she needed to speak with Pauli the next week, and there was much to-do about when, with Pauli saying she couldn't take off from work, and the worker calling her uncooperative; Pauli saying she got home at four o'clock, the worker saying the office closed at four o'clock: the meeting finally got set during Pauli's lunch break—and then unset.

Miss Jefferson called to say, " 'Tst, Mrs. Mason. We need to see you in your home right now. Today.'

"I said, 'Well, that's fine with me. I'm home. I told the other lady she could come anytime I was home.'

" 'Well, we'll be there by three-thirty.'

" 'That's fine with me. Do you want the kids here?'

" 'Yes.'

" 'Then I'll have to go get them. They're still at the babysitter's. So if I'm not here, I'll *be* here.'

"So I went and picked up the kids. They were all angry because they didn't want to talk to them. And I told the kids, 'Well, it's something you have to do, and you don't have to be afraid. All you have to do is tell them the truth.' I didn't say anything more about it. I took them home. And Miss Jefferson came with the other woman, Miss Kane. And we all sat in the dining room, while the kids played in the living room. And that's when Miss Kane told me that she was gonna read the charges off to me. And she wanted me to refute them. She read them out—with me, her, and Miss Jefferson sitting there.

"The first thing she said was that Laura was sexually active. I said, 'She probably is.' I said, 'And if that's a lie, Miss *Jefferson* told me that.' I told her all the things Miss Jefferson had told me about Laura. I said, 'Is that not true, Miss Jefferson?' She said, 'Yes.'

"So then she told me that Laura had been raped—in my home. I said, 'No. Laura was raped while she was *living* in my home. That was up the street, and I called the police, and it is all a matter of record. One of the boys has been to court and convicted.' I say, 'Is *that* not right, Miss Jefferson?' The woman was shocked. Miss Jefferson had told her none of these things. And Miss Jefferson said, 'Yeah.'

"And then she told me that Laura steals; that Laura had stolen from 7-Eleven. I said, 'If Laura stole, nobody reported it to me.' I say, 'Laura has never stolen anything from me.' I say, 'But if she does steal, that's another thing she was doin' when she came here—that she has improved on.' I say, 'Miss Jefferson, didn't *you* tell me not to lay my pocketbook down around Laura because she steals? And the reason you knew it is because a social worker caught her goin' into her pocketbook?' She said, 'Yes.' The woman didn't know that either.

"She told me she wanted to talk to the kids. Again, I said, 'All right. Do you want me to leave the room?' She said, 'Yes.' So I went into the other room. And she talked to the kids. And when they were finished I went back in there—they were getting ready to leave. And Miss Kane said, 'Well, that's all for now, Mrs. Mason. Thank you. And if I have any more questions, I'll let you know.' I said, 'All right.' And they got up to leave.

"But Dana told her, 'We have one more thing to say.' And Laura said, 'Yes, we do.' So they said, 'All right.' And they sat down. Dana and Laura told them, 'Nana has not neglected us. Nana has never neglected us. And we wish you would let us alone.' And the two ladies just stared at each other. And then they say, 'Well, we're not accusing anybody of anythin'. We got a complaint and when we get a complaint, we have to investigate.' And they left."

There was also what is referred to in caseworker manuals as

a "lateral investigation." "Ruby was taking them to people's houses who she thought might say something against us. That's when Mr. James started tryin' to get a judge to hear the case on an emergency basis—so that they could keep them from removing the kids from my home."

However, no charges of neglect had been made pertaining to Dana and Ali, and Laura had only been with Pauli four months, so the judge determined no bond had been formed, and therefore there was no emergency.

"Dana and Ali's social worker (yes, they had a separate social worker) told Pauli that she also had been asked by her supervisor to say she found neglect. She, however, had refused. She told Pauli they'd had a big meeting—which she'd been left out of because of her refusal. And she said, "Mrs. Mason, you're gonna have a big fight—if you fight. Because it's the whole Department of Social Services. It's a big power play. And you and the kids are right in the middle of it. Plus, Miss Jefferson is the reason for all of it. Social Services has gone along with her so far. They can't back out—especially with Legal Services on it."

This was something else I was to hear frequently: that once Social Services has made a mistake, embarked on an erroneous course, they will go to the wall to defend it. Partly, it seems then to be a power issue—that old territorialism. But also it is very likely an issue of potential liability, as suits against protective service agencies become ever more common.

"So," Pauli says, "they had this big meeting. And they took Dana and Ali—that Thursday. Didn't take any clothes. They just took the kids from the babysitter's—just as they were.

"Laura was the one that the complaints were about. She was the one I was supposed to have been neglecting. They didn't take her—until the following Monday evening.

"I didn't see Dana and Ali. But Laura, her face just cracked, and she just fell into my arms and started cryin'. Dana and Ali didn't know about the system. But Laura had been in it before. I was the only one who had ever kept her. And she didn't want to go."

Dana and Ali were put in separate foster homes; Laura was placed in a run-down hotel outside of town that was being used as a sixty-day home for kids. Meanwhile, Mr. James had gotten a court date, though Pauli didn't know that. (So despite the kids' removal, the pressure on the system continued.)

* * *

Friday night, Laura called Pauli from the hotel-turned-group-home and asked that she come to get her.

"I said, 'Laura, you know I can't do that without permission.' She said, 'You can get permission out here.' And she sounded so strange. I said, 'What's wrong, baby? What happened to you?' She said, 'Nothing, Nana, I just want you to come and get me.' I said, 'But I can't do that without permission. They can't let you come with me unless your social worker says so.' I said, 'I don't want to do anything to hurt my chances of getting you back.' She said, 'I didn't talk to Miss Jefferson, I talked to her supervisor, and I asked her if you could come and get me, and she said yes, she just had to decide on the day.' So I said, 'Well, you can't get in touch with them on weekends. But what you need to do is call her first thing Monday morning and ask her what day did she decide on. And then I'll come and get you.' She said, 'Okay, Nana.' And she asked me for all these telephone numbers for my children—she calls them aunts and uncles. So I gave her the numbers—and she called all of them."

Laura ran away that night.

It was a holiday weekend and the Department of Social Services was closed through Monday. So they never knew Laura had run until Tuesday morning. Pauli is not certain where Laura was for Saturday and Sunday, but she knows that on Monday night Laura was at Maria's, telling her that they had been nasty to her, that they had mistreated her, and that some girl out there had tried to make her "kiss her body." Maria, who at this point did not have telephone service, ran to bang on Pauli's door to ask her what to do. But Pauli, sleeping, did not hear the banging.

Tuesday morning, Miss Jefferson called to say that Laura was missing. By now, Pauli was frantic. Then Maria called from a pay phone:

" 'Nana, don't worry. Laura's with me. Laura's with me.' And then she started tellin' me all these things. And she said, 'I'm takin' Laura out of there and I'm not callin' Social Services, and I'll run away to South Carolina with her.' So I said, 'Maria, you can't do that.' She usually does what I tell her. She doesn't listen to them at all—and they can't understand that. I told her they'd have police all over the place lookin' for her. And what she needed to do was call Legal Services and talk to Mr. James, and he would tell her what to do.

"So she called. Mr. James wasn't there. But some lawyer told her what they would do to her if she didn't call, and how they would put all these charges on her. And that she was to call Miss

Jefferson and tell her that she had Laura, and could she keep her until they found another place for her.

"She called me back. She said, 'Nana, I don't want to talk to Miss Jefferson. I want to talk to her supervisor. What's her number?' So I gave her the number, and she called and told her what was happening. Maria said to her, 'Well, can't Laura stay with me?' The woman said, 'Well, Maria—that's probably what will end up happening.'

"Then Miss Jefferson called me. All at once she's so worried about me. 'Mrs. Mason, I just called to let you know that Laura's with Maria. I know you were upset, and I just wanted you to know she's all right.' So I say, 'Well, Miss Jefferson, what's gonna happen now?' She say, 'Huh?' I said, 'I mean what's gonna happen now, 'cause Laura's not happy out there.' She say, 'I know. That's why I want to put her in ———' She called out the name of some kind of place. I said, 'Miss Jefferson, what kind of place is that?' It's another one of these same kind of places.

"Meanwhile, she say, 'I have an appointment to take her out there at ten o'clock this morning.' She said, 'But I have to talk with my supervisor first. I have to talk with her right now—and then I want to see Maria and Laura before I decide what to do.' "But evidently her supervisor didn't give her a choice.

"You know what they did? They gave Laura back to her mother."

"Because?"

"With Laura back with her mother there's no reason to go talk about all that's been goin' on—in court."

Astounding (isn't it?). Remarkable.

"All this time," Pauli says, "they have been tellin' Maria she's not ready for these children—she has seven children with Protective Services. All this time they've been sayin' she's not ready for her children. And they've been going to court, fighting, to keep her from getting her children. *Now*—to keep this from going to court—they don't want it known what they have not done for her—they give her her children back. And they tell her that she has improved so much that she can have Laura back, and by December she will have all of her children back, and they will go to Section 8 to get her a house.

"And Maria told me, she said, 'Nana, they said I had improved so much. But *how* have I improved?' She said, 'Nana, I'm worse than I've ever been. And I don't have the patience that you have. I'm not gonna be able to deal with Laura.' "

"That's very nice in some way," I say. "Very honest, very smart."

"Yes. Uh-huh. It is. But what I try to tell her is—and this is how Mr. James feels—that she has one thing now that she never had before. She didn't have any support at all before. And now she has me."

# LAURA
# SPEAKS

$\blacksquare$

It is arranged that I will meet Laura. "Do you think she will talk to me?" I'd asked Pauli.

"I don't know. We can try. She's different. Before, she was belligerent and defiant. She was getting much better, and she was learning to obey—before she left my house. But now she's—too quiet. She's too cowered down. It's all right to be afraid. It's not good to be cowed. It's like every soldier that goes into battle, if he's not stupid, he's scared. But he fights. Laura—that's how she was before. She was scared, but she fought. Only she was learnin' to do it in a different way. She was learnin' to do it with discipline.

"But now Laura is—I don't want a child to be scared to death. It's all right to be scared, but you've got to meet the challenges that life is going to throw at you. You can't just sit back in a corner and draw up. And this is the way she is now."

As I walked toward the restaurant where we were to meet, I

didn't have any idea of what, if anything, I would learn about Laura's experience from Laura herself.

They were waiting outside, Pauli in slacks and a crisp shirt, leaning lightly on the cane in her right hand. The girl standing next to her was almost as tall as Pauli, about 5'5". She looked to be about sixteen. Her face was impassive as we were introduced. Pauli had told me, "She looks older than she is. She's eleven, but Parker says developmentally she's really nine." Still, her midteen appearance was disconcerting. I had to keep fighting incongruous expectations.

Seated, menus served, Pauli asked Laura what she wanted. "Burger and fries." That was just about all she said during the lunch. (Except to the waitress; she said, 'Vanilla shake,' when asked if she wanted something to drink.) Pauli talked for her, trying to engage her: about how she was doing in school, about her passion for burgers and fries. . . .

I gesture to her Run DMC T-shirt. "They your favorite group?"

She looked up from the french fry in her hand briefly, and nodded with some enthusiasm. And went back to the fry.

Thus, when, back in my room, Pauli asked Laura if she wanted to talk to me now, I was surprised when she vigorously nodded her assent. I turned on my little tape recorder and handed it to her, showing her where the microphone part was.

"Okay, if you were to read that Laura is an eleven-year-old girl, and this is Laura's story, what would that story be?"

"Not living with my mother. Living in foster homes." Silence.

"What's the first thing you remember?"

"The first thing I remember—when the police came to my house. They thought my mother was beatin' me. And then the police check on us and they saw some bruises on us. And then they took us to the police station. And then—we was hungry—they bought us somethin'. Hamburger. Fries. And then they checked us one more time.

"And then—we went to a foster home. Me and my sister. They was like mean people. Angry. Treatin' their kids better."

Laura's voice is so low I can barely hear her. (I will be amazed, later, when I can actually get what she said from the tape.)

"Then—I went to a foster home by myself. And I liked that foster home. It was a sixty-day foster home. I left the first home because I told the worker I didn't want to stay there. And then I went to a group home—for sixty days. And then my sixty days were up. They were nice in that group home—they checked my clothes and everything so kids wouldn't steal them. And would let us go anywhere we want. And then I went to this place—like where the sisters're at? And they go to a Catholic church. And that were sixty days. And when my birthday come up they bought me a lot of presents. And when Christmas come up they bought me a lot of presents. Sixty days. And then I moved from there.

"And then went to one more sixty. Then I went back to the sisters for sixty days. Then I went to this other group house for sixty days. I went back to the sisters for sixty days.

"It was nice there. They had us some volunteers—like teenagers—that come and get us and take us everywhere—and we can go shopping and everywhere. And then they have this nice lady, Miss Nancy—and she took me everywhere.

"And then after my sixty days were up I wouldn't go. So they had me stay sixty-*one* days.

"And that's when I went to my aunt's house. I was not there sixty days. I had a new social worker and she took me out of there because she did not want me to be with my family. She didn't like my mother. And then I moved to Nana's house."

"What made you maddest when you lived with your mom?"

"When my mother made me, 'Be quiet, you're gonna get punished.' I ran away from her. I didn't like being punished. If somebody say, 'Laura, you're gonna get punished today,' I'll run away."

"Did you get hit a lot?"

"Mm-hmm. But I didn't care about that. I went outside after the beatin'—because I liked it outside. And I'd tell my mother, 'Now you don't have to punish me. You can just beat me and get it over with.' And then you cry a little bit and you go outside. I only got punished two times, and the rest of the times she beat me and all that stuff. I didn't mind about the beatings. Hands and belt. I just cry. And later—they was tellin' a story about my mother was beating me with extension cords and stuff. And I don't remember her beatin' me with extension cords. She beat me with the belt and her hands. And she punished me two times. I didn't like the punishment."

"Punishment being . . . ?"

"Be by myself. Don't go outside. No TV. Stay in your room. Eat in your room. I didn't like that. So I got punished two times, and it was three days—my punishment. The first time I got punished, that's when I ran away. The second time I got punished—that's when I ran away too. To my aunt's. But my mother came. My crazy friend told her.''

"How did you feel when you first were taken to foster care?"

"I'm not gonna live here. I'm not gonna live in nobody's house. They fooled me. They said, 'Come on, you all goin' to court and then you goin' home.' And my mother said, 'Come on, Laura. You can go.' And I said, 'They better watch out because I'm gonna be runnin' away. From a lot of places.' That's why they took me home now. Because I ran away.

"I wanted to see my baby sisters. They never let me see my brothers and sisters. Till one time I said, 'I don't care what y'all say. I'm seein' my brothers and sisters. And I wanna see 'em *now*.' And that's when I see 'em. And see, when I say that, my brothers and sisters start treatin' their workers wrong too. Like they treat us. So we start treatin' 'em wrong.

"And when they try to make me go out of state, I say, 'Miss Jefferson, if you can fuss I can fuss back and I don't want to go out of state.' I told my brothers and sisters first off, 'You go to her supervisor and start fussing at her.' So my brothers and sisters—they do like me. They bounce her around. Because she do whatever they say. I say, 'My brothers and sisters, I want to see them tomorrow and I want to see them at five o'clock.' She say, 'Okay.' So my brothers and sisters all copies me. They learn by the oldest. My little sister be doin' that too. She's four. She's in a foster home. She's in a group home.

"Every time I could I fuss around. Because my little baby sister—she was in a foster home since she was two months. And she don't know me. I was holding her. And then she was crying. Miss Jefferson say, 'Give her to me here, give her to me.' I say, 'If you take her, I'm gonna hit you. Watch.' I say, 'If I don't go home—before next Christmas—bet y'all not gonna see me no more. I'm goin' far, far away.' ''

"Where did you go the last time you ran away?"

"I ran to my grandma's house. She wasn't there. Then I ran away to my uncle's house. He was there. He kept me for three days. Then they grabbed my mother. My mother took me. Then my mom talked with Miss Jefferson's supervisor and the supervisor say, no, I can't go home. But I start fussin' her. So that's when they let me go home. Why? I don't know. They didn't want me runnin' away or anything like that.''

All during these recitals of her imaginary power in the situation, Laura has grown progressively more animated, her voice stronger—though still far from loud. As she talks, I remember something Pauli said to me: "The fact that she is back, I think, will mean a lot to her. Because I kept promising her that she'd be back home. That, 'All you have to do is listen to Nana and do the things I tell you.' I tell her that I was fighting hard for her—but that it was up to her. She had to prove to these people that she had improved."

How very strange. Laura's improvement had nothing to do with whether she could go home. Yet here Pauli fell into a pattern of thinking I was to encounter over and over—wherein the problem the child *has* becomes viewed as the problem the child *is*. A pattern of thinking that helps account for the drift of kids from the foster care system to the mental health system to the juvenile justice system.

In Laura's perception, of course, it was not her "improvement" but her running away that helped get her home.

In reality, it was simply the Department of Social Services' desire to avoid a challenge in court by Mr. James, Laura's attorney, that got Laura home: it was simple expediency, based on DSS's wish to avoid scrutiny.

Laura is continuing, in fine voice now: "I say, 'Miss Jefferson, let me tell you one thing. My brothers and sisters coming home. My mother goin' get a big place. They coming home.' Miss Jefferson say they could come home if my mother did that. I say, 'Not *if, when.*'

"My mother gettin' a place after Christmas. My father helping her. He gonna take some money out of the bank. Stepfather. He say he gonna take a lot of money out of the bank, buy a new house, buy another car. And buy new clothes. So we can get away from Miss Jefferson. If I ever see Miss Jefferson, I'm gonna turn her to dust."

"Laura, what would you say to other kids?"

"You should never go away from your mother."

"No matter what? Ever-ever?"

"Un-unh. They shouldn't take you from your mama. And treat them like they own kids.

"See, they call themselves smart. But in the car I asked Miss Jefferson what is the three elements in earth. She said it was spirit, water, and earth. It was atmosphere, humisphere, and litmosphere. She say, 'Oh! I know it!' Later I say, 'Miss Jefferson, see how smart my brother is. I bet he's smarter than you. I say, 'What is the three elements of the earth?' And he said it right. He said atmosphere, humisphere, and litmosphere. 'Okay.

What does atmosphere mean? Do you want me to tell you? Atmosphere is air—like you breathe?' I say, 'What does litmo-sphere mean?' She say, 'Um, litmosphere . . .' I say litmosphere is air plus light. And humisphere is nothing but rocks and stone. And guess what that is. Land! I told her. And she said, 'Atmo-sphere is air. Litmosphere is land . . .' I told her, 'No, humisphere is land. Lady, you don't know nothing. You're always saying that you're smart, but you're not smart at all.' I say, 'I bet you're not smarter than my mom.' ''

''Wow,'' I say, ''you're pretty tough. Were you always a tough kid? Or did you used to be scared?''

''Tough. I think. Every time I fell when I was a baby, I don't cry. I just say, 'Ow.' My brothers—tough. Very tough. They was fightin', they didn't cry like the other kids. They was fightin' over the chairs. It was a chair higher than them. The smallest one fell. He didn't cry. He just laughed and got up and started playin' again. That's how they is—when they fall. They stop a minute and then, 'Are you all right?' If they don't be all right, then somethin' might be the matter with 'em, because they always get up. They don't stay down there cryin'. They get up and laugh. And start playin' again, that's all. They are some bad kids. And they say, 'Well, shut up, Laura. You was that way—when you was small.'

''What do I do after school? Go outside and pick on every-body. 'Cause it's fun pickin' on 'em and just—makin' 'em cry. Somebody pick on me, I just laugh. I don't cry. And when I turn around and pick on 'em—n-n-n-n, boo-hooo, n-n-n-n-n—and everybody pick on me, I pick on 'em—en-*heh,* en-*heh*—and I'm still laughin'. I don't cry. They pick on me and I'm un-*huh,* un-*huh,* un-*huh,* that's-true-that's-true. And they crackin' on me, and I don't cry. They crack on me or my brothers and sisters I can crack on them and make them cry.''

Laura has gone off to the bathroom. Pauli and she are about to leave. Pauli says, ''Laura loves her mother to death. That's where she really wants to be—with her mother. She wants to be with me only when she can't be with her mother. And then—after being with me this length of time—she sort of wants to be with both of us. She keeps asking me, 'Nana, can I stay with you this weekend? I want to stay with you every weekend. I want to stay with you every night.' She wants to be with both of us, and that's impossible.

"But when things get too rough for Maria she can say, 'Nana, come and get her.' And I can take her off her hands for a while.

"The only thing is—Maria doesn't want her at any time. She really doesn't."

As Laura and Pauli go off down the hall toward the elevator, I find myself wondering whether this, also, qualifies as a "happy ending." Certainly, if somewhat ironically, Laura—at least at this point—is part of that statistic meant to show the success of intervention: that most children in foster care are reunited with the family.

As it will turn out, my musing is premature.

I will learn later that this is not, yet, the end of Complications at all.

# LA MADRE

Carmen, Maria, and Agata are three Hispanic social workers, former employees of Connecticut's Department of Children and Youth Services (DCYS) in Bridgeport—a poor city with a heavily minority population.

Carmen is from Puerto Rico, Maria from Cuba. Agata grew up in Madrid. I encountered them first at a conference in New York City, and they responded eagerly to my invitation to come visit, to talk about what they'd seen of the system as it affects the Hispanic population.

The picture they paint is of a world of women, often battered, in grave financial as well as physical distress. These women turn to a system that says it is there to offer them help—and do not understand, from then on, what it is that has hit them; do not understand, in fact, what is going on. If the language of foster care/child welfare requires decoding by English-speaking natives, both the language and the system are undecipherable for the most part within the Hispanic community.

"Hispanic women start out believing the system," Maria says. "They trust."

Carmen says, "Because it's authority. Hispanics believe authority."

Maria says, "If it's orderly, if it's neat, if it's government—most Hispanics trust. That in this country—things are going well—and they are not gonna hurt me."

"I had a mother," Carmen says, "and she was being battered. And she requested help. And when she went to the Mental Health because she was saying she wanted to kill herself to—ease the pain—it was a very difficult situation.

"What agencies were doing was working against her. She was at day treatment at Mental Health and there was a nurse there and staff that was Italian. She had a therapist at the Mental Health that said to her, 'I don't believe you.' What would the therapist ask her every time she would go in session? 'Did you drink? Did you use drugs? What did you do to the kids?' This is the therapist she is supposed to work with.

"The kids' counselor would say, in a session with the mother's counselor, 'This woman is psychotic. She's very sick. She really hates her kids. She could explode any minute.' All of this.

"Well, this mother, one day, said, 'You know, I'm feeling depressed.' She was trying to figure out whether she should apply for a divorce from her husband, whatever; what to do. And she was very frustrated this particular day, and she said, 'I just want to kill myself.'

"She knew when she said that in the meeting DCYS was gonna be at her door within minutes. Exactly so. When I arrived, she told me, 'Okay, here I am waiting for you. I knew you were coming. Here's the chair. Do you want a cup of coffee?' This is how she treated me.

"She made me a cup of coffee and says, 'Now you're gonna hear me.' And she was screaming at the top of her lungs: 'It's unfair. I was asking for help. And I am being labeled. It's *unfair!* I asked for help—and look at what has been happening to me!' And all she needed—I didn't say a word—all she needed was—someone to hear her and not judge her."

Maria: "She's lucky she got you."

Carmen: "She's lucky she got me. The kids could have been placed that same night—because she says she was gonna kill herself."

When, later on, the woman went to an inpatient unit, the agency did place the children. However, Carmen says, "When she was out of the inpatient unit, the kids were returned. I was the social worker—so they were returned.

"I requested a meeting to confront everyone in the matter. Within three months, Child Guidance closed the case. Within two months, the mother was out of the day treatment. Why? All of a sudden, she was healthy. This woman was able to find a job. Go to school. Her kids are living with her."

In other words, what this woman needed was practical and emotional support (a service): someone to hear her and encourage and trust her.

Maria says, "And for a Latin woman to be labeled unfit, that is . . ."

Agata: "Terrible!"

Maria: "Terrible."

Carmen: "It is even worse. And here you're working with a system that has no resources. Another woman—spoke some English, but mostly Spanish. Here I had to bring two non-Spanish-speaking women to her house to try to help her. She did not want their help. Obviously. She could not communicate—with the helpers. So she did not 'cooperate' with anybody. So what's the next step? Remove the child. Because she did not cooperate."

"This is not a trick question," I say. "But—one need not like all the people one deals with, and that still doesn't mean they should lose the right to their children. The first woman you described—did you like her? Did you feel sympathetic to her?"

"I felt truly sympathetic for her," Carmen says. "I really did. And I saw her limitations. And especially now—that I have been working with family violence—I see the low where this woman was. She's a battered woman, being labeled, first of all. You are 'depressed'; you are 'alcoholic.' You are a 'drug addict.' You 'cannot take care of your kids.' You are a 'bad mother.' And it's instilled on and on—by everyone."

"She is told over and over again," Maria says, "that she is a bad mother, that *she* is depressed, that *she* doesn't know how to take care of her kids."

Carmen says, "So she's believing that. And now the system's telling her that. The system is reassuring her on and on and on, on a daily basis: the school, the hospital, the place where the kid has to go to receive therapy . . ."

"The reality is that you have a beaten woman . . ."

*"Exactly*. And a woman that is—stuck."

Maria says, "And the motherhood issue is, I think, stronger for Hispanic women."

Carmen: "It's my opinion that's the pride. That's the pride. You are a mother, and however the kids are—bright or whatever—it's to be a 'good mother.' To be a 'mother.' The worst thing that you could do to a Hispanic mother in the system is remove the kids. And *label* her as an 'unfit mother.' "

"There's a kind of motherhood—cult," says Maria. "It's like *La Madre*. If you want to fight with an Hispanic, you go to the mother. In English, it's become a joke. But blacks and Hispanics, you don't mention their mother. Because it's an honor—the society has an honor cult. Based on the sanctity, the purity, the goodness—of the mother. So each woman's identity, what she has—is motherhood. Her claim to fame, her glory, is on her children. So when the Hispanic woman hears this stuff, it's even more devastating."

Agata, who has been sitting quietly, now enters the conversation enthusiastically. "When I came here, one of the things that amazed me—because when I grew up, the respect is so important in our culture—I was amazed when girls answered back to their mother. How could they lose their respect? And by removing the children—what's that for? What's for the mother—after the children? How are the children looked upon? So they are hurting. And the resentment that I see that they have is that—knowing they suffer all these things—but, 'They took us our culture away.' "

She continues, "I don't know about other cultures, but like in Spain—it was like when you're talking about *my* family, and no matter how you are, you know that they are going to take care of you. And they all come. You know, like something happens to you—and you are 'my daughter' or you are 'my son'—they protect you. It's unbelievable."

"Then," I ask, "would you say that all the expressed feeling in this country about caring so much about children is less than authentic?"

Agata: "I agree with you."

Maria: "This country doesn't give diddly-squat!"

Agata: "Right now, the state is going through some cuts. I was reading in the newspaper, DCYS is gonna have about eighty-five to a hundred thousand dollars cut in programs for children—it's going to affect the larger cities."

Carmen: *"Which* of the larger cities? Starting with Bridge-

port, New Haven, and Hartford. *Where* are the biggest group of
children that need these programs? *Exactly* in these three cities.
And what color are these children?"

Maria: "They're partly black. And the color that was invented
in this culture—which is Hispanic. We don't know what color
that is yet. But we know it's another thing."

Carmen, ruefully: "It's your otherness. It's your otherness."

"What," I ask, "do you see the point of all this intervention
as being?"

Maria: "It's called intervention without end."

Carmen: "It's nothing really concrete—to really help the
family. Again—no resources. Nothing really solid to offer a
family when you go into their house and start asking these
questions."

Agata: "You have to really get into the training. Because
that's another thing—you're training to an ideal. It's like Nazi
Germany."

Maria: "It's indoctrination."

Agata says, "What I think is an example—the mother is the
one that is portrayed as the bad one. The cases go by the mother's
name. Even if the father is the perpetrator they write down her
name."

Maria says, "She's responsible. The fact that the case goes
by her name—she's the responsible party. No matter what. This
is a patriarchy, not a matriarchy. Usually, in everything else in
the culture, we go by his name."

"I remember one of the things that came up from the training," Agata says. "If you see that the father beat the hell out of
the kids, or the wife—you have to tell her she is responsible.
That was in training. Even with my supervisor. You just tell the
mother, 'You are responsible. If your husband beat the kids, you
are still responsible. And they may take your children away from
you. Because you are allowing that to the children.' And that's
clear. Very clear."

"That's why I quit my job," Maria says. "That's why I was
driven into years of therapy. Just to deal with what that whole
situation was. I quit my job because I couldn't deal with that.
The biggest issue is resources. What resources are we really
offering? Because if you have a woman who is battered, who can
hardly get her own soul out of bed in the morning—and you have
this psychopathic maniac—where are the resources?

"And the major thing I hated so much about our job—when
you're doing a study, you are in their soup. They know you're

checking with every reference that each spouse gives you. You're supposed to be part Sigmund Freud and part Sherlock Holmes. And for Hispanic people that's also a very difficult aspect. That people come in and they invade your family space. Family is much more important. The impact is so much more magnified in the Hispanic culture. It will rock a woman much harder off her feet.''

Carmen: "It's a personal insult to their integrity when a person comes into their home—social worker, investigator—requesting a study. It's an assault.''

Maria: "And at the same time compliance—from Hispanics—is so much easier. Hispanics are accommodating. And that goes against them. Because they accommodate themselves right out the wazoo.''

Carmen: "Exactly. They don't realize. They trust the authority because the authority knows best. But once they are found in a situation in which they are betrayed—then you are not gonna get someone who is gonna cooperate with you. And then—so what does the system do? Poom! Label. 'Uncooperative.' ''

"What," I ask, "would you call 'abuse'? And how much real abuse did you see?''

"I really did not see much real abuse," Carmen says. "What we would say was real abuse—would be a child that was burned, with hot water. Or severely physically abused, with broken bones. I do not recall seeing one case of, in quotes, real abuse in my caseload in six years working with DCYS. Me, as an Hispanic caseworker. I dealt strictly with Hispanic clients.''

"But," I say, "if you're saying that in virtually none of the cases you saw, the kids were removed for abuse—what were they removed for?''

A momentary pause, then Maria says: "Disorderly conduct.'' And there is general hilarity.

Carmen: "Excellent point! Disorderly conduct. Kids that would decide to mouth off at their parents. Or stay away from home one night. Kids acting out their anger at what was happening at home—for example, if the mother was separating from the father, the kids would be furious. So the mother would call the agency for help. The agency would immediately label the kids: this kid has 'problems.' The labeling issue is immense. *Im-mense!* In order to remove the kids, they would label: 'The kid needs psychiatric treatment.' 'This kid needs a foster home.'

"One kid, told she would be placed in a foster home for three months, kept track of every single day. Once the day came and she was not returned back home—she stopped eating as a means to say, 'I wanna go back home.' Well, what did the psychologist label? 'Anorexic.' Put in a petition, sent her to an institution for six to nine months. Then from there she had to go into a group setting. Her mother, a single mother, working, that could not get to New Haven by train—by the time she would get to New Haven, she would not have a train back. And so she could not make a lot of the appointments. Well, 'This kid should be adopted. The mother is not cooperating.' "

Agata says, "I see it as a mistake. It's usually a group that is chosen—to be used—for the purpose of trying to say, 'We have all these programs. Put all this energy in this group. That's where the abuse is.' Let's decide to detach from this specific group. It might sound cynical, but after ten years of experience in this field with DCYS and Bridgeport in general—this is my opinion of what all these supposed programs, or foster care or whatever, is about."

Maria: "The thing is to identify Hispanic and black people as the ones to whom unhappy childhoods happen, and unstable families are characteristic of. Because—just speaking for Hispanics—the love, the commitment to children, is much higher in Hispanic culture. But if you look at this country, you would think from the clients we have—that Hispanics and blacks are less human than other people."

"You know what that's called?" Carmen asks. "Institutional racism."

# THE
# GREAT
# LEVELER

"WILL LISA STEINBERG MAKE A DIFFER-
ENCE?"[1]
"CHILD ABUSE CASES DRAW NEW ATTENTION"[2]
"WANTED: A PERMANENT HOME"[3]
"CRIMES AGAINST CHILDREN: THE FAILURE OF FOSTER
CARE"[4]

The current crisis in child protection/child welfare is variously
attributed to the growing number of homeless families—single
women, that is, with children but without housing. To the growing
number of children born to crack-addicted or AIDS-infected
mothers. To the growing population of female-headed households
and the resultant poverty.

(It is also attributed—as it has long been attributed—to inadequate funding, inadequate staffing, caseworker burnout, etc.)

Listed also, and perhaps most interestingly, is the rapid

177

growth in the number of reports of child abuse, most particularly
child sexual abuse. "Among the three major child maltreatment
categories, physical abuse, sexual abuse, and neglect, reports of
sexual abuse rose the fastest. For the 29 states providing complete information, sexual abuse increased 57.4 percent between
1983–84, and increased 23.6 percent between 1984–85."[5] In fact,
reporting tripled between 1980 and 1986.

Child sexual abuse in the home—incest—in overwhelming
number by males, fathers and stepfathers, brought an entirely
new piece into the puzzle of child protection. And it brought
down a backlash against protective service intervention that sent
the system reeling—from lawsuits, threats of lawsuits, a major
publicity campaign, and powerful lobbying efforts.

Incest was an issue born in the late 1970s when, for the first
time in known history, women by the tens of thousands began
speaking out about what had been done to them as children. The
shocking discovery was made that paternal child molestation cut
across all socioeconomic lines. Virtually on impact, the bomb
dropped in society's lap (that the sexual exploitation of children
within families at all class levels was so prevalent as to mock the
label "deviant") was defused by referring to it, as to child
battering, in medical terms, as an "illness," a "problem of family
dysfunction." Along with physical abuse and the ever-expanding
"neglect," incest was placed under the domain of protective
services. This had the intended consequence of largely avoiding
the potential issue of criminality. But it had the unintended, and
entirely unprecedented, consequence of threatening to bring middle-class American families, most especially middle-class American *fathers,* into the state's purview and power.

With the media saturation of stories on child sexual abuse/
incest, and the alarm generated, the public was barraged by
public service announcements imploring them to report any
suspicions. Prevention programs were funded and mounted to go
into schools—not just into ghetto schools—to teach children
about "appropriate touch," to admonish them to tell if they were
being abused. Inevitably, what was termed "prevention" turned
into case finding.

A proliferation of magazine stories carried sidebars on the
sexually abused child's behavioral "indicators"; and sidebars on
how to report, where to go, what to do. As with the stories of
children killed, and the general upset about physical abuse, these

stories ran side by side with stories on the system glut and breakdown already existing.

If anyone foresaw what was coming, it was probably the collection of academics and professionals who, in 1981, were labeled the "pro-incest lobby," one of whose members stated that incest was "so prevalent as to make prohibition absurd."[6] Prevalent, that is to say, in "nice" homes where the male perpetrator had an exemplary work record and all of the trappings of social respectability and social responsibility.

Kadushin and Martin write: "The perpetrator of child sexual abuse is generally a white male in his late thirties or early forties. . . . The perpetrator group is better educated, more continuously employed, at a higher income level" than those reported for either child battering or neglect.[7] Aside from the incestuous activity, that is, he is a law-abiding, socially stable, normal citizen.

Like most generalities in child welfare, this should be sprinkled liberally with salt, suggesting as it does that in the arena of child sexual abuse the poor, minority, unemployed male is perceived (for the very first time) to be somehow morally superior. What it tells us, though, is that for the first time the respectable white male was at risk of being identified as an offender (together with his wife or ex-wife, who would come to be called, rather begrudgingly, the "nonoffending parent"). White males were at risk of being offered the only "service" available to protective service agencies: the removal of the child to state care.

It is popularly assumed that the incidence of physical abuse belongs to the lower classes, as does the incidence of that potpourri of behaviors or lack of same that get loaded under the term *neglect*. No one really knows. It may well be that what is class-specific is not the incidence, but the reporting and intervention. It is far more possible for a child in a home situated on an acre of land to scream its head off with no one knowing; far more possible for the middle class to use private doctors and not hospital emergency rooms; far more possible for them to have credibility about "accidents" to the child. (I mean—Joan Crawford? Who would have believed . . . ?) It is also far easier for them to dump an inconvenient child—a child who is threatening to tell, to call for help—into private mental health facilities; to quash the complaint by shifting the focus onto the child as "disturbed."

And—curiously if you think about it—no one ever thought to go into schools and teach kids about "appropriate hitting."

It is equally possible for the middle class to avoid the appearance of neglect. (Although psychologists and psychiatrists would be far less comfortably supported were there not psychological and emotional neglect and abuse among the middle class.)

Child sexual abuse hit the child welfare industry like The Great Leveler.

It did not hit without consequence.

Ripples of backlash, of real outrage, began to be heard. In 1983, the sexual abuse scandal in Jordan, Minnesota, in which numerous children told of sexual abuse—by parents and others; middle-class persons all—culminated in the formation of Victims of Child Abuse Laws (VOCAL). The group soon had 30, then 60, then 120 chapters across the country.

While VOCAL's major thrust was against what they called False Accusation Syndrome—allegations of sexual abuse committed by solid-citizen, law-abiding fathers, most particularly attendant on (or causative of) or following divorce—the bright spotlight they turned on the protective service system could not help but throw many of the system's inadequacies and errors, its whimsicalities, into relief.

In blunt terms: The poor, accused of neglect or abuse, had no voice and few resources to do battle with the state. Women, mothers, poor mothers, almost universally the target before, had nowhere to turn; no weapons with which to fight back. Middle-class *white* fathers had the wherewithal—and the passionate sense of indignation that this system, designed to "serve" the poor (and women), would dare to touch *them*—to organize, to lobby, to sue.

Among VOCAL's membership, there may well be those whose outrage is entirely justified. My point is that the juncture at which well-organized and politically effective pressure was brought to bear on the system was the point at which the system tangled with middle- and upper-middle-class men. Placing the issue of sexual abuse under the mandate of child welfare services willy-nilly violated a tacit covenant the state had with its respectable citizenry: to stay out of their homes, to stay away from their children, to allow them to "breed up their children to be ornaments or disgraces"—at their own discretion.

Faced with this impossible dilemma, the system often inclined to do what it does with such impunity: it lied. Where it was forced to intervene, it quashed all mention of incest, and removed the child as herself the "problem."

\*   \*   \*

Linda was a protective service worker in a midwestern community of about seventy-five thousand—a mainly white, mainly "normal American" community—from 1980 to 1984.

"I went into it at twenty-two years old," Linda says, "not knowing what the hell incest was. Not having a lot of training. I had a degree in social work, but they taught us everything but what incest was. I went into it without knowing what any of the child protection laws were. I felt like I was put in a situation where I had to grow up real quickly. And be responsible—for things that, at twenty-two years old, you didn't know how to be responsible for: kids' lives, placing kids, and making recommendations to the judge about 'This kid is in danger and needs to be placed.'

"There were a few workshops, and the state booklet—what the child protection laws were, how you go about placing, and when to remove. When not to."

"What did you learn about 'when to remove'?"

"That was pretty inconsistent. Sometimes it felt like it was whether it was the judge's good day or bad day. With sexual abuse, if I had a report that the child was being sexually abused by Dad and it was going on right then—once we got that statement then we would go out. My way of doing it was to always go out with a deputy [sheriff]. And we'd talk to the parents. We walked in and we said, 'I'm so and so from child protection, and we have a report that you have been sexually abusing your daughter.' Generally, they would be, 'Oh, that's bizarre.' Or, 'That's not true at all.' There were some occasions where Dad would admit it—right there."

I ask Linda if she felt she really could "protect" the kids in those circumstances. And I tell her of another young worker—also from the Midwest—whom I'd met at a conference. She'd told me she'd gone into protective services work two years before thinking she could protect children. She'd said, "I'd tell them, 'Trust me. You can tell me the truth. I'll protect you.' Now," she'd said, "I still tell them, 'Trust me. You can tell me.' But—now I know—I can't protect them."

"Yeah," Linda says. "I went in with the assumption that I would help families. And that families would really appreciate what I was doing for them—in helping. And left feeling like—nobody's ever gonna come and say, 'Thank you for removing my kids.'

"The hardest part for me—the thing that I always felt was the most ugly—was the way the court system would treat the kids.

Basically, one of the things that the court system would do—in the case of an incest kid—would be rather than say, 'This is an incest kid,' they would take the kid into court on a 'dependency' petition, saying, 'This child is being truant. This child is running away. This child cannot be handled by the family. And therefore the family is saying they cannot keep this child. And therefore we are gonna place this child.' But never saying the words, 'Incest was going on.' It was making a deal with the parents. Making a deal that—'You place your child and we're not gonna say what it is.'

"And it looks like the kid is at fault. It looks like the kid is delinquent."

Whatever else this is, it is clearly and unmistakably different from what our New York City "permanency-planning worker," Mark, has told us about the system's positive eagerness to affix blame and labels to the parent—when that parent is a single, poor mother. In those cases, as he suggested, the tendency appears to be to pile on the labels. However, where a sexual abuse allegation arises, implicating an otherwise respectable father, there is a very strong inclination to entirely switch accountability—from the alleged perpetrator to the child.

Ignoring for the moment what this does to the kids, like Carol's former foster-child, Lila, who are so labeled and stigmatized, it also renders these children entirely vulnerable to the ministrations of the system in *all* its guises: juvenile justice, mental health. . . . All of these systems are contiguous—foster family care, group homes, residential treatment, juvenile justice. It is the label placed on the child that determines which "door" he or she enters the system through.

As a nation, we have a mania for mental health "solutions" to social problems; and the child welfare system, particularly, carries the mania to the point of virtual fanaticism—counseling for everybody! The fact of that mania, and the illusion of "solution" promised by the concepts of "treatment" and "cure," has encouraged a boom in such placements. In 1987, for instance, in California, there were nine thousand children in seriously restrictive, intensive residential treatment facilities at a cost of $220 million a year.[8]

Linda says, "I remember one kid I felt was responding pretty normally to what was going on at home. It was a sexual abuse case, but the kid wasn't making any statement about that. Basically, she was refusing to go to school. She got caught drinking. Driving while intoxicated. She didn't have a driver's license.

"And she ended up being placed in a treatment unit at a state hospital—for her behavior. They call it an adolescent treatment unit. It's one of your typical 'residential treatment centers.' I'm assuming there was a psychiatrist on staff who would provide medication for kids. I don't agree with medicating kids, period. It was real obvious that she didn't need to be there. I really felt that was a totally inappropriate placement. That what this kid needed wasn't 'treatment.' The kid needed someone to care about her."

As easy as it is, then, to mask the actuality of a father's sexual abuse by relabeling it to blame the child and her behavior, it is equally—in fact, increasingly—easy to reinterpret (relabel) the sexually abused child as "sick." Even if evidence of this "illness" is a status offense—an offense that can only be called an offense because of your status as child—the Juvenile Justice and Delinquency Prevention Act of 1974 restricted the use of public facilities for the incarceration of status offenders. So instead of a secure prison facility, the sexually abused child is now at risk of finding herself (or himself), instead, in a secure "treatment" facility; even in the lock ward of a psychiatric hospital—where the "treatment" consists of restraints, coercion, and medication.

Michael Robin worked as a psychiatric assistant for three years in a Minnesota hospital. He writes, "Status offenders are often children who have been abused, yet in this hospital they are treated as offenders . . . most patients are diagnosed as having behavior or conduct disorders, like status offenses."[9] (If nothing else, this sentence illuminates the uncanny way in which the English language, when used in a child welfare context, is no longer even expected to mean anything: it is now possible to speak of "diagnosing" an "offense.") Nevertheless, the point is important. In 1980, 47 percent of juvenile psychiatric admissions to American hospitals were for "preadult" disorders—adjustment reactions, emotional disturbances of childhood and adolescence. . . .[10]

Status offenses now become "status disorders": this has been called the "medicalization of deviance."[11]

In this Wonderland, the language of help and "treatment" can be used to camouflage aggressive maltreatment and extreme cruelty, in comparison with which the placement of juveniles as "offenders" in secure punishment facilities looks—if not benevolent—at least candid. In the correctional facility, at least the child is clear that she is being punished for what she has *done*. In the "treatment" facility, she is being tormented for what she *is*. "Many child-rearing practices," Robin writes, "that would be considered abusive if done in the family are legally and socially condoned by our society in the name of discipline and treatment."[12]

Whatever legitimacy there may be to focusing on the abused child as an object of mental health ministrations, our readiness to buy into *incarceration* for "treatment" points to an extraordinary gullibility. That the smoke screen of language can convince people that the abused child's "disorder" requires the draconian environment of a locked and heavily guarded (by "helping personnel") facility, is nothing short of extraordinary.

As in child protective services, the point for many of those employed in these institutions quickly becomes power-over-others (as distinct from the power to help). As Linda said to me, "I saw that happen to me when I was in the system. That I went in with the sense I could help people. And I ended up being real controlling. To the point of just doing things like, 'This, this, and *this* need to happen before this kid can ever go home.' I look back on it now and I think, 'Oh *God!* I can't believe I did those things. I can't believe that was me!' I didn't like myself when that was happening."

Robin writes, "My initial reaction to this program was quite positive. I was caught up, like many others, in the power I had over children." As disillusionment set in, "I came to reject the system."[13]

In many ways, the experience of "treatment," for the children, is akin to the experience of hostages: Stripped of their belongings, of anything familiar, they are subject to demands that they meet incomprehensible "treatment goals." They are required, in effect, to confess to their shortcomings, incorrect attitudes, wrongdoings—in order to gain release. They are required to accept as truth (and appear to embrace) constant negative and critical appraisals. In short, they are held in captivity by adults who see them and treat them as though they were an inferior enemy.

Chronic and severe abuse by a parent is—among other things—mockery of the child's autonomy, a routine degradation ceremony. For the child, then, this "treatment" facility is simply the apotheosis of, the clincher for, all that has gone before.

The techniques used by staff are remarkably similar to those used by hostage takers as well: the threat of isolation; depersonalization; routine searches, not only of space but of mind. Kids are subject to the threat of bondage (termed "restraint"). And the kids must submit to a regular litany of coerced call-and-response about their feelings and faults that amounts to brain-washing.

Previously ordinary things, like listening to music, are held to be "privileges"—earned by conformity and continuous confession. This, it seems to me, is a terribly high price to have to pay for having been raped by your father, and for believing the system that told you "help is available."

As Robin writes, "The attitude of the staff toward these children is markedly ambivalent: they claim to be nurturant and child-centered, but they are also hostile and demand disciplined and controlled behavior. The concern for order and obedience leads to denial of the children's needs and often to abuse."[14] In short, this "therapeutic environment" is only the far end of the continuum of the system's demand for acknowledgment of its own total and unchallengeable power; its demand for obedience and conformity.

What is it like for the child so "treated"?

# MAL-TREATMENT

"Tracy," I am reading, "has received seventeen ricks of wood at camp. These ricks are for major rule infractions. The camp average is seven so she has exceeded this number."

To "receive a rick" of wood, it is explained to me, means to have to split that amount of wood.

"Tracy has an abusive attitude toward other people, and often her behavior is disrespectful. Many of the ricks resulted from this poor attitude. Tracy received these ricks for such things as calling a teacher 'smart ass,' screaming in class, being out of control, having a poor attitude, antagonizing another peer, being assaultive, throwing a canoe to the ground, not following directions, breaking the camp's no-smoking rule, and throwing a tantrum. Tracy also received 70 minus points at camp. These minus points are consequences that result from minor rule infractions."

*Consequences* (it is explained to me) is the term used for

187

punishments assigned by the staff at the camp. It is a funny euphemism, carrying with it the connotation of God-ordained inevitability, of a law such as gravity (the consequence of tripping is falling), when, in fact, the "consequences" are determined by nothing more than the will of those running this "camp."

The report goes on: "She received these minus points for such things as being loud, 'yelling,' being late, not following directions, swearing, and not keeping her personal items picked up in the dormitory. . . . Tracy also received 28 days of dorm restriction. This dorm restriction results from accumulating too many minus points in a one-day period or by failing to cut ricks by the assigned due date."

Under "Relationship with Peers" it is written: "Tracy often has a hard time understanding how she has come to be involved in a situation, and it's more difficult for her to feel like she needs to do something to resolve the situation when she is unable to see that she has helped to create the situation."[1]

Let us try to see what Tracy, they claim, does not see: how she helped to create her situation.

She's a slim, smiling girl, handshake to the ready. From the first second of contact I can feel her taking a reading on me: a person with a keen bullshit detector. The reading accomplished, she proceeds—forthright and outgoing.

"My mom and dad—how do you describe my mom and dad? My mom and dad have a real bad relationship. They think it's excellent. My mom is sort of locked in the house—she won't go anywhere. She has to have my dad's permission for *everything*.

"I can tell you for a fact that my dad didn't want me as a kid because of the fact I was a girl. He said it to my mom many times. My mom told me he said it. He said it to me. He wanted a guy because of the fact that he does carpentry—so he wanted somebody to take over that.

"He was kind of a power freak. He liked having power over everybody in the family. And I'm a really rebellious person, right? So that didn't work out too well.

"The first time he molested me I was nine. And when it started out it was actually innocent. He told me about all the parts and all this kind of stuff, and what happened. And then, after a while, he said, 'Well, you got to see how this *works*.' And so it just got worse: it progressed. It was routine. This is so funny; it sounds stupid. He'd always go to work at the shop. And

he'd ask my mom for me to come over because he needed my
help. And he had this attic at the top—where he stored all kinds
of tools. And he'd go up there, and bring me with him, and it got
so that every time we went up there that's what he'd do.''

"What made him sure you wouldn't tell?"

"The fact that he knew I was scared of him. Physically. He
was physically violent ever since I was born. He used to just yell
in my face all the time. And grab me by the shoulders and just
claw me. And he used to spank me a lot. And when he spanked
he wasn't like a normal human being. The more he spanked me,
the angrier he got. He was always threatening me with a board
with a nail in it. And the belt. He did that once, and he never did
it again. I don't know why. He used to push me around and I'd
end up banging my legs. I have a lot of scars on my legs. Which
pisses me off. Because he always said that I'd remember him
forever. I have lasting scars to remember him for the rest of my
life. No problem.''

Tracy was thirteen when she blew the whistle on her father.

"At the time I was wondering: How long is this going to go
on? Before he's going to have intercourse with me? And I'm
going—'I don't want to be pregnant by this crazed idiot.' That
was what really scared me: What if—it goes too far? What's to
say he isn't going to? To think of being pregnant by him absolutely grosses me out. I just got more worried. And I got worse
in school.

"He used to do weird things. You know those Shout caps—
like the caps from cans of hair spray? He always used to come in
those things. And they'd be all over the attic. And once in a
while, he'd remember they were up there, and he'd throw them
out. I just hated it. I was sick of it, I was just sick and tired of
keeping quiet for this screwed-up family.

"One day it just hit me: This is stupid. I'm not like this. I'm
not like my mom. I'm not a little person he could throw around
and, 'Oh, yes, master. I'll do everything.' ''

It was this very spirit, this very feistiness, of course, that
would make its way into Tracy's "case history" record as "dis-
respect for authority": in fact, it was Tracy's long experience
with *authoritarianism* that gave her a fair eye for that. Real
authority she would know and respect when she finally encountered it in her present foster mother, Barb.

"But," Tracy continues, "I didn't even know what to call
this. So I'm like, 'What do I say to people?' I don't want to say,

'Um, my dad's been screwin' around with me.' It was before they'd come out with all this incest stuff, so I'd never even heard of it. It was just before they went nuts, remember? That one year? I think it was 1984. They went nuts and *everything* was *incest?*

"I wasn't sure who to call, so I was callin' all these shrinks. And they wouldn't take the phone. They wouldn't do anything for me. And I said, 'Well, I need to talk to somebody. I'm having major problems here and I don't know what to do.' And they said, 'Well, do you have an appointment?' And I'm like, *'Do I have an appointment?* I can't even get out of the house without begging on my hands and knees, how am I supposed to get an appointment?'

"Finally I saw a notice about this rape crisis center and it said: 'We take collect calls.' And I'm, 'Oh, thank you!' So I called and—I'll never forget the lady's name, Marjorie; I remember her voice too, because she was really soothing. And I relaxed a lot and I thought, 'Uh. Finally.' I told her, 'I don't know what to call this. I don't know. It isn't adultery.' And then she told me, and she said, 'Do you want to tell somebody so that something can be done?' And I said, 'Yes!' "

The next day, two social workers came to Tracy's school and she told them the whole story. They took her down to the police station where she had to tell it all again—this time with her mother present. Her mother was contradicting everything she said.

"I don't think she really knew before. I mean she knew that I was being hit around. That he was violent. But not about the sexual abuse. So of course she didn't believe it. She kept saying I was lying. And I was crying—I could barely make my statement. I wanted to just scream, 'GET HER THE FUCK OUT OF HERE.' It was making it so much harder."

"You never told other kids?"

"No. At the time I didn't trust any kids because I didn't have any friends. Because—my mom and dad went to garage sales for my clothes. So I was definitely out of style. And second—my mom and dad took showers about once a month. So—I smelled. I'll admit it. I smelled. My hair was gross and I couldn't stand myself. My hygiene sucked."

They put Tracy in a foster home. They put her mother in the home with her. And—in what is truly a statistically aberrant move—the police arrested her father. One often hears that kids don't want their fathers arrested, that they feel guilty for "putting their own father in jail." Not so—with Tracy, at least.

"I was happy. It was like, 'Good—he's in jail.' Because I didn't want him on the streets. He did it to another girl that I know of.

"And then—they put my mom back home. And they put me back home—because he was in jail. I was there for about a month. My mom was always driving over to the jail. It drove me crazy. She was always blaming me for everything. 'It's your fault that this is happening.' And, 'We're gonna be poor.' "

So far, everything that is being done in Tracy's case is exactly what one would wish to be done—where there is a protective mother: stunned, perhaps, but able to make the choice of her child over her husband. The fact is, though, that even where that good mother is present, the system is far more prone to charge the mother with "failure to protect," or because she "knew or should have known." So the fact that the system did what was right in the *wrong* instance—the instance where the mother was actually the old cliché "incest mother," choosing husband over child, etc.—seems almost diabolical.

"I remember," Tracy says, "all the time things were for dad. I'd come home after school and there was these bars there— cookies? And I walk in and I have a couple of bars and then she walks in and she goes, 'Where did the bars go?' 'I ate 'em.' She goes, 'Those were for your father!' And I'm like, 'The whole fucking pan? For my father? Is he the only person in this family— that everything goes to him?' It's really stupid that something as little as bars can get you into shit like that.

"Finally, I said to the social worker, 'I can't handle this anymore. Get me out of here.' She said, 'We can't right now. Unless she does something that's against the rules.' So this is how I got out of there. I have to admit—I did this on purpose.

"I'm going nuts. This woman is driving me crazy. She said, 'Do you want to go with me to see your dad?' And I thought, 'Ah! Here's a way to get out of here.' I wasn't supposed to go with her when she went to the jail. So I went with her, and I stayed in the waiting room. Then I went back to the social worker. I said, 'Peggy, I went with her to the jail.' She says, 'Did you do this *on purpose?*' 'Oh! *No!*' But I had to get out of there."

The first home Tracy was placed in was similar to her own: mother stayed home, father went out to work. "And they were really religious. They had Bible verses hanging all over the place. They had them hanging on the door to the bathroom so when you

sat down to take a shit you could read all these Bible verses. I
remember that—I wasn't real impressed.

"And I had real bad hygiene, so she had to fight with me
every morning to take a shower and wash my hair. And I refused
to do it. Because I hated it. I hated water, for some reason.

"I hated school. I hated people. I hated a lot of things. And I
just started running away. So they put me in this other home after
two, three months."

This home Tracy liked.

"The only problem was they put me in a sexual abuse program. We had to drive about sixty miles every Monday to get
there. And I was feeling, 'Why am I getting punished for this
crap?' They're preaching at me all the time about how this isn't
my fault. That's what bothered me. They're all saying, 'This isn't
your fault.' And I'm—'Fine, I think I got that point now. I know
that.' Every time I said anything: 'This isn't your fault.' 'GOD, I
*know*. Would you just tell me something *besides* that all the
time?'

"It was such a contradiction: 'It's not your fault, yet we're
gonna put you in treatment.'

"It wasn't really helping me out a lot because the program
was set up for families. My family situation was *no* situation.
There was no family. And I started becoming suicidal because I
felt nothing was working. Nobody can help me because all this
shit's set up for families, and I don't have one. I started feeling
sorry for myself all the time.

"So they sent me away to further treatment."

By now, Tracy had received another label besides "sexually
abused." The label was "runner." The place where they sent
her? The adolescent treatment unit of a psychiatric hospital.
What happens to "runners" in this rather draconian institution?

"When you're a runner, you can't wear your own clothes.
You have to wear a gown and robe. You're locked on this one
floor all the time. You can't go anywhere when you're in gown
and robe. You can't go in your room except to sleep. You can
only eat at certain times, and if you're not done by the time that
they're ready to take the food away, tough shit. You can't have
your tape player unless you have a certain amount of points from
the last day. Points for your behavior. Like if you sit there and
say, 'Yes, ma'am. No, ma'am.' And just sort of kiss their ass.
Then you'll have great points."

By now, I have come to like Tracy very much indeed. Her
candor, her vigorous self-assertions in the face of an authority

with virtually total power over her—with no family, no support from anywhere—seem almost inspirational. Winding up on the lock ward of a psychiatric hospital at the age of thirteen, solely because it is taking you a few minutes (or months) to come to terms with the fact that you really don't have a family, that you feel sort of lousy about that, that you don't have the information to know what is possible for you—and fighting still? To me, that seems heroic.

To those in power, however, Tracy's strengths are grounds for ever-greater repression. Outside of juvenile prisons, the mental health system offers the greatest number of facilities that are tooled up to provide kid-control. As I listen to Tracy, I think: "The goal of the adolescent treatment unit is to 'rehabilitate' you from—adolescence." (Keep in mind what you know of a "normal" thirteen-year-old; what you know is important to a "normal" thirteen-year-old.)

Tracy says, "I feel violently toward treatment, as you'll soon tell.

"I sat there for almost a month. That's a long time for a place like that. You're not supposed to be there that long—that's what they kept telling me. The whole time I was there I was in gown and robe, except for maybe the last two days. And they'd said that after a couple of days they'd let me get out of gown and robe. And I kept asking.

"My psychiatrist kept saying no. And finally I said, "Fuck this, I'm getting pissed here. I mean, you said that after two, three days I was gonna get out of gown and robe.' I *hated* being in gown and robe. This stupid gown has a thing in the back—so you feel like everybody can see your ass all the time. And then you have this robe that never stays on. And everything's big and baggy and you look gross. It was disgusting. They wouldn't let me have my makeup. I just got more angry and more aggravated. And then finally one day I just let loose. And that was it.

"I 'went off' is what they call it. 'Went off' is you get violent, you scream.

"Actually, it started off rather innocent. I was really aggravated: The colors were starting to aggravate me. Everything was earth colors. Everything. The walls. The ceilings. I started to hate earth tones so bad—all those oranges and browns. Gross. And the people were gross. These old ladies who were going insane were gross. All these weird people were gross. And I hated myself. 'I hate these clothes. I hate it.' You have to walk around in these stupid socks all the time, that have little no-slip things.

So you sort of stop real nice.'' With her hands, Tracy illustrates
an abrupt fall on your face. "I was just sick of everything. And
this one day a nurse said, 'Go to your room.' 'Cause she thought
I was being obnoxious. I didn't think I was being obnoxious. I
was just asking her when could I get my clothes. I must admit I
got a little pissed, but I tried my best not to show it—because I
knew that would down my points and I wouldn't be able to do
anything the next day.

   " 'Go to your room.'

   " 'Why should I go to my room? I haven't done anything.'
And she says, 'I want you to go to your room.' I said, 'No! I'm
not going to my room for doing nothing!' She says, 'Do you want
the orderlies to come up?' I go, 'Sure! I haven't met *them* yet.
I've met everybody else in this damned place. Why not?'

   "So the orderlies were trying to get me to go down the hall,
and it just got really bad.

   "The funny thing is they give you these slippers, right? And
they sort of defeat the purpose. What they want is for you to go
in this little 'time-out' room—with the little doors locked, and
padded walls and shit. And you couldn't go to the bathroom
while you were in there; the bathroom was locked. You have to
knock on the door and look through this little peephole and go,
'Hey-y-y, I've gotta go to the bathroom.' So I'm sitting there in
the hall and it's like if you go like this"—plant your feet down—
"there's no way you're gonna go anywhere with rubber soles.
Defeated the purpose totally. I thought it was rather funny.

   "So I'm crouching there like this, and there's five orderlies
behind me trying to push me—and I ain't going nowhere. Finally,
they just had to pick me up. And then they put me in there and I
got really violent.''

   I try to picture five orderlies pushing and shoving at this girl
who, even at seventeen, is only 5'1" and perhaps 105 pounds.
And I wonder: Suppose this were a scene in a movie. This young
girl, sexually victimized for years by her father, and who has
committed no greater a sin than aggression against her own
bewilderment and sense of displacement—running away, feeling
awful—finds herself summarily trapped in a psychiatric hospital,
all the outward trappings of her identity, her possessions, removed. When she asks how long she's to be here, they do not
tell her anything, except that she's been here too long already.
When she asks to have her things back, they tell her nothing,
except she cannot. I cannot believe that the entire audience,
adults as well as adolescents, would not be enthusiastically

rooting for Tracy, were this a scene in a movie. Why is it, then, that in hearing of Tracy-the-real-girl, I sense that people will want to back off; to reach for an "expert" to explain her "pathology"? Is it because we believe, in real life, kids are not in mental hospitals *for no reason?*

"The more they screw with you, the madder you get. That's the thing. They think it's gonna calm you down if they put you in there. But when you're in there, you're locked up. You can't do anything. There's nothing to throw. There's nothing to do anything with. The madder you get. So I'm flipping out on this nurse—I hated her. Through this little window, I'm going, 'Mmmmm.' And every time I flipped off, I got twenty more minutes. 'Mmmmm.' Twenty more minutes. 'Nnnng.' Twenty more minutes. Twenty more minutes. Twenty more minutes. And the more I did it, the madder I got.

"It was ironic in there.

"And after that they had me in four-point. 'Cause I started slamming the movable bed they had in there against the door. And I kept thinking, 'You bitch, you bitch! You bitch! You *bitch!*' It was so great. I got my adrenaline up real nice.

"So then they took the bed out. And they take you, and they have these little things that go around your wrists and your ankles—all four points. They have you spread-eagled.

"I remember lying there. And I started crying because I was so mad, and, 'My tears are going back in my eyeballs.' I kept thinking that. My tears were running back in my eyeballs. And I started *laughing.* I couldn't help it. They thought I was going nuts. And they started giving me drugs and shit to calm me down."

Drugs? "They do that?"

"They do that all the time. They give you drugs the whole time you're in there. Elavil. It's supposed to be an antidepressant."

Well, that makes sense. I'd certainly be depressed in a place like that.

"And then when you're freaked out they also have a drug for you. To calm you down.

"I stayed in four-point for I don't know how long. But I remember it was a really long time. I would say it was about four hours.

"A couple of days after that, they put me in A-2, which is an adolescent treatment unit, separate from the whole thing. I was there for about nine months. There were different 'steps.' So if

you were in a certain 'step' you couldn't go into the cloakroom
where you could play music. You'd have to stay in the hall and
dayroom. The place where I was, there were two cottages—for
the guys and the girls. And the part where I was, the girls', there
was this one part where the guys were that were locked up. PCU,
they called it: the protective care unit."

More protection. More care.

"What were the other girls like?" I ask. "Crazy?"

"No. They weren't crazy. Most of them were in there for
sexual abuse. Rape. Because of stuff like that, they get emotionally screwed up, then they end up doing things like drugs, running
away. That's the aftereffects crap. 'Because I've been sexually
abused, I can take these drugs and it doesn't matter because I'm
already screwed up.' " Well, yes. But is it not the *system* that's
telling them they're screwed up, they need "therapy"?

"Would you say they needed to be there?"

"Some. I'm not gonna say all because I don't think that
anybody—*needs*—to be in 'treatment' like that. I mean they
called it an open unit. But—if somebody ran, the whole place
was locked."

"In order to turn everybody against the kid who runs away?"

"Supposedly. But it doesn't work that way. They get pissed
because of the fact that the doors are locked. You can't go
outside to have cigarettes. But it's regarded as real cool to run.
Because then—you can see something besides the goddam treatment unit. It's like, 'Hey, man, what'd you *see*? What did you
*do*? What-did-you-do? What-did-you-do? Did you get drunk? Did
you do anything bad? Did you rip off anything? Huh?-huh?-huh?'
Anything that was exciting to us was—'Yeah!' 'Great!' When
people went off, it was big excitement. Our 'news' system was—
mouth to mouth. And our news wasn't: you get a new girl, or a
new guy. That was news but it wasn't big news. Big news was if
somebody left—bad. Meaning, they had a bad discharge. They
couldn't handle them anymore."

Discharge. A "bad" discharge. Where else can you get such
a thing besides in the military?

"Where did they go from there?"

"A lockup place. Most of the time they get put in Southfield.
I was there too. Or big news was if somebody ran, somebody
tried to cut themselves. Anything like that was excitement. 'Oh
my God, man, you should have seen that, man. It took five staff
to take him down, man!' 'Wow, what a trip.' "

It's a very interesting concept. You take kids you decide have a "problem with authority" (or with the authoritarian), and you put them in places of ever greater restrictiveness, ever greater and more apparently arbitrary authoritarianism. You take kids whose parents' abuse of them has robbed (or has tried to rob) them of any sense of autonomy or control—and put them in a situation where they are totally disempowered. What can the expected result be? To finish the job of destruction of dignity and will that their parents started? Or to turn them into a gang—engaged in guerrilla actions against the system?

"What," I ask, "did you do all day?"

"Went to school for a little while. We smoked. We listened to tunes. Talked about running. Everybody used to talk about 'the outs.' 'What're you gonna do when you get out?' 'When you getting out?' 'I don't know.' Nobody knew. 'They *say* I'm getting out in July.' Nobody ever expected to leave when they said you were going to.

"I was in 'treatment' for four years. The first time, I was in that place for nine months. But there's people that are there a very, very long time. There were girls who were there the first time I was there—who are only just now going to be leaving."

"Was there any reason you could see?"

"Well, in one girl's case, she was sort of ding-y. Meaning she acted stupid a lot of times. And she didn't listen real well. But she never tried to do anything bad. To me, it didn't seem like she needed to be there. I know she was nervous about things a lot of times. But then—who isn't? I felt that a lot of people who were there shouldn't have been there. Either because they weren't that bad. Or because they were very very violent toward themselves or others. There was this one girl who kept cutting herself. She should have been somewhere they could help her. Because the dayroom isn't going to help you. They supposedly don't have knives around, but you can get them. Just about anywhere you go you can get them.

"See, the thing that bothers me is—kids who don't do anything bad aren't even going to be talked to. In effect, they're just sort of ignored. Because there are other people who are just about trying to kill themselves, so, 'We have to go out there and watch *them* all the time; give them attention.' "

"Was there therapy attached to this?"

"Yeah. Supposedly. I don't call it therapy. I don't know what I call it. We had a sexual abuse group there. And there's no way I'm going to participate. 'Why—am I going through this—again?' I told my social worker, 'I'm not gonna do it.' So I sat there in the group and I didn't say a damn thing. And they said, 'Well, you're not gonna get out of here doing that.' I said, 'Fuck you. I'm not gonna sit here and tell you my whole life story, when I've already told fifty million other people. And it hasn't helped me much, has it? Otherwise, I wouldn't be here.' "

"How did you get out?"

"I guess they considered I was fulfilling my 'goals.' You had these goals you had to fulfill. Like, no running. And like mine were—for a long time—'Do your laundry.' "

"A fourteen-year-old doing her own laundry sounds like a contradiction in terms."

"We had to do our laundry every week. That was one thing. And the other was, 'Don't flirt with boys.' So—I couldn't flirt with boys, couldn't run, and I had to do my laundry. I got a point every day, not running, not flirting with boys. And seven points a week when I did my laundry."

That is some basic moral economy.

"Seven points! Wow! I couldn't tell you what I did that got me out of there. I guess I wasn't as obnoxious. I wasn't as— 'playful,' as people called me. I wasn't as spontaneous. I was more boring. They—may call it that I was 'treated': I was being a good little girl. Which is the way you get out."

Perhaps it was nothing Tracy did or didn't do the first time. Suddenly, an aunt turned up, claiming she had just found out about Tracy, claiming she cared, and took her home with her. Tracy was put in charge of minding the aunt's ten-year-old daughter. Fracases erupted. It lasted three months. The aunt took Tracy back to the "treatment" center. For another nine months.

The most exceptional thing about this period was that Tracy asked that her mother's and father's parental rights be terminated. They had made no effort to communicate with her during all of this time, claiming that once out of the home, she was no longer their responsibility. Finally social service workers prevailed on them to visit her. Her father said he didn't want to discuss "feelings." Tracy did talk about "feelings." They walked out. She then asked that their rights be terminated. She signed an affidavit as a state ward—not wishing to be adopted.

This, truly, is unusual. Most kids, I am told, will want to keep returning and returning to even the most abusive parent(s). 'Now am I all right? Now are you the parent(s) I wanted?' How much of this is real feelings, how much a response to the stigma of alternative placements (not to mention the frequent errors of the alternatives)?

Barb, the foster mother Tracy now lives with, makes Tracy look like a big person: Barb is 4'10", small boned and wiry. She has come into the room while Tracy is talking with me and seated herself cross-legged on the floor by the couch Tracy and I are sharing.

She says, "I got Tracy last August. I wasn't going to take any more placements. I've had a couple of really tough, really heavy placements. But when the social worker read Tracy's workup papers, she really felt that I'd be interested in her. And the reason why is Tracy's the only kid I've ever worked with—that she asked that her parental rights be terminated. Tracy asked.

"And—all of the kids that I've ever worked with, no matter what has happened, no matter how bad it is—they always want to go back to their parents."

"Why?" I ask.

"Because they still have these fantasies about the nuclear family. They feel like they've been denied things. They feel like they've got a right to it. And so this is the first kid I've ever worked with in my life—even when I worked with sexual assault, and I've been working with young women for about fifteen years—this is the first young woman that I've ever seen that has enough guts to say, 'They're dysfunctional. I want out.' And I think that's real fascinating."

I wondered then, as I was to wonder any number of times, how much of the anguish children in state care suffer is socially constructed? How much of it results from the shoulds that are, even today, ever-present about the family, and ever-present as well in the words of the system? And how curious the juxtaposition is: the concern expressed for the "family" and the virtually exclusive focus on women, as mothers, as foster mothers.

"What we're trying to do in foster care is fantasy," Barb says. "It's let's pretend: 'This is what a good nuclear family is.' " Barb is a social worker with a private agency. She tells me she wanted to start a unit with just single people. "They were really threatened by that. Some of it's real patronizing. 'If there was a male around, he could put his foot down.' Well, there's not a male. The fact is, there's not a whole lot of males around to do that. And our lifestyle is different. Like I tell the kids, we have a whole different family structure. That doesn't mean we're not a

family. And the message they're still getting—like from Social
Services and stuff—is what we're *not*."

We turn our attention back to Tracy. "Your aunt?" I say.
"What happened there?"

"All of a sudden she turns up—at this time in my life where
I'm feelin' I have no family, right? So I'm sitting there and I'm
like, 'Who are these people?' And they're like, 'Oh, we care.'
And, 'We didn't know what was going on.' So she takes me.

"I hated living with her. I hated it. I hated her rules. I hated
everything. I was a rebellious person and I hated a lot of things.
I didn't accept a lot of things. I have to admit some of it was fair.
Some of it was not fair. I was supposed to stay home and take
care of my cousin all the time. She was ten years old, and she
smoked. She drank. But she was an a-a-a-angel, according to
them. And guess who got in trouble for ripping off the cigarettes.
Ripping off booze.

"I got in trouble. I tried to tell her, 'Your daughter smokes.'
And she's like, 'No, she doesn't. I know you smoke.' I go, 'Well,
*I* know that. I never told you I didn't. I told you that the first
thing when I got here. I said, "I smoke." And if you can't handle
it, then I'm not living here.' And she said, 'Okay.' And finally,
one night, they said, 'Well, we're gonna bring you back.' This
was after three months. And I said, 'Oh, hm.' "

Back to the adolescent treatment unit for another nine
months, then. "When you got there? Were the other kids happy
to see you?"

"Yeah! I think that was the neatest thing. I had been there
before so when I come in, it's like, 'Oh my God! Where'd *you*
come from? Are you visiting?' 'No. I'm back.' And they go, 'Oh,
what'd you do, man?' Then you make up all this shit that you
didn't do. 'Oh, man, I got so fuckin' stoned every day, man.'
And they're like, '*Really?* Oh? God!' You do that kind of shit to
say you're really cool. 'Man, I was fuckin' every guy in that high
school.' 'Oh, wow, was it *great,* man, huh-huh-huh?' 'And I went
to these wild parties you wouldn't *believe.*' Stuff like that.

"Some of my old friends that were in there before were still
there. And then some new girls. And of course all the old people
that I'd known: 'You should see these new witches. They are so
stupid.'

"So—I was already in this cool group. To be cool you have to
be there for a long time. Seniority. And you also—have to be
with certain people all the time. I had that, too—from before. So

I didn't have to work. I knew all the staff. So I was being a hotshot."

Like Laura, Tracy is taking her sense of being in control where she can find it. Wouldn't we all? Don't we all?

"I had to go through school all over again."

"Why?"

"Because you have to go up. You start out in orientation, and then you go from Orientation 1 to Orientation 2, and then from there you go to Intermediate 1, Intermediate 2, Intermediate 3. If you *make* it to Intermediate 3, you're very lucky. You can go to the school 'out there.' The real school." As in the school for real kids, who have real families, or appear to.

"If you're Intermediate 2, they bus you down to a school where you can do more interesting things—like art, sewing, photography. The first time I was there I got to do that. But it was a lot different the second time around. Because they changed the rules on me.

"So then I bullshitted my way out of there again. By kissing ass, and all that kind of stuff."

Tracy then was returned to foster home #2. Actually, it was working rather well in the home. Until:

"After a while, it got like the town just hated me. They knew everything about me. They hated my family, they hated me. I got a lot of criticism from everybody. This was the same town as where my parents had originally lived. I couldn't handle it. I said I wanted out of there.

"They sent me to this foster home in the middle of nowhere. I got no rights. I was worked—I felt like I was their chore person. I did chores at five o'clock in the morning. I fed the cows. I had to separate the cows to feed them. You have to feed these certain cows this, and those cows that, and take two bales of hay out, and then you had to go and feed the chickens. Pick eggs. Then I had to slop the pigs.

"They had their own kid. But she didn't do anything. She was like five years old. Still, I thought, 'God, she could at least feed chickens.' My dad had me doin' shit by the time I was three.

"There was another foster girl there. She was like the sheriff's daughter, or his niece. And she'd been there like a month, and she'd been ripping off cigarettes from them and she wouldn't tell them she smoked. Whereas I did. So she was a good little girl. She got easy jobs like cooking, working in the house.

"She had been wanting to run for a long time. And one day I

decided I was gonna run. I was very sick of living there and getting nothing.

"Where I got into a lot of trouble was that I ripped off money from them. Well, how else are you gonna get anywhere? You've got to have money.

"So I ripped off about sixty dollars. I sort of felt bad about that because I had to rip off the little girl's piggy bank. But then— she had more money than I did. I didn't have any. They got money every week for taking care of me. But I never saw any of that. And they're supposed to put some of that into us. Supposedly. That's what the deal is. For allowances, clothing. . . . I never saw that. They never bought me clothes. They fed me— that's more or less what they did.

"Finally, I said, 'That's it. I've had it.' The girl helped me rip off the stuff. She was sittin' there, singing; she was real happy. She hadn't had an allowance for so long.

"And she got the mace. I guess she thought that way she would protect herself? I couldn't figure it out. She ripped off kitchen knives. The kind that don't even scare you.

"The next day she put most of it in her backpack. We were going to go to school. Run from there. That didn't work out too good. We ended up coming back. And—she put all the stuff in my locker. I got caught with it. She had nothing to do with it— supposedly—according to her. I said, 'Hold it, here! It was her idea to rip off anything.' And I felt really bad about ripping off money.

"I got probation for that. Then they put me in—it's like a group home, but it's treatment. Like they had all these groups, and you had to sit there and tell them all your problems every day. And they have this basic list of problems—they had a problem sheet. So you could classify your 'problems of the day.' One of the things that made me mad was—anything you did— like if you forgot something?—that was an 'authority problem,' because you knew you were supposed to do it."

"My kids," I say, "wouldn't have made it."

"Nobody, as far as I'm concerned, would make it. You have to be almost perfect to get out of that place. You had to sit there every day. You went to a normal school. Fifty cents was the most you could bring to school. You had to do your homework every day when you came home, first thing. You had to ask the group if it was okay to ask the staff if it was okay to have a cigarette. Or go to the bathroom. You'd have to sit there and ask the group if you could ask the staff if you could—like take out money. I remember you always had to say 'excuse me.' And they'd be sitting there, watching us. And you knew damn well they were listening. And you had to go up there and say, 'Excuse me, so and so, but may I ask you something?' And they'd already know what you were gonna ask them. And then they'd say yes or no. And you'd have to say, 'May I please . . .' and then the question.''

If there is a point to this exercise besides authoritarianism and diminishment of the object of your ''therapy,'' it eludes me. It is one thing to punish people; something entirely other to call it help. What is served by calling it that except our own sense of *our* benevolence? ''More, sir, please, sir.'' I look at the peppy, direct, no-bullshit kid sharing the couch with me, and I think that to the extent the system is about kids at all, it is about inducing their absolute conformity by punishing all nonconformity. This is done by incarceration and the enforcing of compliance in trivia: by ''points'' and ''privileges'' and ''steps.'' It is ''Solomon Says, 'Do this, do that . . .' '' at its most transparently mindless.

''How long,'' I ask Tracy, ''did kids stay there?''

''One girl had been there eleven months. And one girl was going to graduate. She was so happy. I would be too. But then she was so perfect—she was like a robot.

''The people that got out of there looked like robots. They didn't fight anymore. They were walking around the school and they told everybody everything about them. Someone'd ask them a question and they'd give this long, 'Well, I *feel* that . . .' They sounded like a fucking social worker. And that isn't a person to me. They had no personality.

''This one girl that was getting out—she'd sit down in group, and I couldn't believe it. She was constantly saying how she was still 'fronting.' It was almost like a disease.''

I look baffled.

'' 'Fronting'? Putting on these fronts for people? And she'd never put on acts that I'd ever seen.

''I used it against people. This one girl I couldn't stand, I'd sit there and say, 'Well, you're fronting.' She'd say, 'No.' I was really good at this—I'd be all calm and sit there and, 'Well, I think—that you are doing blah-blah-blah by doing blah-blah-blah. . . .' And you could always get them in trouble because it was easy: anything anybody did was bad. People would always be saying, 'You have a problem.' And every time they said you have a problem, they're checking your behavior. So I'd always be checking their behavior all the time.''

This begins to seem worse than mindless: it is setting the hostages (or inmates) up so they will do your thought-policing for you.

"Yeah. And me and Ellen and Fran came in and, 'We're gonna turn this place upside down. These people are robots.' And Fran becomes like them. So that was it with her. Me and Ellen were constantly running away. I was on probation. This was not good.

"We'd run away. We'd party. We'd come back and we'd say, 'Okay, I state the whole problem.' They say, 'No. We have to state the problems separately.'

"My P.O. [probation officer] was getting a little p.o.'d. He said, 'What's the problem?' I said, 'It sucks here.' He goes, 'Well, I know that.' And I go, 'Fine, why did you put me here?' It ended up he said I had to go to court. Well, we can't have this happen. So I ran away again, and this time I was gone for a month and a half.

"And then I got caught. Ellen was in California. But I stayed in the same town the whole time. I remember I used to go up to these cops who were hanging around, and I'd say, 'Are you looking for somebody who's on run?' And they'd say, 'No.' And I'd go, 'I'm on run.' I just did it to be obnoxious."

By now, I have learned that *obnoxious* is Tracy's word for tugging a bit on the system's tail, tweaking its ear. So I say, "It doesn't sound obnoxious to me. It sounds like a funny kid."

"For me, it was fun."

Barb breaks in proudly, "She's got a 4.0 grade point average."

"When they caught me, they put me in jail. Because I ran away while I was supposed to be waiting out my court date. They had a warrant out for my arrest."

This is when the court ordered Tracy to go to what we will call The Camp: the one with the "ricks of wood." She had to wait in a lockup facility about a week for an opening.

"They put me in The Camp. The Camp is—hell on earth."

Barb: "It's for rehabilitation, mostly. It says you are somewhat incorrigible. And won't follow the rules."

"It's a place in the middle of the woods, in the middle of nowhere. They took my makeup. They took my stuffed animals. They thought you could hide dope, drugs, knives in your stuffed animals. They tear the stamp off your mail all the time—because they thought you could hide acid under it. It's true. I've seen people do it."

"Like you?" Barb asks.

"I've never used acid, man. I'd never touch that stuff. No way. Your mind's screwed for a month."

"What did you do at The Camp?" I ask.

"You went to school for the morning and part of the afternoon. The rest of the afternoon you worked an hour to four hours, depending on how bad or good you were. Then you went on 'activities'—which meant doing more work. I hated 'activities.' Chopping wood sometimes. Hauling wood a lot. Cutting grass around the grounds—they have a lot of grounds.

"And if you ran? You had to wear these orange—bright orange? like that hunting orange?—sweatshirts and sweatpants all the time. That way they could see you wherever you went. It said 'The Camp' on the back. It was real funny—everybody liked the orange for some reason. Because that way you could show how cool you were.

"And you could get what The Camp called Limbo. That's where you're not in a group anymore."

"You're nothing," Barb says.

"Yeah. You're nothing. You're separate, on your own. The staff tells you, 'You're in Limbo.' You walk around going, 'Ohmygod, I'm in Limbo.' "

Barb: "It means you're not allowed to participate in the group. You lose the support of the group. You are now isolated—in limbo. They took something away from you: your peer support."

"Then there's Panthers. Wildcats. We were the Cougars."

"How long were you there?"

"Three months. You know you're gonna be there three months unless you screw up and run. Then you get ten more days. Which *is* like jail, isn't it?"

Barb says, "You should tell her about Expo."

"Expo? In the shortest definition, it's a pain in the ass. You get ready for this the whole time you're out there. It's a very big ordeal. You do all this stuff to build up your muscles. So you can go out in the middle of nowhere and commune. For seventeen days. And eat dehydrated food. And sit with this group you can't stand. Every day. And then you have to go on this thing called Solo. It's just that. By yourself. Take care of yourself. Do everything for yourself."

Barb says: "It was incredible. How many portages did you do?"

"Forty-five."

Barb: "Carrying these giant fifty-pound backpacks . . ."

"About twenty-seven miles. And not on very good food, either. Well," Tracy says, "the next challenge was me and Barb."

Barb has told me that what must be the hardest thing in the world for a kid is the "preliminary interview" with the prospective foster parent. Thus, she decided to go up to The Camp to see Tracy, rather than wait till Tracy had completed her time and have Tracy come to visit her.

Tracy says: "She made herself so tough!" To Barb: "When I first met you, I thought, 'Fuck, I'm going into a goddam jail.' I'm serious! Because you were like, 'I like my power.' " To me: "She's sitting there like a king or somebody: 'If you do this, boy . . .' "

Barb says, "I told her, 'You come into my house with a clean slate.' "

Tracy: "But you sure made yourself sound tough, didn't you? The first time I saw her at The Camp she comes down, she's got all this fancy stuff on. To me, this was like—I mean, here I'm dressed in these grubby old T-shirts and shit. And I *thought* I was dressed up. I'm lookin' at her, and I'm goin', 'Ohmygod.' But she was short. That's the thing that killed me most. I thought, 'All *right*. Finally they're finding people who are—like me.' And then she talked to me, sounded all tough and everything. . . ."

Barb: "I laid out the basic ground rules. And those have not changed, have they?"

"No. But you made them sound a lot worse, the way you were talking."

Barb: " 'If I'm going to share my house with you, there are certain rules. My things are my own.' Because I don't want to have my house under lock and key. And I would never allow the girls to be exploited by older men. They had to date within their age group.

"I told Tracy I'm not gonna be her policeman."

Tracy came down to Barb's for a "preplacement" trial. Barb says: "There was this kid, really nice, came from a good family. I knew him, used to be my paperboy. He wanted to take Tracy out on a date. Well, I knew one thing you don't do, you don't let your kids out of your sight; you've got to be a policeman. So I talked to him. He came up and said, 'I'd really like to take her out.' I took Tracy to the side and I said, 'Look, you want to fuck it up, this is the time to do it.' I said, 'If you want to go out and have a good time, these are the limits. And I expect you to follow them.' And I let her go out on a date on her preplacement. It just blew her mind. I said, 'You're seventeen years old, you're gonna be dating, you might as well find out.'

"The kids were about three minutes late. I almost had a heart attack. But I let her go. The social workers were in shock."

"You're still in school, Tracy, " I say. "What happens next?"

"Well. My birthday. This is the first time I've ever been out of treatment since I was thirteen. And I actually spent Christmas in a normal home. So this is a major deal. It was—overwhelming—but great! I got a lot of presents and stuff, and it wasn't a sweat. And you don't have somebody snapping at you all the time, 'Do something!' "

Barb says, "She did everything she possibly could to take the joy out of Christmas. And finally, I just fucking blew up. It was the twenty-third of December, and I told her I was tired of her takin' my joy. I was tired of her attitude. And I went to bed about seven o'clock at night, because I said, 'You want to fuck it up, fine. Just start right now. And I'm not going to talk to you anymore. I'm not gonna play any more fuckin' games with you.' And I went to bed.

"She can be a bitch. It's all real sabotage. Kicky. Whiny. She's a master at it. She really is. And she'd made my life miserable for about two or three days. It was just—nothing was right, nothing was good. And I tried to decorate the house and get the tree and do all this . . . No matter what I did, she could find fault with it; she could say how stupid this was. How superficial this was.

"So I went to bed. I refused to talk to her. I woke up at four o'clock the next morning, and I got her up. She sat up in bed, she wiped her eyes. And she said, 'Barb, I really feel bad. What you said yesterday made a real impact on me.' She said, 'I'll try to enjoy the day.' So we went out. We had a wonderful day, and then a beautiful Christmas, and we went over to my sister's and the tree was beautiful and the house was beautiful; my whole family was there.

"It was just like all of a sudden she realized that she had really offended me. That she had really taken something away from me. And Christmas Eve—I suppose we'll always refer to it as 'Tracy's Christmas'—and it was like, *'That's* what Christmas is supposed to be all about?'

"And my son, who is probably the most hard-assed, jaded individual you ever want to meet, he got Tracy a watch. And it was just—it had been real hard for my family, because there'd been a lot of loss, a lot of deaths. It really blew my mind to stuff stockings. Tracy never had had a stocking.''

Tracy and Barb: a match. They look at each other fondly. Barb says, "Santa Claus was very kind to her." To me, she says, "I think Tracy had a difficult time in traditional homes—with authority."

Tracy says, "Traditional homes are bullshit. A lot of the kids who are in foster care don't have traditional homes because they have problems, the family's torn up. So they go to this 'traditional home'—and they're not gonna live like that. So: I'm not gonna get out of a traditional foster home and go back to my 'family.' Because I didn't want to."

A few weeks after I'd flown home, I got a long letter from Tracy. In part:

"Louise,

"I have been debating here for a while as to exactly what I want to say to you. The first thing that comes to mind is, 'God, I hope that your book can change the system!' Not that I'm holding my breath.

"I was going through some old papers of mine and I noticed something rather interesting. They (staff in ATU) wrote about me: 'She seems to want to be in charge of adults or at least be regarded with equal status. . . .' Then they go on to say, 'Tracy will have to work on this problem by designing appropriate short-term goals dealing with awareness of her voice tone and body language. . . .'

"It's so hard for me to believe that these people who are supposed to be our saviors in disguise are so frightened of a young girl who wishes to be treated as an equal. This really frightened me when I read it. I guess I never really paid that much attention to my reports because they were just more of the bullshit you'd get in treatment. I just wanted to try and ignore some of the crap that was going on around me.

"The more I read, the angrier I get. 'Tracy has often complained and protested about her placement at ATU.' Of course. I was *angry!* I get punished all my life for being born and then I get more punishment of a sort, while my father gets free room and board.

"And the language they used! 'Conforms her conduct,' 'responding,' 'progress,' 'observed.' They talk as if I was a fucking lab experiment.

"If only these people could realize that we don't need conformity and 'progress' to be loved or to live a normal life. I've always wondered why they must always *change* the abnormal instead of *living* with it and *learning* from it and *supporting* the people.

"Obviously, their so-called 'centers' aren't doing any good for the 'emotionally disturbed' adolescent. Otherwise, I wouldn't be seeing such a variety of treatment centers and such a long list of treatment friends that I see so often as I get switched from institutions. Or, shall I say, as I *got* switched from institutions. For the first time I realize more what bullshit it all was and I'm doing something about it."

# A PROFESSIONAL'S
# VIEW

I t began to be creepy to listen to story after story, like Tracy's, where the child-victim of parental abuse is removed only to find her- or himself redefined after removal as the problem and then subject to sometimes drastic mental health intervention or, almost arbitrarily (quite possibly depending on where the funding is at the moment), "chemical-dependency" intervention.

Before becoming an attorney for the Minnesota Mental Health Law Project, Kathy Kosnoff was involved in an effort to propose legislation in Minnesota that would be more stringent about child and adolescent admissions to mental health facilities. She says, "The fury and the strength of the industry we were talking about regulating was just something to behold. We knew it would be strong. But it was beyond our wildest dreams. I wish I could remember the exact figure, but just the adolescent chemical-dependency business was something like a ten-million-dollar industry.''

Minnesota, of course, sees itself as a ''progressive'' state. ''Help'' is meant to be progressive: it is meant to be ''understanding.'' As a result, Minnesota's laws governing admittance for ''help'' are relaxed. As a result of that, kids are sent to Minnesota for placement from states that have more stringent laws. As with so much else in the world of protective services/child welfare, hard numbers do not exist (or did not exist at the time of this writing). However, Kathy Kosnoff says to me, ''I can tell you, for example, that in working with the people in the adolescent treatment industry, that is, the people who run the chemical-dependency hospital inpatient units and the facilities for the emotionally disturbed, they have told me that anywhere from 75 percent to 100 percent of the children that they treat have been physically and/or sexually abused.''

I mention Tracy, and a number of other kids I'd spoken with, who'd fallen into the mental health system—after physical or sexual abuse, certainly—but for what amounted to simple adolescent nonconformity.

''Right. It's called adolescent adjustment reaction. A large percentage of kids who are put in adolescent treatment facilities—that is the primary diagnosis.''

There are, she tells me, a lot of private placements by parents. There are situations where the child is privately placed, where it becomes clear that the child has been sexually abused—and is being conveniently gotten rid of. And then returned, eventually, to the same situation.

''But,'' I suggest, ''labeled crazy, so she can't complain again?''

''Well, yeah, I think that's an effect. People—adults, and especially children—get so used to not being listened to and not being believed.''

''I have been told by some psychologists,'' I say, ''that there is no such thing as a chemically dependent adolescent.''

''I wouldn't go so far as to say that. But I think it's overdiagnosed. I think there are a lot of kids who are displaying very typical adolescent drug or alcohol use. Which is certainly not to be encouraged. But on the other hand does not rise to the level of chemical dependency. And sometimes it's not the primary problem. The kid who's got other problems does not need to be sat down in a room and told they're not getting out of that place until they say, 'I am an alcoholic.' ''

Why, I wonder, is it so virtually automatic to perceive children who have situational problems as being, themselves, the problem? Probably because it deflects attention from the issue at hand as a social issue, a social problem, and turns it into an individual's problem. And more important, probably because—as was true almost a century ago—there are folks who have noticed there is money in them thar hills.[1]

I had been told that, if I could get myself to New Orleans, I should talk with Dr. C. A. Cowardin, a child psychiatrist: that she had been extremely active on behalf of children involved in the world of foster care.

It was time to do that.

Dr. Cowardin is quick to explain that the only system she knows is the one in Louisiana, and that Louisiana is an extremely poor state that has suffered tremendous cutbacks on all social services, not least protective services/child welfare. Still, money is far from the only problem.

"I was in court this spring on a case. I had a copy of the *Manual for Permanency Planning* that I had gotten several years before, when I was on the Permanency Planning Committee of one of the parishes. So I was quoting them chapter and verse from the manual. And I was told—in court—'Oh, that doesn't apply anymore. There's a *new* manual.' Which I could accept. But getting a copy of the pertinent information was very difficult to do. I had to go to somebody that I knew in the system who thinks the same way I do.

"And, having gotten it, I felt sad. There's one item in it that I think is just—wrong. It says, 'The following are maximum amounts of time it ordinarily takes a child to form a new psychological tie when the old psychological tie is not maintained. From birth to two years: several days.' Well, that's just not true. If you take a two-year-old away from its parents—or say an eighteen-month-old child—that child does not form new parental attachments in a few days. Anybody who's ever seen an eighteen-month-old child would know that after a few days it's waiting for Mommy to come back. That reality implies that the previous relationship is not completely destroyed. And then the manual says, '. . . when the old psychological tie is not maintained.' And that's so vague.

"Foster care sets up visits to, quote, maintain bonding, you see. They're under the impression that you can let a kid eighteen

months of age visit every third week or every second week or
something like that and that 'maintains the relationship.' Of
course it doesn't. It's so vague that it can become an excuse for
a judge to say, 'Well, it's perfectly all right to take this two-year-
old child who has been with foster parents since he was five
weeks old and put him up for adoption or return him to his
parents. Because he's going to form a new relationship in two or
three days. Or a week.' Because it's not specific. And this is
something that—if these things weren't kept secret, I think it
might be shared with, for instance, the Council of Child Psychiatry, which is a local agency. There's not much we can do because
we're generally excluded.

"About five years ago we were having so much miserable
distress about what we were seeing happening to children in
foster care that we finally got people from Baton Rouge to come
down and talk to us. Well, all the big muckety-mucks came down,
and we had a big conference. And they were all surprised because
they didn't realize we were having all this problem. They were
just bending over backwards wanting to cooperate and all we had
to do was write recommendations up and so forth. So we set up
a committee and I chaired it. I spent days and days and days with
a number of other people on the committee writing up a very
extensive report that specified areas that we would change,
rearrange, and so forth: big areas of concern. And it was never
even acknowledged.

"There is that kind of territorialism. I don't think any of the
child psychiatrists in town are the least bit interested in trying to
run the agency. But we do have information that should be
pertinent."

There it is again, that word: *territorialism:* turf.

"There are many people in foster care and protective services
that do want to listen. But they are not the people who have the
power. They're not the ones that call the shots."

And the people who call the shots are a million miles from
any contact with any real children, or biological mothers, or
foster mothers. The shots are being called in a place so remote
that the real shots—at children and women—cannot even be
heard.

"There are," Dr. Cowardin continues, "some very difficult
issues. For instance: it is really grossly unfair of society to say to
child protection workers, 'If a child is abused, it is your fault for
not taking the child away.' Now that gets done. And that's not
fair. Because there is a basic dilemma about child protection, and

# 215 A Professional's View

that's where a lot of foster care starts. The basic dilemma that society refuses to look at is—on the one hand, we have all the media out braying about 'Report child abuse' and how terrible it is, and you can get something better. And on the other hand, if everybody that somebody in the world might possibly think had abused a child had the child taken away, it would affect such a staggering number of children—it would destroy so many children—I mean that's already happening to an extent.

"It's like—what would happen in society if you said to the policeman, 'If anybody gets murdered, buster, it's gonna be your fault. And we're gonna get you for it. Because you didn't arrest him.' We'd all be in jail."

"Preventive detention."

"Preventive detention. And it's kind of preventive detention with the protective services. And it's not fair.

"It's easy to say when a child gets killed, 'Isn't it horrible that protective services didn't protect this poor child!' But you never, ever, ever see anybody say, 'In this case, it was probably impossible.' And that if we removed all the children where we had that piece of information available—and that was all—we would be damaging far more children than is legitimate—on the chance of protecting a very small number. So there's that. And that, of course, makes it very difficult for these workers in the field to say anything.

"But I don't think there is any excuse for the fact that the agencies do not provide adequate guidelines. The people in the agency, by and large, do not really understand the principle behind their 'permanency planning.' So that they leave children in placement until the placement is permanent from the child's point of view. And then it's absurd. It might as well not be done. It makes no sense once a child has become permanently attached somewhere to remove them and place them somewhere that's going to be a 'permanent placement.' Because permanency in itself is of no value. We can send somebody to jail permanently, and it's certainly not 'placement.' It might be permanent, but it's not advisable."

"Then you're saying that the eighteen months to two years which the current legislation [P.L. 96–272] sets as the limit is too long?"

"Well, that's another problem. There need to be special rules for under-three-year-olds. Because there are so many things changing between birth and three years of age that all the guidelines that are quite appropriate for school-age children—don't apply. And it does untold damage. It really does. I see over and over again children who have been taken away at three, four, five months of age—allowed to stay too long—become attached to the foster home. But then it's still within the guidelines of eighteen months. So they're sent back to their parents. And they're sent back damaged. Because they're damaged by the separation from the foster parents who've become psychological parents. And then the parents can't manage, so they reabuse. Or the child gets into the mental health system. It's just the beginning of one bad thing after another."

The children, Dr. Cowardin tells me, are referred to her because the state facility can't handle the cases. And there are very few mental health centers in Louisiana that have child psychiatrists.

"But there is," she says, "another whole area of difficulty. And that is the agency uses psychiatrists in the most incredibly stupid manner. They send us children for a number of reasons. They may ask for a psychiatric evaluation to find out whether a child needs to be removed from a foster home and put in a more restrictive environment—meaning a group home or a residential placement of some kind.

"And there's a whole major problem there, because the state does not differentiate between group placements—which are in lieu of a home—and group placements which are for treatment. Long-term hospitalization. Or long-term residential treatment. That is a perfectly legitimate psychiatric maneuver for certain children who are developing personality disorders or significant conduct disorders.

"But the state doesn't differentiate. They have 'group facilities' that are a kind of admixture of the two. What happens is, if you don't have an available foster home, you send a child to a psychiatrist, so that the psychiatrist will say they need to be in a group facility—so you can put them somewhere to have a roof over their head.

"It is an absolute disaster because those two things are very different. You cannot treat a child who doesn't have a home. You have to have a home if you're a child. It's like—if somebody is starving—there's no point in giving them psychotherapy. They have to have food, you see. You can't talk to them about food. You have to feed them. And a child whose family has just fallen apart—supposing the father's just shot the mother or something—some horrendous thing has happened to them. And they have no home. It's ridiculous to send them to a psychiatrist to decide whether they need treatment or not. First, you need to get them a home.

"There are many older, school-age children, adolescents, who do much better in group facilities than in an individual foster home. But you can't put them there because—in this state at least—all of the group facilities get labeled as residential treatment. So in order to get in you have to have a 'diagnosis.' Or you need to have a psychiatrist say you need to be in. And as soon as you stay there long enough to really start feeling comfortable and let your hair down and start behaving yourself and doing well—then somebody says, 'Aha! He's been "treated."' So now we better go find him a permanent home.' So you take him out and you find him a permanent home. But of course that doesn't feel like home—because the treatment facility or the group facility has begun to feel like home."

This is such a bizarre picture: a situation in which the reality sounds Dickensian, but the mind-set sounds utopian. I say this to Dr. Cowardin.

"That's what I'm saying here. Human services has a utopian outlook. The utopian outlook is, 'We will take this child. We will "treat" this child because this child is behaving badly and having difficulty in getting along, adjusting. And we will send this child to a psychiatrist who will pin a label on the child. And then we will send the child to a, quote, treatment center. And then after the child is all glossied up and treated, we will send the same child out to a foster home. And then after we've had a chance to look around a little while, we will be able to find an adoptive home for this child, or send this child back to its own home—if we've flossied up the parents and got them back.' But it doesn't work that way. A child can't wait five years for a home. So they make a home. They settle in wherever you put them. Unless it's really awful. Even if it's pretty awful, they settle in.

"The problem I see in this state is there is this strange group of residential facilities that is not a hospital. And is really not under medical supervision. But somehow or other, for some strange reason, requires a psychiatric diagnosis to get into. And where what is called treatment really is not treatment at all. It's usually behavior modification. But all these places bill themselves as 'treatment' centers. I think they're kind of bastard institutions. And there's a pressure to get children who don't do well in a foster home into a residential placement. Whereas the reason they don't do well in a foster home may have nothing to do with psychiatric illness whatsoever. It might have to do, for instance, with loyalty to parents. It might have to do with the foster homes that are available. You see children who have been in four or five appallingly bad foster homes. Or been in two bad ones but gotten into a good one, but the foster mother has cancer and they had to take the kid out. And after that's happened for a while, they really don't want to let themselves become attached to foster parents. They would do better in a group facility. But there's no reason why it needs to be termed mental health."

Yes there is. It is called money. In Minnesota the cost of keeping a child in a welfare group home in 1984 was $55 a day. The cost (or the price paid) for the child in residential treatment was $102. Funds available for 'treatment' include Medicaid. The label of "special-needs" child always seems to trigger higher payments: and a child with a "special need" for "treatment" will do that, where a child who simply needs a place to be will not.

Dr. Cowardin continues: "They don't have to be 'ill' to need that kind of care, in other words. People send their kids away to boarding schools—if things are kind of rocky at home. They aren't labeled 'sick.' It just means that they do better if they get away from their peer group, or they get into a structured boarding school or something.

"A lot of it has to do with the complications of the system. I've had a lot of contact with this. And there are a lot of people that care—about the children. And it's easy to find fault with them; some of these cases are horrendous.

"But the system itself doesn't function. That's the thing that bothers me. The system has acquired a life of its own. I mean, I can get angry at people and get something done. But I can't do any good here. Because I have to get angry at 'the system.' And it's not a thing. I can't get anything done because—the system is wrong. There are areas in which the system itself doesn't work. And it's very complicated—the fact that it involves the courts. For instance. I don't think there's ever been a clear decision from the Supreme Court that says, in effect, a parent doesn't have the right to . . . or the parent's right stops *when* . . .

"I guess my feeling is that there are some really bitter pills that have to be swallowed by society. If we want to get the mess cleaned up.

"One of them is to recognize that you're not going to be able to keep all children from being abused. That the price of doing that would be to take a staggering percentage of them away from their homes.

"I don't think there's any question that there are cases where children need to be taken away from a rotten home. But I don't think there is any question that it is much fewer cases than are actually acted on. And that, having done it, they ought to stick with it. Because what we see is children who are taken away and kept away—and then given back. And actually nothing is really accomplished."

But there is, I say (again), an obvious difference between the parent who, based on actual behavior, could be said to be homicidal toward the child and the mother who simply doesn't have enough. Even if part of what she doesn't have enough of, in the circumstances, is patience. One augurs return, and the other doesn't.

"This is certainly true. And I think one of the huge areas that I have found myself in the past in conflict about is—especially young children—is taking them away. For example: Say a woman has four children, is pregnant with the fifth. She has a brutally abusive husband who's not working, hasn't worked for years. He dumps her out on the street. Maybe she has a relative, and they all crowd in with the relative. Eventually OHD [Office of Human Development] gets involved. And their solution is to take all the children away and place them.

"But really—there has been no neglect on this lady's part. She didn't have any money because she had four kids, and she's pregnant—so she didn't have a job. That's hardly the state in which to get a job. She needs—money is what she needs. And it would cost less money to give it to her than to give it to all the foster parents and whatnot.

"Now it can easily take her five years to get her children back. But by then—one of them shouldn't be given back. Because that baby was taken in infancy—and was four years with substitute parents. OHD may *think* that child is doing fine. But that child is very likely to have problems.

"It's inexcusable. Because that child should never have been taken away in the first place."

Help, please, King Solomon, wherever you are.

# COMPLICATIONS.
# AGAIN.

A number of months had passed since I'd spoken with Pauli. One Monday, early in October, I decided to ring up. When one of her daughters answered, I learned that Pauli had died, of cancer, just the Friday before.

And that is how *I* came to meet Dana and Ali's mother, Pat.

"You're the lady who's writing the book," Pat says when she's called to the phone and I introduce myself.

I tell Pat how sorry I am about Pauli; how I feel I know *her* to some extent because Pauli had talked about her so often, about Dana and Ali—and about Maria's daughter, Laura.

"Tell me," I say, "I realize I never did learn what happened to Dana and Ali."

"Oh well, I got custody back of my children. In November of 1987. They're fine."

"Cheerful and happy and going to school? And you?"

"I'm fine. I'm gettin' my life together. Right now, I just finished vocational assessment. I'm in a vocational rehabilitation program. And within two weeks, I should be in a training program."

"Has the system been helping you—or have you done this mostly on your own?"

"I've done this mostly on my own. The system really hasn't helped me at all. When I first got custody back, the system just completely ignored me. They didn't send me any money for three months. That's how I wound up back in Miss Mason's home. Because they didn't give me any documents stating the children were back in my custody. And when I went to Social Services to apply for AFDC—that's the first thing they asked for: 'Do you have any proof that the children are back in your custody?' Well, Protective Services or the lawyers or the courts didn't give me anything—so they had to take my word. And then when they kept running the children's social security numbers up on the computer—it kept coming up 'active.' That means they were still under Protective Services. But—they weren't. They were with me. And AFDC wouldn't give me any money as long as they thought Protective Services was giving money to a foster parent. And there wasn't *nobody* receiving any money.

"So finally—I was explaining the situation to my landlord. And my maintenance worker kept telling him that the check would be in the mail: 'Could you hang in there with her for a little while? It is comin', it is comin'.' But for three months nothing came. So eventually the landlord said that I would have to leave. He said he would rather that I find someone that would take me in. Because he had went to rent court once. And that time Social Service gave me an emergency check—but it still didn't cover all the rent. So he said if we have to go through the court procedure again, he would have to evict me. Put me out on the street. And he asked if I could find someone who would take me in—because he know I had just got the children back, and he didn't want Social Services to see me out on the street again because that might have gave them reason to take the kids back.

"So I called Miss Mason—'cause I really didn't have anybody else. I have some family across town, but that would have meant transferring the kids' school. And they had been through enough of that. So I called Miss Mason, and she took me in until I could start gettin' my money, retroactive. This was in February. And at the beginning of April I finally got all my money."

"When the kids were removed from Pauli, were they given directly to you?"

"No, no. My son was placed in a foster home. And my daughter was placed in a separate foster home. That was in July of '87—because I was in an alcoholic rehabilitation program. My son stayed in that same foster home. But my daughter was transferred to a shelter center."

"What kind of thing is that? A group home, or . . . ?"

"Yeah. A group home. But she didn't stay there long. This was the last week of October they transferred her."

"And they gave the kids back to you because . . . ? I mean, I'm sure you wanted them back, but you probably wanted them back before they gave them back. . . ."

"I didn't even want them to take them. But they gave them back because—most of the things I was doin' I was doin' on my own to get my life together. I had signed myself up into an alcoholic clinic. And then I signed myself up for detox. And the fourteen-day rehabilitation program. And I was still continuing my outpatient alcoholic treatment. And I'm still doing that."

Ali is now nine years old, Pat tells me, and Dana twelve. Pat and the children are moving from Pauli's house in the next couple of days.

"Was Pauli's death a blow to you?" I ask.

"Oh, it really was. We had kind of prepared ourselves when we first found out about the cancer. But not even the doctor expected it to be this soon. And I was holding up pretty good until yesterday—because that was the final good-bye. It's sad—because I never really got a chance to say good-bye to my mother. My mother's dead too—but she didn't raise me. So when she passed it was like a distant aunt or just a relative passing. I was raised in a foster home myself—a family-type thing, not a legal foster home. I was goin' through that bad period of my life, with the drinking. So I didn't go to my mother's funeral.

"Miss Mason was—this is like the first time in my life bein' able to say good-bye to my mother."

"How's Laura doing? And Maria?"

"Laura came to the funeral with Miss Jefferson. 'Cause she's in a group home."

*"She's now in a group home again?* Tell me what happened—because for five minutes there she was back with Maria, wasn't she?"

"Yes. Maria got Laura back, but she had problems with her boyfriend. And so she brought Laura over here to Miss Pauli.

And left her. That's when Miss Pauli went to court and they gave Miss Pauli temporary custody."

This woman never stopped, I am thinking—never stopped trying, for this kid.

"After having said she was neglectful and removing the kids from her . . . ?"

"Mm-hmm."

"So Laura should have stayed with Pauli all the time then?"

"Right. Right. 'Cause they were makin' theirselves look bad. They took the girl because they say she was bein' neglected. And then they turned around and gave Miss Pauli legal custody."

"How long did Maria have Laura?"

"More than two months. Because I moved back with Miss Mason in February. And April, Maria brought Laura back and left her. And in that time that Laura was with her mother she had been raped twice. Once by a friend. And once by her mother's boyfriend. And when Maria left her here she took charges out on the boyfriend. But then she abandoned Laura here. And went to North Carolina with the boyfriend."

` "So Laura was there . . . ?"

"From April until September. Miss Pauli was sick then. And I had planned on moving. And even though Miss Mason had temporary legal custody of Laura, they still weren't sendin' her any money for Laura. They were still sendin' money to the mother. Because Miss Jefferson had forgot to let AFDC know. As a matter of fact—Miss Armstrong—they finally paid Miss Mason her money the day before she passed away. Now you tell me this system ain't messed up. *They finally sent her her money the day before she passed away.*"

It takes me a minute: I am thinking how Pauli would have said this with utter indignation—and then she would have laugh-laugh-*laughed* at the absurdity of it.

"I assume she'd had to stop working."

"Mm-hmm. First she went on vacation in July. And then she got sick, she couldn't go back to work at all."

"And Laura is now in what kind of shape?"

"Well—she adjusts real easily. When you take her from place to place. The only thing she doesn't like is for someone to tell her what— She doesn't like authority." Well, why would anybody, with her experience of "authority," *like* authority? "And she ran away from the first group home they put her in when she left here. She ran away for two weeks. Eventually, she came back here. Miss Pauli had her daughter go pick her up from where she was callin' from. But that was just to keep her from bein' on the street. Then Miss Pauli called Miss Jefferson the next day. And Miss Jefferson, knowing how sick Miss Pauli was, still asked— 'Could you keep her one more day?' '' Amazing. It is (isn't it?)— amazing.

"And then," Pat says, "you know the family just hit the ceiling. 'Cause you know Miss Pauli wasn't gonna say no. But she was just too sick, and she didn't need that worry-ation— having to keep a twenty-four-hour eye on Laura.

"So they came and got her. That was the same day Miss Pauli went into the hospital. And now Laura's in her second group home already."

"What do you suppose will happen to Laura?"

"I don't know. I really don't know. Because she'll never be able to find anybody to care for her like Miss Pauli did. And nobody's gonna put up with her ways or take the time to understand."

"Miss Jefferson—she was not your social worker?"

"Oh no. Mine were very good. They weren't all *that* great, but they were better than Miss Jefferson. They kept up with the kids. And they always kept me informed. But me and Maria are two different people anyway. I care. And Maria really doesn't care."

Exactly what Pauli had said about Maria.

"The first time Miss Pauli came home from the hospital, Miss Jefferson told her they were gonna put the kids up for legal adoption because they had been in the system for over two years. Miss Mason wanted to adopt Laura and her older brother. And the family was tryin' to tell her that 'You're terminally ill. No court's gonna give you custody of the children.' But she didn't want to accept it. We felt that was her way of denyin' what was really gonna happen."

Solomon Says. The longer I listen, the more it seems like some ghastly game with eternally arbitrary and chaotic dictates, and entirely random results.

# ONE

# SOLOMON

# SAYS

■ ────────

During the week of June 20, 1988, a woman, a mother, Tracey Maye, was asked by Judge Gerald Sheindlin whether, on March 20, 1987, she had recklessly caused the death of her child, Baby Tess, "by striking her repeatedly with an electrical wire."

"Yes, Your Honor," she said.

*New York Times* journalist Michael Winerip followed up on the case of Baby Tess—taken into foster care, then returned to her mother. Pam Miller, who had been foster mother to Tess for nine months, pursued the case as well. After six months of hounding the system for answers, the state sent her one of their formal-language letters, sympathizing with her concern. Asked by the New York Times to expand on the letter, a state social services spokesman said that he could not even confirm the letter existed. (Because no file copy existed? Or because even that

227

fact—that a letter had been written—was "privileged information"?) All further information was said to be shielded by "privacy laws."

The *Times* then filed a Freedom of Information request, which
was turned down (based on "sections 372, 422 2a and 87 2a of
state law"). David Emil, general counsel for social services,
wrote, "There is nothing in the statute that suggests that privacy
interests of a foster child terminate with such a child's death."
Pam Miller's response? "That was one of the most amazing
sentences she had ever heard."[1]

Two months later, and not fifty miles away, a young woman
named Cheryl Shahine pleaded guilty in another New York State
court to having bashed the head of her nine-month-old baby,
Valentine Eugene, against the sink until the boy died. The passion
this case evoked in Orange County was every bit a match for the
ruckus raised by Baby Tess's death, and the death of little Lisa
Steinberg.

The fact that all three of these cases occurred in New York
State does not, I believe, suggest there is anything funny in New
York's water supply. Rather, it suggests only that it is far from
uncommon for children to die at the hands of a parent or care-
taker anywhere in the country. The fact that these cases are the
ones picked up by the media serves as ammunition for the system
to shout that the media are interested only in "sensational"
cases. Whatever one's impression of the general media, the fact
is that it is only a *dead* child that the system cannot keep hidden.
And even once there is the dead child, the system is empowered
to stonewall, to refuse information—to sit tight and wait for the
whole thing to blow over from, if nothing else, the lack of hard
information to print.

At twenty-two, Cheryl Shahine had four children—besides
Baby Eugene—in foster care. (She was pregnant with her sixth
as she stood trial.) Eugene had been placed in state custody
within days of his birth. He was seven months old when he, along
with three of his siblings, was returned to Cheryl's custody at the
order of Judge Elaine Slobod, in November of 1987. It was
January 18, 1988, when Eugene died. In June of that year, Judge
Slobod made a virtually unprecedented offer to open her court to
the media. There were provisions put on this offer that the press
found problematic. Still, the fact that enough of a story had
actually emerged despite the system's blockade, the fact of a
judge then opening her court, brought together a number of
elements cogent enough to motivate me to go speak with the

reporter for the *Times Herald-Record,* Lawrence Lebowitz, and with the judge herself.

How, I asked Larry Lebowitz, did you get enough hard information to write a whole series of stories on the Shahine case?

"I got lucky," he says. "The information that we did get that was of official nature, official documents, DSS documents—off the record for now because I don't want to reveal the source—but it was a couple of psychiatrists in the area that had seen the girl. One was a very good source of mine when I worked in Newburgh. That's where Cheryl is from.

"I called around the day after the murder charges were filed against her, trying to get a profile of what she was like, what she was about. I'd heard from one of Cheryl's family members (who was still speaking to me at the time) that she'd seen a couple of psychiatrists, on her own, in an attempt to show the court that she was trying to do all these things on her own with her life—to win her kids back.

"I started making phone calls. And this one psychiatrist gave us more than he should have, and probably violated his own doctor/client privilege. He gave me a two-, three-page letter from DSS caseworkers that outlined a lot of her background. Including her own background as an abused child, who had abused her, and that she was also a foster child.

"That laid the groundwork for knowing where to go for a lot of the other stuff. It gave her history and how her kids got into the system, and that they were in and out of foster care. And it mentioned something I'd already heard on the streets before—but it gave me enough to confirm—that she had been a prostitute when she was thirteen, fourteen.

"The word had been basically that her family sort of pushed her out on the street. The letter mentions that her first child was born while she was walking the streets. And I'd heard from her family that that's how she had met her first husband. At fourteen, she went to New York City to a home for unwed mothers. Mind you—none of this is coming from DSS or anybody in the system.

"Anyway, she met her first husband down in the city. He was a hot dog and chestnut salesman in Central Park. An Egyptian national—only a few weeks away from deportation. And they got married. They didn't live together very long. He moved out on her. But weekend visits, regular visits type of thing. He took a job in Tuxedo Park. She lived in a welfare apartment in Newburgh. Kids were in and out of foster care a couple of times. The letter outlines all that case history.

"I got none of that from the system. At all."

"What did you get from the system?"

"Basically, told that confidentiality laws prevent them from discussing this with me. And I went out of my way to be really polite, without pestering, but persistently enough. I found out from those documents who the caseworkers were. And I got shot down. Their bosses told me to stop calling."

Like Pam Miller, the foster parents, who had been crushed by the (in their minds unnecessary and senseless) murder of Baby Eugene, set about making phone calls, writing letters, in search of accountability.

On June 8, 1988, they were able to read Cheryl Shahine's explanation of what happened in Larry Lebowitz's story in the *Times Herald-Record*:

"That afternoon [January 18], while her husband was at work, Mrs. Shahine was playing upstairs with the three older children while Eugene was asleep. She went downstairs to get some cookies and found the infant, still asleep, lying in his own vomit.

" 'I grabbed him and he started to cry and get excited—I think he was scared because I just grabbed him . . .'*

"Meanwhile, the other three children upstairs were fighting, she said.

" 'Then the kids and that were screaming and the water was running and the baby was giving me a hard time so I banged his head against the sink because I was nervous and I didn't know what to do. . . .

" 'I hit his head hard against the sink a lot of times,' she said. 'I don't remember how many times because I was angry and wanted Eugene to stop crying.'

"The baby eventually calmed down, she said.

" 'And when I realized that I hurt him and what I was doing was wrong I just picked him up and hugged him,' she said."

On June 15, 1988, Eugene's foster parents received a letter from the New York State Department of Social Services, signed by Fredric H. Cantlo, director, Family and Children's Services,

---

*After Baby Eugene's death, doctors discovered an untreated wrist fracture. It is not unlikely that she may have grabbed the wrist.

Metropolitan Regional Office. With (evidently) all the compassion
the state-as-parent could muster, it said:

"This is to advise you that the Metropolitan Regional Office
of the Division of Family and Children Services has completed
the investigation of the concerns and issues brought to our
attention regarding the Orange County Department of Social
Services as it relates to Valentine Eugene Shahine.

"The investigation focused on the following: case investigation, assessment, service provision, preparation and representa-
tion of the case during the court process, administrative case
supervision and the nature of supervision, particularly upon the
child's discharge.

"Based on our review of case records and interviews with
Orange County Department of Social Services personnel, we
have determined that the procedures followed in relation to the
discharge and post discharge plans were in accordance with State
Department guidelines.

"We have, however, informed Orange County of the need to
meet certain Child Protective Service monitoring, investigation
and report determination requirements. Additionally, we have
delineated various recommendations that are geared toward improving case assessment, provision of service, communication
and accountability. Implementation of the requirements and recommendations should better meet the needs of the children and
their families."

And, in what is the most gratuitously fatuous closing to a
letter that I have read in a long time:

"I want to thank you for bringing these issues and concerns
to our attention and am sure that your continued interest and
efforts will benefit the children of New York State."

"What's the answer, Larry?" I ask.

"I'm not an answer man. I just know that the system does not
work. And I'm not sure that any way you fix it will make it
perfect. I'm not convinced that just throwing money at the
problem is going to make it better. But I'm not blind enough to
think it generally works the way it is. Too many people's lives are
torn up by it now. And—I bring to this a personal perspective:
One kid dies, then the system's screwed up. It doesn't work.
Even if the system turns around and says, 'We did everything
right.' Doesn't *prove* they did everything right. It just *says* that
they did. 'We did our own investigation—had a state agency look

at our county agency. And we can't give you the information, but we know we did the right thing.' "

I am sitting in the wait-place of the courthouse. This is not a place where people look happy or smile. It is, however, a place where a *lot* of waiting takes place. A sweet-looking black child, about eight, dressed in his Sunday-best tie and jacket, sits nervously swinging first one leg, then the other, under his chair. He appears to be alone, but this cannot be so: his mother (or someone) must be elsewhere in the building. A young man and woman sit grimly: their expressions reflect both apprehension and the tediousness of the wait. A gentleman who, from his suit-tie dress and his manner, appears to be an attorney strides in front of them, and, speaking to them, says, "There's nothing worse than getting mixed up with the Department of Social Services. Here, *their* life has been disrupted and *your* life has been disrupted—and all because of an allegation made by a woman who's a known liar."

Although I have made my presence and the fact of my appointment with the judge known to the officers on the other side of the door, as time passes, I decide to reannounce my presence. It's as well that I do. They do not appear to have registered it the first time.

The judge's secretary comes out and leads me back to Judge Slobod's chambers. She is there, along with her law clerk, John Cameron—both seated at the conference table.

Like most people who've had little to do with the court processes, I realize I have imagined a "Judge" would be formidable. Judge Slobod, with lively dark hair, rapid-fire New York–style speech, immediately strikes me as forthright and affable.

I inquire first about the reasons family courts have long been assumed to be closed.

Before the formation of family court, she tells me, there was a law that closed the court, completely closed it. But when the family court was established, it was established that it would be open *unless* closed.

"The judge *may* close the court," John Cameron says.

"But they may open it," says the judge.

So then it's different from the whole confidentiality thing surrounding child protection work?

"Absolutely. For the Department of Social Services. Yes. For the protection of the children."

"But," I suggest, "lots of people have told me it's for the protection of the system."

"I am not sure it has not come to that. Which is the reason that I've opened the court. Because I said, 'I wonder if the answers will be the same in an open court as they are in a closed court.' Why *aren't* services provided? What's going on? Why is this child still here? Why is what I ordered not in place for this child?"

"Do you think it will get you better information? The reporter on the story told me there was information you didn't have in the Shahine case."

"I don't know if it was information I didn't have. With what we had, we made that decision. It's the same decision I would have made today—on the information that I *had* at that time. If there was information that did not get to the court, I don't think it's because DSS refused to give it to me, or that some rehabilitation program refused to give it to me. I read in the paper that the foster parents claimed they had certain information. I will tell you that these weren't the foster parents that were in the court. Never did I hear anything out of their mouths. And neither they nor the attorney ever said, 'You ought to know this—before you do that.' If there was anything that wasn't in the records and wasn't in the reports, it wasn't as if it couldn't have come to the court. I want to know what was known.

"In hindsight, we all knew. We're all a lot better judges in hindsight—including the foster parents. They're no better or worse than the rest of us. But I'm not sure if there really was anything more. We had notes from three psychiatrists who saw no violence.

"I don't *know* that any system will ever protect all kids. I'm not sure that, in this particular case, given what happened, *anybody* could have foreseen it. It's one thing in retrospect to say, 'Hey, we should have seen this little piece here. There.' And that's always true in human behavior—that you can pick it apart afterwards. But coming from the other side and *pro*spectively looking at it . . . There are other cases where the child welfare system is failing and failing miserably."

"Like for instance?"

"I think we have a real problem in the sex abuse area. Having enough groups for the kids, enough quality therapy for the kids and offenders. God, sometimes I put kids into therapy and I wonder what's really happening. Are they really getting the services and the rehabilitation they need? Would I send *my* children to any one of these?

"We've seen a tremendous rise in our sex abuse cases, violent sex abuse. A lot of neglect cases. A vast increase based on the drug usage of the parents. When they pick up the parents in the raids, we get the kids. I have four-year-olds who don't put Daddy's slippers out at night, but they can roll a 'cigarette' for him."

"How do you determine whether a case is 'founded' or 'unfounded'? Do you take Social Services' word?"

"All we do for the initial removal is decide that probable cause exists to believe these children are abused, and that the final disposition will be abuse, or that the children are in 'imminent danger.' DSS can't make that removal, only the court. Now if they come back in on a hearing, that's what they need to show us. Which is not a heavy, heavy burden.

"Remember, when we remove kids—we do tremendous damage to those kids. We found out that one of the worst things that happens is when we remove kids and bring them back—because maybe Mom's become supportive or whatever—there's tremendous internal pressure on these kids then to recant. Because of their fear that they're gonna go back into foster care. That's a real significant problem for us. Foster care is like shock treatment: 'I don't ever want to go back there.' Even if it's a good foster home. It's very frightening. They're moved out. They don't understand why.

"I'm sure you've heard from foster parents that, 'Nobody told us what these kids are about.' And then the kids—nobody explains to *them* what's going on. And there are other kids in the house, who are not necessarily nice kids. We end up with kids who are abused in foster care—by other kids."

Again, as I listen to the judge, I get the sense of incredible busy-ness—almost as though child welfare were, at last, the true perpetual-motion machine—powered by children.

"What's the answer?" I ask, smiling.

The judge laughs. "I wish I had it. That's the million-dollar question."

I ask again—I keep coming back to it—"At what level of physical abuse, at what level of neglect, do you remove?"

"Then we talk about the words *imminent danger*. Depending on the child. Obviously, the younger the child is, the more likely a 'neglect' will bring about removal. Because if a mother's neglectful, the child cannot fend for himself in any way."

"Neglect means . . . ?"

"It could be she's not supervising properly. It could be she doesn't feed him properly. Doesn't take him to the doctor. Educational neglect, we are unlikely to pull those kids out today. If we put a homemaker in the home, will that get the kids to school?"

Judge Slobod tells of an easy case:

"The woman was so slow she would put the infant on a countertop and say, 'Now you stay there.' Kid would roll off and bang its head on the floor. No amount of homemaker services short of a foster parent permanently in the home would have helped. On top of which she was living with a convicted sex offender and saw no reason why this was a problem. We terminated her rights, and she went off saying she didn't see what the problem was."

Judge Slobod returns again and again to the trauma that foster care is for children.

"As a court we're just in a terrible Catch-22. Because *we* recognize that once a child has been moved around in foster care, they become so fragile, and so at risk, that even if what's happening in that home—when we remove the child, it's the first foster home. But when it's the third foster home, we better see if there's some way we can keep them there—even if it's not the greatest foster home—because the next step may be an institution. Believe me, it's not something you easily do—and those are horror stories: How did this get to *be* a foster home? How did it happen that this kid got into this foster home?"

Out of the clear blue, I ask, "Do you believe the caseworker records?"

"I think—" She laughs. "The records? Look. They're written with their own agenda. No question. We have never found out-and-out lies in any case record that I've seen. And we have no reason to question their honesty as they do them. We have not. I'm not saying it's not there. That has not come up as a particular problem in Orange County. Do we have the full story? I will tell you that we have a CASA program [Court Appointed Special Advocate*]—unfortunately, it's just a very fledgling program. And we have found that the CASA volunteers have given us information that I believe other people do not want us to have.

---

*The Court Appointed Special Advocate Program is a national one designed to recruit and train community volunteers, appointed by a judge, to advocate for abused and neglected children in court.

Because *their* loyalty is strictly to the court. They're not out to prove the case. They're not out to adopt the child. They're not out to do anything."

I begin, "I was talking to a former worker—because most good workers are former workers—"

"Absolutely. Either way up on the scale—or out."

"—and she suggested there is no question there's an authoritarian mind-set. A power thing. They don't make much money, but they do have a lot of power over people's lives."

"Absolutely."

"Why do I get the sense that antifemale bias is so pervasive?"

John Cameron: "I used to represent a lot of welfare mothers in Rockland County, and I found the bias was—not antifemale— it was anti*black* or anti*class*. The lower-middle-class or middle-class young caseworker who had preconceived ideas of how a family should be raised and was appalled by the fatherless family and these people who couldn't control their own lives. And they were building themselves up by knocking down these other people."

Judge Slobod: "I haven't seen it as a female issue—that doesn't mean it isn't. But I do see it as a class issue. I do see it as a power-base issue. You're absolutely right that there are a number of caseworkers who, '*I'll* make decisions.' And, '*I'll* decide what's best for this child.' And, 'You do not *do* that with a child.' Really giving them no alternative. 'If the child is in the room, it should sit in the chair.' Well, that's what it may say in the book. But anyone who's had a child—they don't really sit. I mean, you've got four kids running around like crazy. That's not an answer. To give textbook little answers of discipline—which is that, 'You will do this.' And, 'You will do that.' 'You should be doing this.' Or, 'You shouldn't have had any children.' Or, 'Your tubes should have been tied.' "

I have hesitated to use the word before: it crosses my lips: "Does it seem a bit of a Gestapo mentality?"

"No doubt. They are very authoritarian. They are very authoritarian also, I think, to the foster parents. And the foster parents are authoritarian. I mean, I wonder about the screening of foster parents. I can't find any screening process, frankly, other than that they have never committed a crime. And have not been charged with child abuse. I've written to the state, and just recently got back a letter that I thought was wonderful double-talk. I wanted to know. Because we have some people who are not bad people but should *never* have been foster parents.

"So I question—there are so many agendas that we're dealing with. And power bases. And for the foster parents, for some of them, it's a power base."

"It's not about children?"

"No! We've often said—they're the pawns. We jump over them. We kick them over."

John Cameron: "Which is not the objective of social services at all. Which is not the objective of the Family Court Act . . .' "

Judge Slobod: "You have power games. And you also have—the players change on such a rotating basis. How could you ever have a continuum of purpose? These kids see more people in one year than a lot of people see in a lifetime. They go into foster care, so of course they're questioned by a caseworker as to what got them into foster care. They may be sent to a therapist. But the foster mother and father don't take them to a therapist. A case agent takes them.

"For the visitation: a case agent comes up; and that even rotates—because they get paid even less than caseworkers. Then—if it's a criminal thing, or a heavy sex abuse—you're going to go see a police officer. Who's a big, burly guy. They're going to see the therapy people in the police department. They're going to see the DSS attorney. Now, from the child protective worker, they're going to go to a foster care worker. And that worker will change every couple of months. And then maybe the law guardian will come out to see them."

John Cameron: "The psychiatric social worker, they might have seen. The psychologist. The 'validator.' "

Judge Slobod: "I find it preposterous."

"Dear King Solomon [I am thinking]:

"I am writing to inform you of the funny thing you started when you got wise with a decision about whose kid was whose. It would have been seriously better, perhaps, if you'd made a terrible gaffe, given the kid to the wrong lady, and then—being the wise old guy you were—issued a decree that no one was to mess around with these kinds of decisions anymore.

"Yrs truly."

Judge Slobod is continuing. "I had called the state and said, 'Look. It seems to me, particularly in sex abuse cases, we ought to have a crisis intervention team that—a social worker should be appointed to this kid, and nobody should talk to this kid without that social worker being there. She should also do crisis therapy for this child. And really walk them through the entire court system.

"Well. I have to tell you there are a lot of people very upset about turf. 'What do you *mean* we can't talk to the child!'

"*Horrible* things happen to kids who tell [about sexual abuse]. *Horrible* things. Seeing what happens if you tell, I'm not sure if *I* would tell. I have to be honest about that. The kid tells, he gets removed. She gets removed. We put her in a foster home. She's gonna be a little aggressive. Maybe a little provocative. If there's some teenage boys in that home, they're gonna take advantage. And even the foster dad may take advantage. And then if she starts to tell—one, nobody believes her; two, foster mom sure doesn't want her there. Then we move her to another home. And she ends up in an institution. Particularly, I would say, that's the scenario for a kid we don't pick up until she's maybe ten, eleven, twelve.

"It's not as if we save these kids when we take them out. The alternative isn't good either. I don't think that when I remove a child I've done anything wonderful for that child.

"And I always say that the only thing worse than not finding abuse when I should is finding it when I shouldn't. I can remember one case. There were allegations of sexual abuse of the daughter, and we severed the father from them. They stayed with Mom. They were not sent to a foster home. The little girl did okay and it later came out there had been touching, not a sexual touching. The child came home saying, 'Daddy hurt me.' She had a vaginal infection and when he picked her up, he hurt her. He truly did. Mom did not make it up. And the father said to us, 'I am not a criminal. I will not visit my children in a supervised setting. I have done nothing wrong, and if I visit them in that setting, it's telling them that I am a criminal. And I will not do that.' The little boy really deteriorated in that three or four months, not seeing his father."

It is truly almost breathtaking, the profoundly different ways in which women and men are perceived and treated throughout the entire world of child welfare. It is so ingrained, so habitual, it seems, to those in the system, entirely unremarkable. Imagine if Kelly or any other mother had issued the statement that the above father did. Refusing supervised visitation, she would immediately have been branded uncooperative, neglectful, uninterested in her children's welfare, abandoning. . . . Yet, reading the father's statement, I fully believe that most readers will empathize entirely. What he is saying is that in the real world, a guy's supposed to have some rights. 'You can't make me tacitly agree that I've done something wrong by acceding to restrictions that can only be there if I've done something wrong.'

That he got away with it, that it never occurred to anyone to challenge him on it or further harass him for it, shows the enormous chasm between what is expected of and tolerated in men-as-fathers, and what is expected of and *not* tolerated in women-as-mothers.

(We do not know where the girl got the vaginal infection. We do not know how we are meant to know that she did not just recant when she saw the number of questioners she would have to face. But all of that is not, to me, the point of this particular story.)

"In the old days," Judge Slobod is saying, "a kid came into foster care, he'd stay forever. We've come a long way in working with natural parents. But there are a whole lot of people now yelling it should be the other way. That it should be a 'best-interests' test."

"What does that mean?"

"It means a lot! It means no kid ever goes home. It means a lot! Because if you have a middle-class foster parent who has never committed abuse or neglect or a crime, and if you *don't* have a presumption that the kid would be better off with the natural parent, you tell me how [the natural parent can] ever overcome having abused their child. I don't know how you get over that. Even if they've gotten therapy, and now the house is clean, and the abuser is gone from the home.*

"I don't know how you ever overcome that if you don't start with a presumption that natural is better; if you're kept to a strict 'best- interests' test."

"You mean—it's in the child's 'best interest' to be rich?"

"I always tell people when they talk 'best interests': 'You know, I have one very bright child. The Rockefellers could have done a *lot more* for him than I ever could have done. They could have afforded private schools in Europe—much more than I could.' I say, 'And then I have another kid who's not—but maybe with lots of enrichment that kid could have done more. I could never compete with that.'

"The Task Force on Permanency Planning has been a wonder-

---

*Notice again the assumption of a male abuser, but a female "client," getting therapy and cleaning house to recover her children.

ful unit that the governor set up. Seminars, making you a lot more sensitive to the issues of permanency. I said to them the other day, 'Wonderful. I'm a lot more sensitive to those questions. But in a closed courtroom, if I scream and yell—who hears? I throw a tantrum—and everybody walks out. I mean—so *what?*' I said, 'But you know—there's a missing piece. Who do I send off the information to? Do I educate DSS? Do I write to the Appellate Division? Where do I process the information I'm getting—on what's really happening?'

"Which is why I decided the press has a responsibility also."

"Because the public has no information?" I ask. "Just knows they're against child abuse?"

"We're all against child abuse. I don't think that there's anybody—there's not a caseworker, there's not a foster parent— they all want the system to work perfectly. And those of us who've been around awhile know that can't be. It'll never work perfectly. But it can sure be a whole lot better than what it is."

"What will make it work better?"

"I think a system where everybody's accountable works a lot better than a system where you're answerable in secret. Because that's not answerable.

"I don't blame the system, and I don't blame the courts, or DSS. I blame society. Because we don't want to hear. We don't want to know what happens in the system. So we can all say the system is no good; we can all go, 'We'll blame the system. Get a new judge. Get a new caseworker. A new mental health worker. It'll be okay. All we have to do is change the players.' And that's not gonna make it okay. If they don't put in some money, some time, some commitment."

I mentioned to Judge Slobod the conversation I had with the Official at SSC—who told me his opinion was that foster care was a bogus system. It was a welfare issue. She looks curiously taken aback, then, to John Cameron: "When we had a foster care meeting—what were you told?"

"I was told," he says, "at a break—by someone who should know—that changes in the law, or any kind of progression, getting a handle on the problem, will never happen. Because it's a racial question. Blacks view further government involvement— as far as abuse, neglect, foster care—is aimed at a kind of genocide. Or diluting their ethnic thing. Taking black kids out of the home. And this is being said by people who are in power. Blacks in power. Who are not going to permit this to be done to their race."

"We thought that was interesting," Judge Slobod says, "because *we* didn't call this meeting. Ding! Call this meeting and everybody will feel better.

"There's very little justice within the judicial system, or outside the judicial system. But society needs this thing—picture—so that people *believe* that things are being done. To take it to the family court, people believe that this incredible social problem we have is being handled. It's very, very, very difficult to handle."

"Why does it seem to me that when it works, it's almost by accident?"

"For those kids that go into foster care and stay in one foster home—those kids seem to come out fairly unscathed. For that group of kids, it's okay. Even if it wasn't a perfect thing, but they lived in a quasi kind of home. I have a hard time knowing how any kid who lives in limbo can be okay. And that's what foster care is—by its nature, by its definition: it is legal limbo. When you're waiting for some kind of decision—be it a health decision, a job decision—I can handle whatever it is. But I can't stand not knowing. And these kids live that way every single day. Am I gonna go home? Am I gonna see my mother? Or am I not gonna see my mother? Will she show up for the visitation? Are my loyalties here? Are my loyalties there? Never knowing where to focus. Because you may be sent home—tomorrow. And the kids are—for the most part—not part of the plan.

"We talk about the foster parents wanting now to be interviewed about the service planning. I'm not saying that they shouldn't be. But the kids are *never* included. And who's there—and appointed—to discuss it with them? Not only just their feelings, but more than anything to let them know what's gonna happen. 'You're not gonna go home now, but it looks like in six months you will be going home.' "

"But not lie to them . . . ?"

"Which is another thing. We lie to them all the time. I've seen that. Not for the purpose of lying—but just—it's easier to deal with. You don't have to deal with the kid. And the kid's own perception of foster care—I will never forget: Before we administer an oath to a younger child, you have to see if they know the difference between right and wrong. And I will never forget saying to this six-year-old boy, 'And what will happen if you tell a lie?' He says, 'You go to foster care.' And that's exactly where he was headed. And I was, 'How can I explain to him that that has nothing to do with it?' Obviously, that's what he'd been told.

'You get up there and you tell a lie and you're gonna go to foster care.' "

And so it begins: lacking contrary information, the kids see themselves, their behavior, their being, as causative of their predicament. And thus they are primed to collude with a system that enthusiastically labels their "problems," emphasizes their need for "treatment."

The judge continues: "Kids who sit in care short term—they don't have great things to say. Because they're in a strange house—even a good foster home. I mean I remember when I was a kid and you'd go to your aunt's or uncle's house—and you're ready to come home after three or four days. Even if it was okay, or it was a great place—you wanted to go home. Even if it was a wealthier aunt and uncle—who gave you lots of things, and did things. These kids are no different."

Judge Slobod has been a family court judge now for five years.

"Does this get old after a while—family court—from the judge's perspective?"

"I can see burnout. I can now see that I'd be a basket case if I'm doing this for the rest of my life—without some interruption. From time to time, I see a criminal case. I think there are a lot of us who would stay here if we could get a break—for a month or two a year. In fact, I had a shot to go over to county, but this is where I think I can be the most use. In retrospect, psychologically, it takes a toll. You're dealing with it. There are so many things—you can't make the world right. I know that. But you can't also not think about these kids when you walk out of here. You say to yourself, 'You can't think about it.' But you do. And not so much for the child who dies and it's over for that child. What about the other kids?"

# EMERGING:
# AN AFTERWORD

$H$ow odd (I am thinking): I leave the real world of foster care reluctantly. However appalling it may be, it is a world of particularity. And I'm all too aware of what awaits us as we emerge: the cacophony of shoulds: a shouting on behalf of children's rights, family rights, and fathers' rights; a noisy fray between those overwrought about intrusions into the "traditional" and "patriarchal" family and those outraged by system failure.

I am aware, also, of how vulnerable some readers may be—in their frustration with the complex realities—to easy persuasion by hyperbole. In fact, delving around in the backlash literature (books and articles expressing outrage at false accusations and wrongful removals), I am repeatedly struck by how simple it is to make a solution of the perfectly reasonable, the quite correct—and the muddleheaded. How simple, then, for good-hearted people to swallow the potable, unaware that some of the ingredi-

243

ents may be less than wholesome and the effect of the solution may be toxic.

It is more than possible, then, to level accusations against the system that are grounded in truth, and to parlay those accusations into something with another meaning entirely; something in the service of another agenda entirely. Thus, while groups like VOCAL claim to be speaking on behalf of those who were falsely accused of child abuse, their actual focus is on those men who claim to have been falsely accused of child *sexual* abuse.[1] While they claim to speak on behalf of all who are victimized by child abuse laws, their literature does not focus on poor single women whose children are removed, homeless persons whose children are removed. While vigorously asserting that real child abusers should be prosecuted to the full extent of the law, the literature assumes that real abusers are deviant, other, not nice "you-and-me" Christians.[2]

It is even possible to weave into the fabric of your outrage the cry that it is not child abuse that is the real abuse at all—but the legal right to abortion.[3]

Alternatively, those impassioned on behalf of the protection of children—often moved by the death of a child like Lisa Steinberg, Baby Tess—are apt to lose sight of the fact that we are not always talking about something as clear-cut as a severely battered child.[4] The outcry that particular caseworkers should be held accountable is certainly understandable. The outcry that they should be held *liable* is less clear-cut unless it can be framed in so narrow a way that it would apply in only the most egregious instances. It is, as Dr. Cowardin said, as though we were to say to the police, "If any murder takes place, buster, it will be your fault."

How, then, can we emerge from the particular to the thematic with reason intact?

Gingerly.

My impulse, indeed, is to go tippy-toe. Yet one cannot write tippy-toe—filling the page with "it seems to me" and "it would appear that" and "it might perhaps be suggested that . . ." However, if anything is clear from the last hundred years of state intervention "on behalf of" children, it is that there is no formulation, no rule, no theory, no policy that cannot be diluted, adulterated, corrupted, substantively altered by a mix of agenda, careerism, the entrepreneurial spirit—and expedience.

Much like the lives that are its subject—Laura's life, Pauli's, Kelly's, Bob's, Tracy's—this book does not allow for tidy conclu-

sions: the call for a(nother) task force; legislative proposals. . . .
I did emerge from this journey, though, with a strong sense that
there were various themes that want the public's concentration
of mind as the issue continues to engender heated dialogue and
controversy.

The first is the critical need for *distinctions*. You cannot lump
together a parent who deliberately or willfully and repeatedly
batters a child, with a woman like Kelly who simply does not
have the wherewithal to be an optimum parent. Indeed, you
cannot talk about "optimal" parenting at all—because it is invid-
iously value-laden; because the conversation is occurring in the
context of such overwhelming state power; and because we don't
really know, for any particular child, what optimum parenting
would be. (Some kids thrive on benign neglect: others do not.)

Indeed, logic dictates that some behaviors do not belong in a
civil system at all. They are behaviors that are covered by
criminal law: aggravated assault, assault with a deadly weapon,
rape and sodomy. They are also, alas, behaviors that have
already occurred—not that *might* occur. At issue is provable—
not "imminent," or potential—danger to the child.

This would seem to me unarguable—yet argument is abun-
dant. "No conflict has caused greater dissension among professionals working on behalf of abused children than the use of
criminal prosecution as a response to child abuse."[5] What is the
nature of this dissension? It is said that, "The decision to leave
the case in the hands of social services generally places an
emphasis on reunification of families, with community interests
deemed best served by not pursuing criminal prosecution. It is
assumed that: the juvenile court can adequately protect the
children involved: proceeding with criminal prosecution would
harm children by making them feel to blame and requiring humiliating testimony and cross-examination in the presence of the
abuser: criminal prosecution would prevent an abuser from con-
tributing to the support of *his* family: *and the political risks
involved in prosecuting an offender who may be a respected
community member are unwise and unnecessary.*"[6] (Emphasis
mine.)

Opponents of criminal justice intervention argue that "the
criminal justice system views children only as pawns under the
authority of a politically motivated district attorney's office which
sets the rules and doesn't care what the victims have to say."[7]
Well, but can anyone, having listened to the voices speaking out
in this book, still believe that the social services system, in the

concrete reality, views children any differently? Opponents "point to evidence that children are sometimes forced to repeat their story over and over, confront the defendant, and endure repeated continuances and hostile cross-examination."[8] But it is axiomatic that children in the world of child welfare will have to repeat their stories over and over—to an ever-shifting bank of workers. If visitation with the serious offender is encouraged, they will have to confront that offender repeatedly. And what is that child's life about except "repeated continuances"—shifts, delays, uncertainty, moves. "Hostile cross-examination" would have the virtue of being something actual and time-limited, as opposed to the ongoing impersonal hostility of the foster care system. Mandy *wanted* to say what her father had done to her, and in court (albeit that was a civil court).

Although much has been done to confuse the public, though images have been presented of innocent fathers, handcuffed and dragged off to jail, fewer than 8 percent of 388 randomly selected child sexual abuse cases (in Fairfax County, Virginia, and Santa Cruz County, California, between 1983 and 1985) went to trial.[9]

What stands in the way, what triggers the outcry against prosecution, are interests—the interests of potentially prosecuted parents in the power group, the interests of turf, the interests of "professionals" who, under the banner of compassion, are in the business of "treatment." Even as the "interest" behind which they take refuge is the "child's best . . ."

Yet it is the absence of this distinction between serious police function and social work that, in case after case, can be seen to lead dismally to a child's death.

In 1986, in Everett, Washington, for example, emergency-room doctors, day-care teachers, and relatives all reported to Protective Services that three-year-old Eli Creekmore was being brutally beaten at home. After the child was killed by the father, there was much to-do about why Protective Services had then allowed the child to remain in the home. Few seemed to question what seems to me most obvious: Why is a brutally beaten three-year-old not more suitably reported to—and the case investigated by—the police? And why, then, is the police report not filed with the prosecuting attorney?

The evidence is that a police officer was present at the hospital the second time Eli was brought into the emergency room. Evidence is that the examining physician saw significant danger of a life-threatening injury, saw clear signs that there was a fracture at the base of the child's skull. Yet back the child went to the purview of Protective Services; and back, then, to the abusive father. Strangely, the railing, the outcry, was against the failure of Protective Services[10]—and not against the entirely weird thought process that would have a social work system practice "rehabilitation" on known batterers and rapists by giving them back their victims to practice on. This is not a "system failure." It is a failure of linear thought.

The same pattern emerged in the story of Joshua DeShaney, who fell into a coma on March 8, 1984. He was not quite four years old. Joshua's father, Randy, was convicted of abusing the child and sentenced to two to four years in prison. (He actually served less than two years.) Like Eli Creekmore's father, Randy DeShaney was known to the system as a violent man. Joshua wound up in the hospital repeatedly, with bumps on the head, burns, bloody noses, a boxed ear, a bruised shoulder. After Joshua's death, the caseworker, Ann Kemmeter, told Joshua's mother (who was divorced from Randy and lived in another state), "I just knew the phone would ring some day and Joshua would be dead."[11]

The question at issue when this case was brought before the U.S. Supreme Court in the fall of 1988 was whether aggravated negligence by the state in failing to protect a child from physical abuse can amount to an unconstitutional deprivation of liberty.[12] Whether, because the case was known to the system, a "special relationship" existed, even without that the state had taken custody of the child. It was argued also that the social worker had deliberately refused to act; that there was egregious negligence.

To the latter, the county replied that Kemmeter was not indifferent, but rather sensitive to the parental rights at stake. She " 'had to walk a delicate line' in order to maintain contact with the family."[13]*

But in all my listening, this "delicate line," this fear of

*As mentioned before, on February 22, 1989, the Supreme Court ruled in *DeShaney v. Winnebago County Department of Social Services* that the State did not have an affirmative duty to protect Joshua from abuse at his father's hands. Certainly, in the context of this case—where the child was well known to have been brutally assaulted by the father before—this decision rejecting system accountability seems wrong, bizarre, and angering. Yet—what *practical* effect would the "right" decision, the one that would seem to satisfy both passion and reason, have? Might it not make removal of children key to the greater personal safety of workers and the security of the system? Might that not then give workers an uncomfortably personal stake in removal? For a brief discussion by attorney William Grimm contrasting *DeShaney* with other court decisions, see footnote.[14]

reprisal, this sense of a need to maintain a conciliatory posture in order to maintain contact, is evident only where it is a white male who is the abuser. In light of the threats of suit, and the well-publicized posture of outrage from backlash groups, this nervousness is realistically placed. All the more reason, it would seem to me, why it should be the police, not a young female social worker, who are called to the task of investigation.

There are definable criminal behaviors directed toward children by parents and caretakers short of outright murder (which often *precede* outright murder). How can we square the outrage when a child is devastatingly raped, or maimed, or killed, with the greater passion for a soft, "service" approach in the most horrendous cases, but not in the lesser, need-based ones?

My favorite argument against prosecution is that children do not want to see their parent jailed. For me, the main interest of this argument is—its irrelevance. Because, in such a circumstance of danger, if the protective service agency were to correctly evaluate the situation, the child would be permanently removed from that parent, would not see that parent (in jail or otherwise) in any case. Such an argument can be made only by adopting the curious logic that says that a parent so disposed to mistreat a child as to repeatedly commit a provably felonious assault (say) will be convincingly "rehabilitated" within some reasonable period of the kid's childhood.

Is this situation—the prosecution of a child's parent—sad? Very. (Though we do it all the time when the crime is, say, burglary.)

But what is the alternative if we wish to strongly condemn the gross maltreatment of children by parents rather than facilely condemn the shortcomings of the needy? Quite clearly, those who take themselves to be members of the power group do not—and on the evidence, need not—take seriously the intrusions of the "helping" arm of the state.

What will it be like for the child who must know that his parent was murderous toward him? Nasty, no doubt. But at least he will know who was in the wrong: he will not have to deal throughout his childhood with the reformulation of himself as the problem.

It bears repeating, this: without distinctions, we are in a closed loop: a pattern of thinking from which nothing can emerge but another trip round. A "social service" can only be that. It can only fulfill a police function when those it is up against are too weak and too powerless to fight back. And at that point it inevitably has less to do with protecting children than with the wielding of power.

As Lucy Berliner, social worker with the Sexual Assault Center at Harborview Medical Center, Seattle, Washington, said to me, "CPS should get out of the business of investigation and leave that to the cops. They should be figuring out how to keep cases *out* of the system, not bring them in." Because by definition, a social work system cannot be geared to proving or disproving: proving, disproving, are neither "service" nor "help." Challenged, should they tread on an otherwise respectable citizen's toes (or should they fail to with dire results), they are driven to a cover-the-ass mentality. This, perhaps, tends to explain why, as things stand, the governing law of protective services, foster care, child welfare seems to be—worse than caprice—perversity.

The worse the abuse, the greater the likelihood that major efforts will be made to "preserve the family." It has been remarked on before. In an article in *Parade Magazine,* journalist Tom Seligson reports: "In some cases, the parent simply needs housing or employment, yet the child-welfare agency makes no effort to help provide it. However, when the problem is as major as a parent's fundamental character, the agencies cling to the belief that *any* parent can be rehabilitated." Seligson quotes New Orleans attorney Richard Ducote: "With the same evidence that would enable a D.A. to send a parent away for 15 to 20 years for what he [sic] did to his kids, some juvenile- and family-court judges are still reluctant to terminate rights. That's what's crazy."[15]

Crazy it is.
A quick scan of the grounds for termination of parental rights in the January, 1988, *Juvenile and Family Law Digest*[16] shows them to be as consistent and logical as the edicts of the Red Queen:

- Willful conduct not necessary for termination
- Can terminate mother incapable of providing care
- Murder of spouse not grounds to terminate
- Cannot terminate for temper outbursts at caseworkers [happily; yet it is sobering that it was tried]
- Cannot terminate just for killing mother if good father

- Can consider prospective neglect without waiting for harm
- Can terminate for psychological abuse . . .

And yet where repeated violence of bone-breaking, skull-fracturing magnitude is at issue, often enough there is not even a removal? Whether or not it is the bias toward fathers and the lesser valuation of mothers (as I more than imply), something is critically wrong here, and that something can be traced to the lack of a fundamental distinction between a crime and a short-coming.

The most compelling question in the Creekmore case, and others like it, is not why "Protective Services failed," but what they—and not the police and the prosecutor—were doing there in the first place.

To begin with, then, I would posit that beginning distinction—between truly policeable and prosecutable actions and those more ambiguous, or *pro*spective. Here, as throughout, humility must obtain. You will not always get a conviction. You will not always make a correct judgment call. *All* children will not be saved. Judge Slobod is most probably correct: nobody could have predicted with any certainty that Cheryl Shahine, who had certainly been less than competent, but had never been violent to her children before, would one day bash Baby Eugene's brains in against the sink.

Suppose there were a mainstream agreement that some behaviors toward one's own children belong in the prosecutorial purview: then what is the role of Protective Services? What is it *for?* I would hardly be the first person to suggest it should be for what its name suggests—"service," the provision of help that can be reasonably supposed to alleviate crisis. Housing, food, clothing, emotional as well as practical support. The need for these things, though, need not be labeled "neglect." In fact, "neglect" as a label might well be dispensed with entirely. Extreme neglect is abuse. To starve a child toward death (where food is available) is not neglect; it is abuse. To lock a child for days in the closet is not absentminded. It is not neglect. It is abuse.

Protective Services should also be for placement—though, as Dr. Cowardin suggested, the need for placement is most likely far less than is currently perceived and acted on, particularly were other real services available and available without the concurrent heightened level of surveillance. Yet there *is* a need for placements, temporary and otherwise. Maria did not want

Laura. Pat, during her drinking days, did not have it together to care for Dana and Ali. Once Tracy blew the whistle on her father, and absent her mother's support, she had to *be somewhere*. There no doubt is a level of what we would all consider abusive behavior—behavior that is short of prosecutable—that wants intervention. But here, on the evidence of much of the literature, we reach a cognitive bog: it is frequently said that you cannot define abuse.

Indeed, this very question—what is child "abuse"; what is child "neglect"?—remains one on which help is still not available (perhaps largely because the question has not been formulated as, What is prosecutable child abuse, and what, then, is left to be considered abuse that requires a less safeguarded procedure for intervention?). Here lies the heart of the matter: the question to which the answer is popularly supposed to be—foster care.

To give a brief tour:

As defined by the National Center on Child Abuse and Neglect, child abuse is: "the physical or mental injury, sexual abuse, negligent treatment or maltreatment of a child under the age of eighteen by a person who is responsible for the child's welfare under circumstances which indicate that the child's health or welfare is harmed or threatened thereby."[17]

As defined by social policy expert and researcher on child abuse David Gil, "abuse is any acts of commission or omission by a parent or an individual or an institution, or by society as a whole which deprives a child of equal rights and liberty and/or interferes with or constrains the child's ability to achieve his or her optimal development potential."[18]

If the first definition is in need of further definition (e.g., what is "mental injury"? Is it not claimed, retrospectively, by every adult seeking any form of therapy or counseling?), the second suggests that children should be removed wholesale from America itself. It can hardly be claimed, after all, that American society does not deprive many, many children of equal rights and liberty; or that society's public education system does not constrain many, many children's ability to achieve their optimal developmental potential.

Sociologists Murray Straus and Richard Gelles write, "Twenty years of discussion, debate, and action have led us to conclude that there will never be an accepted or acceptable definition of abuse, because abuse is not a scientific or clinical term. Rather, it is a political concept."[19] This is interesting because their formulation of abuse as a *political* concept is quite different from other formulations that it is a *socially constructed* concept. A socially constructed concept is one that we may all agree about now, though we did not agree to that concept—did not agree that such was abuse—a hundred years ago.

The idea of abuse as a political concept introduces the idea of power: the power of one group to enforce behaviors of conformity on another group. It implies, not that we cannot define abuse, but that that definition, that intervention, will always be challenged when those behaviors are found in the power group. Straus and Gelles continue: "Abuse is essentially any act that is considered deviant or harmful by a group large enough or with sufficient political power to enforce the definition."[20] The idea of abuse as a political concept also suggests the reason for the reticence of the system to label the male as abusive; the preference for labeling the woman who fails to impede his violence as neglectful, as having failed to protect the child. It suggests, as well, that abuse will always be defined—tacitly; in effect—by those with power as something *other people,* less worthy people, less powerful people, do.

And it suggests why there continues to be, despite reason, such heavy emphasis, in removals, on "neglect."

Neglect. Definitions are far more hazardous here than in the area of abuse, although—because of the vagueness inherent in the idea of "any act of omission or commission"—they often tend to be more loquacious. Indeed, our "permanency-planning worker," Mark, told me how often he hears that one of the key checks conducted by protective service workers is "enough food in the refrigerator." (By that standard, we agreed, they could nail us both on alternate Thursdays.)

"Emotional" neglect, "psychological" neglect—both allegations that, despite "shared parenting," I have never encountered applied to a father—are positively perilous to define, although they are often grimly pronounced to be the most damaging.

Take emotional neglect. As defined by the National Clearing House on Child Abuse and Neglect:

Emotional neglect is the "failure to provide the child the emotional nurturing or emotional support necessary for the development of a sound personality, as for example subjecting the child to rejection or to a home climate charged with tension, hostility and anxiety-producing occurrences, which result in perceivable problems in children."[21]

Emotional maltreatment, then, includes: scapegoating, denigrating, rejecting, ridiculing, humiliating, ostracizing, undermining the child's self-esteem through perfectionist expectations, parental detachment, emotional indifference, lack of involvement or interest, and affective coldness in relation to the child, failure to provide necessary and essential psychological nurturance, extreme inconsistency, inappropriate control, dictatorial over-control, failure to provide controlling guidelines. . . . All of this sounds as if a bunch of adults have been set in a room to recite every single thing from which they feel they themselves, as children, suffered.

By these constraints, in order to prevent emotional maltreat-ment of children, then, you will have to remove them not just from (most) parents, but from this particular planet. If nothing else, this tendency to slip into la-la-land—when wielding such unchallengeable power—should trigger the public's constant at-tention and vigilance. Intervention can be justified outside the prosecutorial system only so long as deliberate harm to the child's basic health and safety are at issue. It would seem to me that there needs to be a surgical excision of the language of social work and psychology from the factor of police function.

To coerce mothers into a contractual, time-specific obligation to accomplish sometimes impossible, and often contradictory goals (e.g., hold a job; turn up for numerous mandated working-hours appointments) borders on the sadistic. And, as the former protective service worker, Linda, suggested, the permission for sadistic practice engenders a sadistic mind-set that is only thinly disguised by the language that tells us the goal is "rehabilitation." That word is ubiquitous—with no one apparently conscious of its decidedly Soviet connotation: its connotation of the reform of individuals to make them conform to what is politically "correct" (or to what the politically powerful deem, in parenting, to be "correct"): or, alternatively, the word's reference to criminality.

The irony, of course, is that time-specific "goal plans" are an intrinsic part of "permanency planning," and both are *concepts* that cannot be faulted. Yet both have become so wildly distorted in the execution as to now be no more than euphemisms. Surely this is a caution that any good idea in the world of foster care/child welfare can be perverted in its bureaucratic implementation: the language remains, but the intent is no longer even recogniz-able in the practice.

Still, not even the use of clear distinctions solves an inherent anomaly. As long as the protective service system retains its empowerment to petition the civil courts for the removal of children—where no crime has been charged as such, or proved as such—its power to punish exceeds the punishment most often meted out by the criminal justice system. While the protective service system does not have the power to charge you with a crime, it also does not have an obligation to read you your rights, or offer you the right to confront your accusers, or a trial by a jury of your peers—or any due process. Even eliminating the patent falsehood that the coercively intervening agent is your friendly visitor, there to offer help and service, one is left with the fact that the system is the authority that has an immense and unmonitored power to punish. It has the power to take from you—not your personal liberty for a specified period of time—but to take from you your children: to remove them indefinitely, and even, by building a convincing paper trail that will never be verified by any independent agencies, to remove them forever.

From the child's perspective, this system has the power to move and remove you arbitrarily, to shift you from place to place and label to label with no input from you, and most often with no explanation, and no accountability. To be angry at a parent for failings, for injustices, allows for eventual confrontation: allows for eventual resolution—either by coming to understand the parent-as-human, or by rejection of that particular human being—painful as all that may be. To be angry at a system that will afford you little information as to its real motives (and whose real motives may have little to do with you in any case), and that is entirely uninterested in how you may feel about it, is utterly futile. That the system then converts your experience of its confusions and shortcomings into evidence of *your* problems, your failings, is insidious.

Implicit in these pages is another theme: beyond obvious race bias, the entwined class and gender bias. One cannot turn in any direction in the world of foster care/child welfare anymore without confronting the ticking bomb that is the issue of child sexual abuse—the issue that inescapably focuses attention on these biases. Even if, nationwide, there were any public or professional consensus that incest should be prosecuted (and there is not), there will not always be enough evidence to do so, and the sheer weight of the incidence of child sexual abuse in the home tells us there simply cannot be that amount of prosecution.[22] Yet attempts at secondary, protective service intervention, when directed at men—most especially middle-class men—are bound to be legally embattled.

The weapon of choice in the accused fathers' war against the system is the lawsuit. Alleged offenders are claiming the violation of their civil rights. Even the threat of such reprisal by the well-heeled, well-regarded father is, I am told by workers, often enough to set the system backing off.

According to psychiatrist Roland Summit, who has been intensively active on this issue for over a decade, "By this time, even if no individual muscles the agency, the agencies are getting chary of saying anything, and of appeals decisions. In California, we've got appeals decisions now that dismiss as rank hearsay the careful report of a social worker, having talked with the child, and everything that has ever been done to support a complaint. The appeals court judges are, I think, would-be criminal court judges who don't make the distinction that you need a different standard of proof for the protection of the child. So they're not only throwing out the social worker reports, they're also finding reasons to keep out of court any expert testimony on behalf of the child."[23]

See what is happening here. Courts that will, should a mother's "neglect" be the issue, summarily remove the child with little evidence, little testimony—in the name of the "best interests of the child"—are balking at removing children from fathers without they can know "for sure"—i.e., beyond doubt—the abuse has occurred.[24] It is here that the idea of child welfare as *politically* constructed becomes luminous. Abruptly the idea of "probable harm" to the child becomes less important than *possible error*. In *this* circumstance, even the strong possibility of serious ongoing damage to the child weighs less than a *possible* wrong to a member of a power group.

When I ask Dr. Summit what he thinks is going to happen, he says, "If it [the issue of sexual abuse] just kept going with the ability of the courts to believe in this, I think it would be put away. Or it would be so diminished that we'd go back to, 'Gee, wasn't it awful in the seventies and eighties when everybody was believing the kids? How crazy we were then.' I think it would get to a very rigid standard of de facto not acting on any case that didn't have adult corroboration."

It is glaring. If the removal of a child from a man whose child has disclosed that he is molesting her provides grounds for a viable argument that his rights have been violated—because no crime has been charged as such, or proved as such—then why would a similar argument, put forth by a mother whose child has been removed because she has been accused by the agency of "neglect"—provide any lesser grounds? The *effective* difference lies solely in the fact that the one is a member of a power group that does the defining. The other, the mother, is perceived to be a member of a disempowered group; a group that is targeted by the defining.

These issues—of race, class, and gender bias—seem to me crucial ones, and ones likely to make the greatest number of citizens uncomfortable; likely to make the greatest number of folks reach for the comforting language of "help" and "services." Bias is, in many ways, the rock and the hard place of child welfare.

In an interview with Professor Kadushin, we had been to-and-fro'ing about whether child abuse should be more or less narrowly defined.

"Either it should be more narrowly defined," he says, "or more broadly defined. Then give the agencies the resources to deal with a greater population of children who are identified as needing services. One or the other."

"Would you also say," I ask, "that if we were going to more broadly define it [to include sexual abuse, for instance], and we were going to put the funds into that, and there were services instead of things that masquerade as services, or are named as services but don't exist—that it should be class-undifferentiated? I know the rubric is—and you've said, except for sexual abuse—this stuff doesn't go on in the middle class. Well, we really don't know this. . . ."

"Okay. It should be undifferentiated. I'll say it should be undifferentiated. But how are you going to undifferentiate? What goes on in middle-class homes is not subject to referral. It is protected in some measure. Would you then ask that the agency be provided with the prerogative of going into homes, defying the autonomy of the family? Have access to middle-class families?"

There it is then: in a neat little coda—exactly what the Official from New York City's SSC said to me when I set out on this journey.

"I'm asking you," I say, "are you comfortable with saying that the poor are then necessarily the focus of an intrusive intervention?"

"I'm not comfortable, but I see that this is inevitable. And I'm comfortable with the fact that if we can't deal with all of the situation, we can at least then deal with some of the situations that become accessible to us. I'm ready to opt for half a loaf. With the certainty that I'm not gonna get the whole loaf. With that, I'm comfortable."

"I hear what you're saying—that half a loaf, and at least you're doing something. But are you comfortable that those who need a hand up are getting a boot down? Losing practically all they have left—their kids? There's a reason for some discomfort in targeting people who are already victims."

"It's done all the time. The school does it constantly. If you take a look at your disciplinary problems—at who is removed from school, or who's put in which classes. I'm not comfortable with it, but it's part of the way the social organization is set up. And I'm not gonna change it, and you're not gonna change it. And I'm uncomfortable with it, but I'll live with my discomfort."

Will you, the reader, live with yours?

It may be that Professor Kadushin is correct (and certainly the evidence suggests that he is): that there cannot be such a system allowed to penetrate the autonomy of middle-class families. But if he is correct, the public has a great deal of thinking to do—or a great deal of burrowing deeper to avoid it. Not only is this clearly heavy-duty discrimination against a "suspect class," but—when said out loud—it is morally queasy-making as well.

Additionally, the open admission that the middle class and upper middle class are out of bounds will force a general retraction on the issue of sexual abuse. As elsewhere, the system here can be seen engaged in folly. The greater the evidence becomes that the system cannot protect children who disclose sexual abuse by fathers and stepfathers, the more intensive the efforts to go into schools, to implore kids to tell: in other words, the less effective the intervention, the more vigorous the case-finding. However, if you really and truly do not want to identify sexual abusers in the middle class, you cannot go into middle-class schools and tell children to disclose. You cannot tell middle-class women that their job is to protect their children. What you must tell them to do is shut up. (And continue to remove to foster care only the children of poor women because they "failed to protect," or because they "knew or should have known." Children whose actual abusers have either no interest or no clout.)

Interesting problem, yes?

It is ironic that an issue—child abuse—that was so warmly embraced during the 1960s by politicians as an issue of "low-cost rectitude," an issue that seemed to allow for no dissension (who can be *for* child abuse?), should turn out to be even more volatile and controversial than raising the public's taxes to deal with it would be.

* * *

The next two themes that emerge in these pages are linked: the preposterous degree of language abuse in child welfare, and the issue of confidentiality. Indeed, one of the things that seemed clearest to me from this journey is that if we have been thinking crookedly about child welfare/foster care, it is to a large extent because the language we have been given to use is itself crooked. To call someone you are harassing to accomplish on her own what she *cannot* accomplish on her own a "client" is not only muddleheaded, but actively deceitful. To call that harassment a "service"—equally so. To tie financial assistance for those in dire need to chronic surveillance may be inevitable, but it is nonetheless unsavory. To call it "help" is monstrous.

Curiously, it is on language abuse that the rationale of confidentiality lies. It is only by asserting itself in the language of "professional-client" relationship that the state can legally defend its "privilege" and right to "nondisclosure": confidentiality. It is interesting that the two legal sources I was able to find to help illuminate the issue of confidentiality primarily addressed the concerns of professionals about reporting abuse and about testifying—thus risking the violation of lawyer-client, doctor-patient, social worker- or therapist-client relationships.

However, what I was able to eke out of these pages corroborates my premise that confidentiality is entirely dependent on the idea that what is occurring is "help" and "service." Stanford law professor Michael Wald and assistant law professor Robert Weisberg link general social services with public mental health institutions, drug and alcohol treatment programs in their right to "nondisclosure." "If the legislature creates health and welfare agencies because it believes they give valuable services, it must ensure the privacy of clients' confidential communications to encourage them to use these services."[25] But as we learned from the cases of Baby Tess and Baby Eugene, what is being kept private are not the clients' confidential communications (whoever you believe the "clients" in these cases to be)—but the caseworkers' records; their writings-down; the official perceptions of the situations. And, as we learned from Kelly's story of losing her two kids to the system, even these do not always match the event.

Wald and Weisberg continue: "The instrumental argument for the nondisclosure laws might seem weaker than that for the privilege laws. The professional relationships governed by the nondisclosure laws might seem less voluntary than those governed by the privilege laws. *Some clients protected by the nondis-*

*closure laws are seeking services they are relatively powerless to refuse.*"[26] (Emphasis mine.)

If this last is so, one must again ask, why are they "clients"? And why is it put to us that they are "seeking" services? You see? If you call black green, you cannot think about darkness. You wind up thinking about fields of grass. And eventually you may well convince yourself that fields of grass are what darkness is.

Wald and Weisberg continue: "The patient in a public mental health institution may have suffered involuntary commitment. The welfare client seeking financial assistance or food stamps might have such a compelling need for the service that no fear of invasion of her privacy could deter her from seeking help. But the difference does not significantly weaken the instrumental argument. In the case of other programs, even if the client's fear of invasion of privacy does not or cannot deter her from initially *forming* the relationship, it certainly might deter her from *cooperating* fully and candidly with the professional."[27]

To me, there seems no way to convincingly relate this formulation to the reality of child protection/foster care. The woman on whose doorstep the protective service worker appears, claiming allegations that the woman has abused her child, is not a person with whom the woman is "forming a relationship," even involuntarily. The caseworker is an agent of a system, sent to scrutinize this woman. Whatever may deter her from "cooperating fully and candidly," it will almost certainly not be the comforting promise of "confidentiality"—if only because there *is* no such promise in any meaningful sense. It is this worker who may very well testify against her; may testify toward the permanent removal of the child. At this point, any number of mothers I spoke with would have been extremely grateful—not for confidentiality but for its opposite: for the opportunity to expose to the public the full facts and course of what they perceived as a ferocious injustice.

The whole defense of confidentiality here depends on the shibboleth that what is going on is a relatively harmless, nonadversarial, parlor "helping" game.

Additionally, this formulation brings into play, once more, that word that has been so mercilessly pejorative throughout: the adjective for *cooperating: cooperative:* the word that has been relentlessly used to fault mothers for failing to succeed at arbitrary or impossible tasks.

This situation suggests not only that mothers "seeking" involuntary intervention and removal of their child should be read a Miranda warning, but that mothers seeking *financial assistance* should be read such a warning as well.

I am reminded of a university social work professor who said to me that she always tells her students not to believe two things: One is, 'The check is in the mail.' The other? 'I'm a social worker, and I'm here to help you.'

Next, and conclusively: "Measuring the instrumental argument for privilege and nondisclosure laws would seem to call for empirical research, but such research has rarely been attempted. *Rather, the laws of privilege and nondisclosure have evolved, or stumbled along, as legislatures and courts have made fairly crude general guesses about social behavior, and have responded to an uncertain mixture of unsupported instrumental assertions and the politics of professionalism.*"[28] (Emphasis mine.)

That would seem to be it, then. At the end of the many roads I traveled looking for the origin of that which was said to be sacred, immutable, carved in stone, dictated by God and reason, we discover that, in fact, confidentiality just got itself written into statutes. It just grew—like Topsy. And the laws grew based on the language of help and the language of professionalism, and the language of service—in the service of the "politics of professionalism." But this professionalism, as Professor Ira Schwartz suggested when we set out, is an emperor without clothes. In the end, King Solomon steps out from behind a screen and is revealed to be—the Wizard of Oz! (Only Dorothy, in this version, does not necessarily get to go back to Aunt Em.)

Despite this, confidentiality is ordained. "In order to be eligible for federal child abuse funds, the state cps [child protective service] system, by law or regulation, must have 'methods to preserve confidentiality of all records in order to protect the rights of the child, his parents, or guardians.' "[29] There are specific exceptions as to who may gain access to records. None includes the public or its real (as opposed to decreed) representatives.

And there is something else that reverberates oddly: "In addition to confidentiality restrictions noted above, cps workers should be alerted to civil liability which may result from improper disclosure of information. The person injured by your disclosure could bring a slander or libel action against you . . . that you orally, or by writing, communicated false, damaging (defaming) information about the plaintiff to another person."[30]

What this suggests is that to make known publicly the specific reasons you have removed a child from a parent could constitute grounds for libel: could be attacked as false and damaging. But the removal of the child in itself—keeping the reason and the records entirely secret from the community whose agent you are said to be—is perfectly correct.

There is something very, very, very, very strange here. It would seem to point to a grave nervousness about the inherent structure on which the system is built. Is the parent from whom a child is permanently removed (or from whom permanent removal is threatened) an *"alleged* perpetrator" in perpetuity? Is the standard of evidence for removal—lower than the standard for criminal sanctions—that shaky? Is the only real proof we will ever have that a removal was correct the fact that the removal occurred? ("Kids are not in foster care for *no reason!"*)

I presented the problem this way to Mary Lee Allen, director of child welfare and mental health for the Children's Defense Fund.

"I have hardly talked with anybody," I said, "who bothered to pretend that what the system was protecting with confidentiality was not children but itself. And to the extent that this is apparent to me, through listening, I think it should not be . . . that the system should have this kind of power, so that it can do anything it wants, write down anything it wants, and whatever it writes down is the only testimony you've got."

"I'd say that's true," she said. "That the system does protect itself. That the system isn't open in terms of sharing, with the individuals who should know, very basic information. And I think the question is— Unfortunately, the solution to that often gets interpreted to be that all confidentiality laws make no sense at all. It often attempts to go to the extreme. And I think the important thing is to try to be specific, in terms of the sorts of information that should be clearly accessible to certain individuals. That's different than making that information available to everyone—even though those individuals may have no interest in the system. . . . I think sometimes people hide behind the veil of confidentiality, obviously."

That, certainly, is reasonable. The problem is—who are the individuals who have "no interest in the system"? If the outcry every time a child is maimed or killed in state care, or maimed or killed in the absence of state intervention, is authentic, then we *all* can claim a legitimate interest. (And what can possibly account for a level of "confidentiality" that extends beyond a child's death, such that even the *New York Times* will be turned down on a Freedom of Information petition?) How can exclusions possibly be made without turning out to exclude (as the statutes now do) people who have no *vested* interest in the system? And if whichever people do gain access to the truth—by being able not only to see the records but to speak with the affected parties to get their view of what happened—are in turn subject to gagging, prevented by law from disclosing publicly what is going on, then adding a few more select groups to the list of those now permitted access will accomplish nothing at all.

As Judge Slobod pointed out, the landscape of child welfare is dotted with groups pursuing their own agendas, grinding their own axes, covering their own behinds. Even the courts, should they make a mistake, have an interest in not admitting it; an interest, often, not in rectifying the mistake, but in insisting there was no mistake. Hundreds of outfits and organizations have a financial stake in the child welfare industry as well: they are selling the service of problem management. (I had dinner one night with a professor of psychiatry who had been active in foster parent groups for years. What he wanted to do, he said, was *franchise* group homes. Right? McKids?) There is far too much leeway for serious damage to great numbers of human beings in this area—absent all accountability—to allow the secrecy to continue as it is.

To allow any level of coercive intervention short of the occurrence of a prosecutable behavior—toward a greater good—is to accede to some compromise with privacy.

As I have suggested, what I encountered was any number of people who, feeling a gross injustice had been committed, wanted to seek—not shamed anonymity—but public awareness of what had been done to them. In the past few years, I have noticed any number of people more than willing to go on national television to speak of how they had been falsely accused, their children or foster children wrongfully removed. The whole idea of privacy in the late-twentieth-century TV talk-show world, in any case, has an odd cast.

The children. Does confidentiality protect them? Judge Slobod told me that when the *Times Herald-Record* printed the names of Tracey Maye's other children—those in other foster homes—the one child who was school age, at least, was ridiculed and tormented mercilessly by other children. That surely is something that child did not need. But kids can be kind as well as cruel. And without any empirical evidence, how can we assume that the benefit of confidentiality outweighs the cost: the vast number of children presently hidden, in circumstances of which we cannot know?

As Wald and Weisberg told us, there is no such empirical evidence to tell us that confidentiality—certainly the total confidentiality that now obtains—is a good. There is plenty of evidence to tell us that it can be an evil, that the potential for that is extremely great. *Particularly* if the system is a compromise with the basic tenets—both real and those to which we give lip service—on which our society is structured, it wants watching. *Particularly* since this is the state acting in the name of good intentions, it wants that old vigilance.

Another theme that emerges from what we have heard is the practice that results from the nature of the language used to express those good intentions: the language of mental health. This seems to me at once of considerable urgency, and yet formidable to present lucidly to a public so steeped in the pervasive imagery of "illness" and "cure." An imagery that carries with it a subtextual presumption that—whether or not there is real cause for grief—misfortune will be reversed by tinkering with the individual's psyche; and that whatever is presented in the "scientific" language of therapy as curative is also socially (as well as individually) redeeming. The fact is there is an alarming increase in the number of children dumped in mental institutions.[31]

What is being increasingly normalized is the acceptance of dubious forms of "therapy" as punishment ("rehabilitation"). Not only is it not "voluntary"; but the alleged "illness" is childhood itself.[32] As Tracy's experience illustrates, "treatment" is based on the principle of confession of your "problems," in the way that much religion requires confession of your sins (and in the way that totalitarian regimes require confession of your "false" beliefs). The "steps," the "points," the "privileges" are signposts on your path to redemption.

As Dr. Cowardin pointed out, first and foremost what abused children who have been removed need is a *home,* a place to *be.* They *do* need care, and caring. They *may* need psychological help. *Some* psychological intervention may even *be* help.

But to frame everything in these victim-focused terms—the reality of poverty, the reality of need, the reality of abuse by a parent and consequent orphanhood—is simply to empower a professional group, carrying the banner of "help," as wardens of people: custodians of adults and children who are as effectively condemned to the custodians' judgments and evaluations as convicted persons.

It is also to ensure that those who have something vital to tell us—what really is occurring in our name: in the name of "public policy"—will not be given credibility. They are the sick ones, the psychiatrically labeled, the troubled. Do not trust them, says the system. Trust our (estimated) data.

There is, as well, reason to suspect the labels themselves can be held accountable for some of the damage we perceive in child-victims. As Bob said, "If I tell you you're an emotionally troubled person and I keep telling you that you're an emotionally troubled person—'You're emotionally troubled, you're emotionally troubled, you have problems, that's why I'm talking to you'—pretty soon it starts to groove into your thinking. And it narrows your vision. It narrows your capabilities. . . . You're a cripple."

Along with various themes, certain concrete conclusions are suggested by what those speaking out here have said—many far from news. The most obvious derives from the enormous gap between all our pieties about the sanctity of childhood, the value of children—and the resources we actually commit to the improvement of life for children of the poor. What else *can* this mean but that we do not really care as much as it pleases us to say that we do? Or, rather, that we so deplore the parents in poverty that we will put up with the fact that the children must share that level of desperation—rather than "indulge" the parents with meaningful aid. (People are not poor—for *no reason!*) Rather than dignify the real need of the parents—a need resulting not so much from their personal inadequacies as from our societal circumstance and structure—we would "solve" their plight by removing their children (and make that morally all right by claiming it to be in those children's "best interests"). In practical terms, real services and moneys for services must equal or surpass funds triggered by removal.[33]

Other conclusions seem equally obvious, though somewhat less often recited: You cannot treat foster mothers with contempt—and then wonder why fewer and fewer women volunteer for this treatment. How much easier everyone finds it to blame the women for not volunteering—because so many are now in the work force—than to challenge the inherent attitude of the system toward those over whom it gains power.

Equally dippy is the idea that mothers in need can be treated with complete dislike, be labeled, berated, judged—and then be expected to "cooperate."

The children, as well, are treated as so much product—to be warehoused, cataloged, inventoried—and ultimately blamed and punished for their failure to make an adjustment we find socially acceptable: their failure to be like other kids; like kids who have been given a valued identity. I was told, often, that there is a stigma to being a foster child. But that phrasing assumes that a stigma just is—something there. In fact, it is something we as a society place on that condition, and it is an utterly upside-down idea. An equally obvious response to the condition would be that it trigger greater respect, greater valuation for the intrinsic difficulties that must be overcome. It could easily be posited that a child in this circumstance of need deserves more, not less, socially created advantage; more, not fewer, chances.

All of which leads to the one, bottom-line theme that, for me, informed the whole journey: the need for humility. The issue of endangered children, of predatory, brutal, or severely inadequate parents, is the stuff of myth and fairy tale. In real life, these circumstances do not lead to a happily-ever-after, but only to best-guess choices—which are themselves limited ones. Cases where children are killed by a parent tend to play out among us like morality plays—with public passion about the particular instance leading to a bloodlust for "them" to be punished: those who are not-us, those who are other. Complacently, we egg on a policing mechanism to "do something!"

Yet, if anything came clear to me as I listened, it is that we have not thought. We do not know what it really is we want done.

The world of foster care/child welfare is a world we have constructed (or permitted to be constructed) for a great number of children. We must think. We must know. We cannot, morally, responsibly, continue to indulge in the luxury of outcry—all the while empowering others to play at the game of Solomon Says.

As I write these concluding pages, the trial of Joel Steinberg for the murder of Lisa is in progress. Nussbaum's testimony is being televised in the New York area, and is being watched by an enormous audience. In an editorial titled "Wallowing in Misery," the *New York Times* says, "If Hedda Nussbaum were poor and unlettered, a broad middle-class audience would find it harder to relate to the horror and to her. Viewers might feel that she'd been battered by poverty and life experience as surely as she'd been battered by Joel Steinberg. But Joel Steinberg and Hedda Nussbaum are middle-class, educated. They could be the neighbors.

"Recognizing that, we try to distance ourselves from her crumpled face and his chilling impassivity with observations about their sanity. But to do that reduces the tragedy to cruel soap opera. Thousands of kids are battered every day. This drama offers, beyond wallowing, a redeeming possibility: reliving on television one child's terrible death can arouse in a large audience the will to prevent the death of many others."[34]

Yes. But along with the will, we need the reason and knowledge and the hard information that temper unrestrained passion.

In particular, we yet need to know more about:

- the intricate structure of the various bureaucracies; the barriers in communication and effect between them, and the competition for funding.
- where the money is going. There may *not* be enough money. But there is a lot of money.
- where and what, precisely, the vested interests are. What are the various agendas fueling the language of child protection?
- where the kids are. *Who* are the kids in various systems? What do *they* have to say?

The goal of this book has been to stand as an introduction; as an access route for the reader to an easier familiarity with the realities of the world of foster care/child welfare that exist vividly and in the specific; realities that have been masked both by distancing language and by periodic incitements to manic emotion. To correct for the fact that the public has been effectively locked out of this conversation.

All we have heard tells us, in my opinion, that the role of King Solomon has not been solidly and reliably cast—it has been improvised. In the end, I think, the only correct actors to fill that role—are us.

# Notes

## SETTING OUT: AN INTRODUCTION

1. Robert Mulford, "Protective Services for Children," *Encyclopedia of Social Work* (Washington, D.C.: National Association of Social Workers, 1977), p. 1115.
2. Alfred Kadushin and Judith A. Martin, *Child Welfare Services* (New York: Macmillan, 1988), p. 228. (Hereafter, Kadushin and Martin.) "Defining child maltreatment is, in effect, an exercise in deciding the limits of legitimate state intervention into family life; the reciprocal, relative rights and obligations of parents and children, and the kind of adults a society regards as its valued model (assertively democratic, individualistic, socially conforming and so on). The definition relates to the way parents need to discipline children to achieve the model. . . ."
3. Consideration of the issues from this value viewpoint can be found in the landmark work, Joseph Goldstein, Anna Freud, and Albert S. Solnit, *Beyond the Best Interests of the Child* (New York: The Free Press, 1973).

267

4. See Trudy Festinger, *No One Ever Asked Us . . . : A Postscript to Foster Care* (New York: Columbia University Press, 1983).

5. Michael Wald, J. Merrill Carlsmith, and P. Herbert Leiderman, *Protecting Abused and Neglected Children* (Stanford, Calif.: Stanford University Press, 1987)

6. Kadushin and Martin, p. 258.

7. Kadushin and Martin, p. 267.

8. Goldstein, Solnit, Freud, *Beyond the Best Interests of the Child*, pp. 5–6. "How, the question then becomes, can the law assure for each child a chance to be a member of a family where he feels wanted and where he will have the opportunity, on a continuing basis, not only to receive and return affection, but also to express anger and to learn to manage his aggression?" Cited in Michael Wald, "State Intervention on Behalf of 'Neglected' Children: A Search for Realistic Standards," 27 Standard Law Review 985 (April 1975), p. 987.

9. Kadushin and Martin, p. 246.

10. Cited in Nicholas Kittrie, *The Right to Be Different: Deviance and Enforced Therapy* (Baltimore: The Johns Hopkins University Press, 1971), p. 9.

11. Kittrie, *The Right to be Different,* p. 59.

12. Judith Areen, "Intervention Between Parent and Child; A Reappraisal of the State's Role in Child Neglect and Abuse Cases," *Georgetown Law Journal,* 63:88 (1975), p. 899, n. 68.

13. Kadushin and Martin, p. 347.

14. Kittrie, *The Right to Be Different,* 112.

15. Anthony Platt, *The Child Savers: The Invention of Delinquency* (Chicago: University of Chicago Press, 1969), p. 105. Also, Louise Armstrong, *The Home Front: Notes from the Family War Zone* (New York: McGraw-Hill, 1983), p. 120.

16. Barbara Nelson, *Making an Issue of Child Abuse: Political Agenda Setting for Social Problems* (Chicago: University of Chicago Press, 1984), p. 10.

17. Kadushin and Martin, p. 223.

18. Kadushin and Martin, p. 224.

19. Nelson, *Making an Issue of Child Abuse,* p. 17.

20. "Continuing Crisis in Foster Care: Issues and Problems." Hearing before the House Select Committee on Children, Youth, and Families, April 22, 1987 (Washington, D.C.: U.S. Government Printing Office), p. 4.

21. "Continuing Crisis in Foster Care," p. 59.

22. "Continuing Crisis in Foster Care," p. 112.

23. Charles P. Gershenson, Ph.D., "An Assessment of Children Reentering Foster Care," *Child Welfare Research Notes #14* (January 1986).

24. "Continuing Crisis in Foster Care," p. 5.

25. Testimony of the Children's Defense Fund before the Subcommittee on Public Assistance and Unemployment Compensation, Committee

on Ways and Means, and the Select Committee on Children, Youth, and Families: Joint Hearings on Child Welfare, Foster Care, and Adoption, May 12, 1988, p. 7.

26. "Continuing Crisis in Foster Care," p. 2.
27. Personal phone interview.

## CHAPTER FOUR: "FALLING IN LOVE"

1. For instance: "A young mother in Delaware voluntarily placed her two children in foster care while she underwent gall bladder surgery. When she found out her discharge date, she called her social worker to find out when she could pick her children up and was told that she couldn't because she lived in crowded conditions.

   "At that time, she was living with her father and her brother. It took two years and a lawsuit for her to regain custody of her children." Testimony of Toni Oliver, consultant and adoption specialist, National Center for Neighborhood Enterprise, Washington, D.C., before Select Committee on Children, Youth, and Families, "Continuing Crisis in Foster Care," April 22, 1987, p. 137. Also, statement of Judy Guttridge, mother, Baltimore, Maryland, before the hearing on "Children in State Care," September 25, 1986, pp. 112–115.
2. According to Janet R. Fink, assistant attorney-in-charge of legal—affairs, The Legal Aid Society, Juvenile Rights Division, New York City, New York State law does not bar foster parents from speaking in court. However, since so many foster mothers I spoke with believed they were barred from speaking, they had certainly been given to understand that was so, whether or not it was the law.
3. Phyllis Chesler, *Mothers on Trial* (New York: McGraw-Hill, 1986), p. 66.
4. Charles P. Gershenson, Ph.D., "An Assessment of Children Re-entering Foster Care," *Child Welfare Research Notes #14* (January 1986), p. 1. "This is a *minimal estimate* of re-entry because children who had been in foster care the previous 13 months or longer were not counted as re-entered cases as well as children who ran away from home or entered a mental health or juvenile justice system's facility after being reunified with their family."

## CHAPTER SIX: THE PERMANENCY-PLANNING WORKER

1. Wald, Carlsmith, and Leiderman, *Protecting Abused and Neglected Children*, p. 5.
2. Kadushin and Martin, p. 101.

## CHAPTER SEVEN: THE "UNFIT" MOTHER

1. "A Report to Hubert H. Humphrey III, Attorney General," October 2, 1986.

## CHAPTER EIGHT: HE WHO "MAKES TROUBLE"

1. *New York Times,* 24 June 1988, B-1.
2. Again, whether or not the New York State law bars foster mothers from speaking out in court, the information they are given seems to be that they may not.
3. *Chicago Tribune,* 14 April 1988.
4. "The fact that, in 72% of the states, the rate of men killing ex-wives also increased calls into question the common assumption that simply leaving an assaultive mate will end the violence [cite omitted]. Studies of men who have killed their partners suggest that the precipitating event is frequently some form of perceived rejection. An investigation by Barnard et al. (1982) found that a mate's leaving or the threat of separation were especially provoking: In killing their wives, these men reported that they were reacting to a previous offense against them (e.g., leaving) on the part of their wives.

   "It may be that more women are now separating from threatening or assaultive men; but that men, perceiving such separations as desertion or rejection, are pursuing and killing them for leaving." Angela Browne, Kirk R. Williams, "Resource Availability for Women at Risk and Partner Homicide," Family Research Laboratory, University of New Hampshire, Durham, NH 03824. Report on research data: 1988, p. 26.

   Also Noel A. Cazenane, Margaret A. Zahn, Temple University, "Women, Murder and Male Domination: Police Reports of Domestic Homicide in Chicago and Philadelphia." Paper presented at 1986 annual meeting of the American Society of Criminology, October 31, Atlanta, GA, p. 16.

## CHAPTER SIXTEEN: THE GREAT LEVELER

1. Nat Hentoff, *Village Voice,* 15 March 1988, pp. 25–29.
2. *New York Times,* 1 January 1988.
3. Tom Seligson, *Parade Magazine,* 31 July 1988.
4. ABC-TV, 30 August 1988.
5. "Child Abuse and Neglect in America: The Problem and Response." Hearing before the House Select Committee on Children, Youth, and Families, April 3, 1987 (Washington, D.C.: U.S. Government Printing Office), p. 3.
6. Benjamin DeMott, "The Pro-Incest Lobby," *Psychology Today,* March 1980, pp. 11–16.
7. Kadushin and Martin, p. 300.
8. "Children's Mental Health: Promising Responses to Neglected Problems." Hearing before the House Select Committee on Children, Youth, and Families, July 14, 1987 (Washington, D.C.: U.S. Government Printing Office), p. 83.

9. Michael Robin, "The Abuse of Status Offenders in Private Hospitals," *Children and Youth Services,* vol. 4, nos. 1 and 2 (1982).
10. Marilyn Jackson-Beeck, Ira M. Schwartz, and Andrew Rutherford, "Trends and Issues in Juvenile Confinement for Psychiatric and Chemical Dependency Treatment," *International Journal of Law and Psychiatry,* vol. 10 (1987), p. 156.
11. Ibid., p. 154.
12. Robin, p. 82.
13. Ibid., p. 80.
14. Ibid., p. 85.

## CHAPTER SEVENTEEN: MAL-TREATMENT

1. Final Adjustment Report of "The Camp," July 14, 1987.

## CHAPTER EIGHTEEN: A PROFESSIONAL'S VIEW

1. For instance, "In 1966, 7.6% of the 145 psychiatric facilities for children and youth in the U.S. were operated for profit; by 1971, 17.1% of 369 facilities were operated for profit—a 125% increase. (Office of Juvenile Justice and Delinquency Prevention, 1983)" "Children's Mental Health: Promising Responses to Neglected Problems." Hearing before the Select Committee on Children, Youth, and Families, July 14, 1987 (Government Printing Office), p. 5.

## CHAPTER NINETEEN: ONE SOLOMON SAYS

1. Michael Winerip, *The New York Times,* September 20, 1988, B-1.

## EMERGING: AN AFTERWORD

1. David Hechler, *The Battle and the Backlash* (New York: Lexington Books, 1988), pp. 110–126.
2. For instance, Mary Pride, *The Child Abuse Industry* (Westchester, Ill., 1986), p. 36. The typical incest perpetrator is "promiscuous, often remarried, and even more often not married (i.e., a live-in boyfriend), alcoholic; often with a criminal record." Also (p. 23), the presumption that we are talking about "bad people" and "skid-row degenerates." It is interesting to weigh the author's apparently genuine outrage at the fact that children are given to the custody of raping and battering fathers (p. 94) against her near-certainty that nice-guy fathers are being "falsely accused."
3. Ibid., pp. 33–35.
4. For example, Nat Hentoff, "How the Press Fails All the Lisa Steinbergs," *Village Voice,* 26 January 1988; "The Short, Terrifying Life of Eli Creekmore," *Village Voice,* 1 November 1988; "Who

Watches the Child-Watcher,'' *Village Voice,* 8 November 1988; ''The Dangerously Passive Caseworker,'' *Village Voice,* 15 November 1988.

5. James M. Peters, Janet Dinsmore, and Patricia A. Toth, National Center for the Prosecution of Child Abuse, Alexandria, Virginia. ''Child Abuse is a Criminal Offense.'' Paper, published in the American Bar Association's Fourth National Conference on Children and the Law, October 1, 1988, p. 1.
6. Ibid., p. 4.
7. Ibid., p. 7.
8. Ibid., p. 7.
9. Ibid., p. 10.
10. Hentoff, ''The Dangerously Passive Caseworker.''
11. Paul Reidinger, ''Why Did No One Protect this Child?'', *ABA Journal,* December 1, 1988, p. 49.
12. Ibid., pp. 49–51. See also 812 *Federal Reporter,* 2d series, p. 300.
13. *ABA Journal,* p. 51.
14. In a personal communication, Grimm points to a footnote by Justice William Rehnquist in the DeShaney decision:
    ''Had the State by the affirmative exercise of its power removed Joshua from free society and placed him in a foster home operated by its agents, we might have a situation sufficiently analogous to incarceration or institutionalization to give rise to an affirmative duty to protect. Indeed several Courts of Appeal have held . . . that the State may be held liable under the Due Process Clause for failing to protect children in foster homes from mistreatment at the hands of their foster parents . . . [citations omitted] 109 S. Ct. 1006 n.9.''
    Grimm writes that although Rehnquist ''goes on to say that the Court expresses no opinion about the correctness of these decisions, there are some significant signals in the Court's recent refusal to hear the appeals of defendant social workers/agencies in two cases which had found that they would be liable for injuries to foster children.'' Grimm cites *L. J. v. Massinga* 838 F.2d 118 (4th Cir. 1988) and Taylor v. Ledbetter 791 F. 2d 881 (11th Cir. 1986), both holding that foster children may pursue causes of action for damages against state or local officials who fail to ensure that the children receive proper care while in state custody. ''Still left to be resolved, however,'' Grimm writes, ''are issues such as what level of negligence is sufficient to impose liability and how far up the ladder of the agency will liability be imposed.'' So (if I'm reading this right), the implied upshot would seem to be that at present the state's greater legal safety lies in non-removal.
15. Tom Seligson, ''Wanted: A Permanent Home,'' pp. 56–59.
16. Ibid., pp. 56–57.
17. Richard J. Gelles and Murray Straus, *Intimate Violence: The Definitive Study of the Causes and Consequences of Abuse in the American Family* (New York: Simon & Schuster, 1988), p. 51.

18. Ibid., p. 57.
19. Ibid., p. 57.
20. Ibid., p. 57.
21. Kadushin and Martin, p. 235.
22. Kadushin and Martin say (pp. 293–294), "The percentage of women in the general population who report having been sexually abused as children varies widely." However, what varies is the numbers arrived at by researchers. From one woman in four, to one woman in ten (and one boy in fifteen). From one woman in thirteen to . . . However, if—as the National Center for the Prosecution of Child Abuse data suggest——fewer than 8 percent of known cases are presently prosecuted, and that is said to burden the system, prosecuting 92 percent more cases must be a horrendous prospect to the judicial mechanism.
23. Personal communication.
24. This is most consistently apparent in cases where the child discloses the abuse to the mother, who then believes the child and acts to protect her. Findings that I have seen, faulting the mother, then, as the "real abuser," often make reference to the fact that no one will ever know "for certain." Yet a frequent outcome of these cases is the reversal of custody—from protective mother to father. And the result of this, increasingly, is that women are being driven to take their children and run, or to face jail when they refuse to turn the children over. For example, Marianne Jacobbi and Rosalind Wright, "Mothers Who Go to Jail for Their Children," *Good Housekeeping,* October 1988, p. 158.
25. Wald and Weisberg, "Confidentiality Laws and State Efforts to Protect Abused or Neglected Children: The Need for Statutory Reform," *Family Law Quarterly,* vol. XVIII, no. 2 (Summer 1984), pp. 184–185.
26. Ibid., p. 185.
27. Ibid., p. 185.
28. Ibid., p. 185.
29. "Confidentiality in Child Protection: An Overview," Trainer Manual, © 1988, American Bar Association, p. 140.
30. Ibid., p. 141.
31. In 1987, a total of 4,547 children in Minnesota alone were admitted to residential treatment centers for treatment of chemical dependency, mental illness, and emotional disturbance combined: "It is interesting to note that while children labelled as 'emotionally disturbed' had an average length of stay of 198 days, those carrying a mental illness diagnosis had an average length of stay of only 90 days." An average length of stay for emotionally disturbed children in Duluth was *815* days. Ninety-five percent of treatment for minors typed as emotionally disturbed was paid for with government funds. The youngest reported age bracket for "emotionally disturbed clients" admitted to adolescent treatment centers was 0–3. There were

three allegedly "chemically dependent clients" treated in residential treatment centers in the 0–3 bracket (!). Source: letter from Kathy Kosnoff, attorney, Minnesota Mental Health Law Project, to Assistant Commissioner Allyson Ashley, Department of Health and Human Services, March 24, 1988.

32. Of the 3,123 children typed as emotionally disturbed in Minnesota in 1987, the most frequently assigned diagnosis was "Oppositional Defiant Disorder" (625 children). *DSM-III-R (Diagnostic Statistical Manual)* describes this "disorder":

"Children with this disorder commonly are argumentative with adults, frequently lose their temper, swear, and are often angry, resentful, and easily annoyed by others. They frequently actively defy adult requests or rules and deliberately annoy other people. They tend to blame others for their own mistakes or difficulties."

The next most frequent diagnosis, "Identity Disorder" ("Who am I?"), accounted for 317 children. *DSM-III-R* elaborates on this one:

"Distress regarding inability to integrate aspects of the self into a relatively coherent and acceptable sense of self. There is uncertainty about a variety of issues relating to identity, including long-term goals, career choice, friendship patterns. . . . These symptoms last at least three months and result in impairment in social or *occupational* (including academic) functioning."

Kosnoff letter. Reference: *DSM-III-R*, pp. 56–58, 89–91, 329–331.

33. For example, from the testimony of Mark Soler, director, Youth Law Center, San Francisco, California, "Children in State Care," p. 118. "It is not a question of appropriating enormous amounts of money. Most of these programs, community-based programs, better services, are actually cheaper than the programs that are being used now."

34. *New York Times,* 6 December 1988, A-34.